Reading Fundamentals for Stu
with Learning Difficulties

Reading Fundamentals for Students with Learning Difficulties is a foundational resource on reading instruction for students with learning difficulties. This comprehensive, practical textbook provides fundamental information related to typical and atypical reading development, reading instruction within K–12 classrooms, and how to identify reading problems and provide interventions to a wide range of students who struggle to learn. Throughout the text, cutting edge research on reading instruction for students with learning disabilities and English learners is translated to practice, making it accessible to even the most novice teachers. Each section concludes with application activities, including self-tests and discussion prompts, to reinforce learning.

Sheri Berkeley is Professor of Special Education at George Mason University, USA.

Sharon Ray is Assistant Professor of Special Education at George Mason University, USA.

Reading Fundamentals for Students with Learning Difficulties

Instruction for Diverse K–12 Classrooms

Sheri Berkeley and Sharon Ray

Routledge
Taylor & Francis Group

NEW YORK AND LONDON

First published 2020
by Routledge
52 Vanderbilt Avenue, New York, NY 10017

and by Routledge
2 Park Square, Milton Park, Abingdon, Oxon, OX14 4RN

Routledge is an imprint of the Taylor & Francis Group, an informa business

© 2020 Taylor & Francis

Library of Congress Cataloging-in-Publication Data
A catalog record for this title has been requested

ISBN: 978-0-815-35290-7 (hbk)
ISBN: 978-0-815-35291-4 (pbk)
ISBN: 978-1-351-13785-0 (ebk)

Typeset in Bembo
by codeMantra

To Peggy, Michael, and Jeremy. Your support means more than you know.

Contents

Acknowledgments

We were fortunate to have talented former and current students make contributions related to their areas of expertise. Thank you to Dr. Leigh Ann Kurz for lending us her expertise in early reading and Dr. Meghan Betz for lending us her expertise in language acquisition. Additionally, we want to express our gratitude to Kelly Liu for helping us with final production tasks.

We were also fortunate to have professionals in the field who assisted us in locating meaningful images and work products that depict literacy learning in action. Thank you to the staff and children of Kiddie Country Developmental Learning Center, and Leigh Ann, Kelly, Julie and Patty. Thank you also to the Ray children and the children of our dear friends for allowing us to memorialize their work and photos in our book.

We were privileged to have a talented artist help us with the development of our artwork and figures in the book. Thank you to Jinny LaBar (JinnyLaBar@gmail.com) for being such a pleasure to work with. You truly helped our vision come to life.

We also want to express our appreciation to Dean Ginsberg and Dean Ford at George Mason University for providing resources that enabled us to complete this professional endeavor.

Finally, we are grateful to our friends and family that have supported us throughout this journey. We would not have made it across the finish line without you all!

Acknowledgments

Section I

Introduction to Reading Instruction and Assessment

Section I: Overview

Reading is a complex, multi-faceted, and integrated process. Teachers need to understand the learning characteristics of students, recognize when they are not making sufficient progress, and know how to effectively intervene. The first chapter of this section contains an introduction to reading, the challenges that some students face with learning, and the school contexts where students learn to read. The final two chapters describe assessment practices used to inform instruction and identify students who need additional assistance, with a special focus on informal reading inventories.

- Chapter 1: Understanding the Nature of Reading and Schools
- Chapter 2: Assessment of Reading
- Chapter 3: Informal Reading Inventories

Guiding Questions

As you are reading, consider the following questions:

- What are distinguishing characteristics of good readers versus struggling readers?
- What factors make students at-risk for reading problems?
- What factors influence reading instruction in contemporary classrooms?
- Why is it important to consider background information about a student when evaluating a student's reading performance?
- What are the two primary categories of assessment and what is the purpose of each?
- What are the steps of the assessment process?
- Why are informal reading inventories (IRIs) used in schools?
- What are the steps for administering an IRI?
- What information can be obtained from an IRI?

Chapter I

Understanding the Nature of Reading and Schools

The Nature of Reading

Reading is a critical component of modern-day society. Reading is a necessity for virtually all occupations, and advanced reading is required for any professions requiring a college degree. Reading is also an integral part of day-to-day life, from reading the news to following road signs. Further, with recent advances in technology, literacy is also required for emailing, texting, and communicating with friends and family on social media platforms. For many, reading is a favorite leisure activity as well. For all of these reasons, reading and writing instruction is prominent throughout K–2 schooling.

There are numerous processes and skills involved in reading that teachers need to understand in order to help students become proficient readers. In turn, proficient reading fosters proficient writing. Like a foundation supports a house, oral language proficiency supports both reading and writing development (see Figure 1.1).

Figure 1.1 Language foundation

Characteristics of Readers

Children enter school with a diverse range of abilities and experiences that contribute to learning success or failure (Baumert, Nagy, & Lehmann, 2012). Students who enter school with solid foundational skills in language tend to have a positive trajectory for successful learning over time, while students who enter school with limited exposure to language and print are at a disadvantage. By 4th grade, 65% of students are reading at or below a basic level and these students continue to fall behind throughout their schooling (NCES, 2013). Difficulties in learning can begin very early. These discrepancies in student performance are exacerbated over time and across all areas of learning. This has been referred to as the "**Matthew Effect**," referring to the concept that the "rich get richer and the poor get poorer" (Stanovich, 1986). In fact, by the 8th grade a quarter of students perform below the basic level in reading (NCES, 2013). It is important for teachers to understand the characteristics of both proficient readers and those who struggle to learn to read.

Proficient Readers

Reading is a complex process that good readers approach strategically—systematically following a plan while reading (Paris, Lipson, & Wixson, 1983; Pressley & Fingeret, 2006). Some of the most effective instructional approaches focus on helping struggling readers approach text in the same ways that good readers do.

Before reading, a good reader will preview how the text is organized and get a sense of the content of the reading through the headings and pictures. This active process also helps the reader to set a purpose for reading, think about what they know about the topic, select strategies to help them meet their reading goals, and narrow their focus while reading.

During reading, a good reader will strategically engage with and make meaning from text by asking and answering questions, making predictions about what will happen next and evaluating those predictions as they read further. As they do this, they make mental notes of whether information read is important, supportive, or unimportant, as well as mental images of what they are reading. Good readers are proficient in basic reading skills needed to access the text as well. They use an array of strategies to identify unfamiliar words quickly and accurately. They also use clues from other information in the text and knowledge from their own experiences to figure out the meaning of new vocabulary and concepts. Additionally, these students recognize how text is organized, which helps them make connections between the meanings of sentences and concepts. Further, good readers pay attention and are aware of when they understand and when they do not. When they do not understand what they are reading, these students make adjustments to the strategies they are using to help themselves understand the text.

Good readers are active and strategic after reading too. These readers will reflect on the content they have read about, summarize important points, and draw inferences. Some students may take their learning further by seeking out additional sources to help them clarify concepts they did not understand. Finally, good readers attribute their learning to their own effort, making them more likely to continue to maintain a strategic approach to reading.

Readers Who Struggle

Struggling readers approach text very differently than proficient readers. Before they begin reading, these students will jump right into the text without considering what they already know about the topic or the purpose for their reading. Doing this causes them to fail to recognize how text is organized and neglect to make a plan for reading based on the text's organization. In addition, struggling readers, and particularly older struggling readers, may not be motivated to read after previous failed attempts with reading.

During reading, struggling readers face a host of challenges. Some students struggle with simply accessing the text. These readers may have difficulty decoding words—and especially words with multiple syllables, which causes their reading to be slow and labored drawing attention away from their comprehension of text. The amount of effort spent on accessing text can be very demotivating to students and even cause them to give up altogether. Struggling readers also tend to lack knowledge of the topic of the text, including a lack of knowledge of novel terms. Additionally, students are often not aware when they have failed to understand a word or concept in text. The focus of these students may be on completing the reading assigned rather than understanding what they have read. Further, even when readers recognize that something does not make sense, these readers lack strategies for problem solving or figuring out unknown words. Because these students are not actively engaged with text, they are likely to be distracted while reading.

After reading, struggling readers are not able to make connections between what they have read and what they already know about the topic. They often fail to reflect on what they have read or mentally summarize and make note of important information. Even when they recognize that they have not understood something that they have read, these students are unlikely to seek out information to help themselves repair comprehension problems. As a result, these students tend to draw faulty conclusions about their reading efforts as well. When students struggle with reading, they often view it as something out of their control. Even when students successfully understand what they have read, students who struggle with reading tend to credit this success to reasons outside of their control, luck or an easy assignment for example, rather than their own strategic effort. This impedes future decisions to put forth effort and use strategies while reading.

Factors that Make Students "At-risk"

Students who have an increased likelihood of experiencing challenges with learning to read are often referred to as "**at-risk**." Students might be at-risk if they are living in poverty, are minority students with cultural differences, are learning English as a second language, or have language-based disabilities. Some students fall into multiple categories, for example being dually identified as an English learner and having a learning disability, which further increases the risk that they may struggle with academic learning in general. Because U.S. classrooms are now more diverse than ever before, it is important for educators to understand the characteristics of these students (Kame'enui, Carnine, Dixon, Simmons, & Coyne, 2002)

Low Socioeconomic Status

Most people think of **socioeconomic status**, or SES, solely in terms of income, but it also encompasses educational attainment, financial security, and subjective perceptions of social status and social class (APA, 2019). "Low SES in childhood is related to poor cognitive development, language, memory, socioemotional processing, and consequently poor income and health in adulthood" (APA, 2019). These students tend to do more poorly in school and develop reading proficiency at a slower rate than their peers (McLaughlin & Sheridan, 2016; Reardon, Valentino, Kalogrides, Shores, & Greenberg, 2013).

Students whose parents or guardians work full time or have multiple jobs may not have as many meaningful early language experiences with that parent/guardian. Similarly, compared to children from more affluent homes, young children living in poverty are less likely to have someone that reads aloud to them at home (Adams, 1994). These families may also lack the financial means to provide experiences for language development, including outings and events that foster conversation. This means that these children are likely to enter school with more limited language experiences and vocabulary than their peers. In fact, a vocabulary gap between children living in poverty and children from affluent homes occurs as early as age three (Reutzel & Cooter, 2019).

As they get older, these children are also less likely to have access to a variety of books and other reading materials in their homes, schools, and public libraries, especially informational books (Neuman & Celano, 2012). This limits their exposure to new vocabulary and opportunity for independent reading practice. Further, these students may have fewer means of practicing their writing due to lack of access to paper and writing instruments or computer software for composition.

Cultural Differences

Students in today's schools have a myriad of cultural backgrounds. **Culture** refers to the beliefs, values, customs, and social behaviors of a group. Culture can include region and class; however, discussions of culture in educational contexts generally refer to nationality, race or residential classification. Teachers need to be aware of the cultures of their students in order to understand the personal values and experiences that these students bring to the classroom. These cultural factors are sometimes conceptualized as an iceberg, with some elements of culture easily visible to others and other elements of culture not visible at all (see Figure 1.2). However, all of these factors play an important role in the identity of that student and their family.

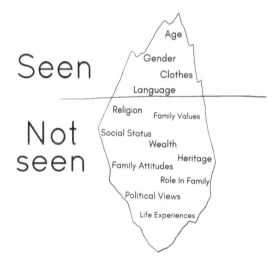

Figure 1.2 Cultural factors iceberg

Culture may directly influence the reading development of some students. For instance, in some cultures, oral storytelling is a valued aspect of family and community life, such as in Native American and Chinese cultures. Students that come to school with these experiences are likely to have foundational tools that will support their ability to read and understand story-based writing, as well as generate their own stories through writing. However, this may also be a limitation because sometimes in these cultures wisdom and knowledge passed down through stories is valued more than current factual information, which is needed for reading and understanding classroom texts. Conversely, families from Asia and India often emphasize academic performance and accuracy, which may help with comprehension of factual texts, but these students may not have been exposed to as many verbal opportunities through oral storytelling. In still other cultures, the emphasis may not be academic in nature at all. For instance, in many Hispanic cultures greater importance is placed on the development, survival, and perpetuation of family and familial customs.

Residential communities tend to have cultural commonalities as well. **Residential communities** are generally classified as urban, suburban, or rural. Students from different communities may have dialectical differences and/or use slang that is specific to the community itself. Additionally, the academic experiences and resources available based on the residential community may have a large disparity with suburban schools that tend to be better resourced than rural or urban schools. Additionally, many urban and rural students have had fewer educational opportunities before entering school for a variety of reasons. However, there may be pockets of students from rural and urban homes that have had the opposite experience with structured and diverse learning opportunities due to family, rather than community, resources.

English Language Development

Some students are from homes where a language other than English is spoken and are learning English as a second language. These students are referred to as English language learners (ELLs) or English learners (ELs). Their first language is referred to as their L1 and their second language is referred to as their L2. There are 4.8 million students in U.S. public schools who are English language learners, which equates to approximately 9.5% of all students. The process of acquiring a second language while simultaneously learning academic content delivered in that second language is quite challenging. As such, these English learners are at-risk for not progressing at the same rate as their English native speaking peers in developing reading and other academic skills. The National Center for Education Statistics (NCES, 2013) reported that 68% of students learning English as a second language fell below basic levels of competency in reading. Students who are learning English as a second language face multiple challenges that students who are native English learners do not experience. Factors that most directly pose challenges for English learners are the differences between the orthography of their L1 and L2 and the natural developmental progression of acquiring a second language.

Orthography refers to the symbols and rules that govern their use in the written form of a language (Coulmas, 2003). English uses the Roman alphabet within its writing system; however, many languages do not, such as Arabic, Russian, and Chinese. Students whose L1 uses a non-Roman writing system have an additional barrier when learning to read and write in English (their L2). Some non-Roman orthographies use symbols to convey sounds while others use symbols to convey longer units like word parts or syllables. Other languages, including many European-based languages, including Spanish, German, and Italian, use the Roman alphabet, or parts of it. However, even learners whose L1 also uses the Roman alphabet face difficulties. Some languages that use the Roman alphabet have a transparent orthography, where there is a one-to-one correspondence between a single sound and a single letter, such as Spanish and Finnish. In contrast, languages like English have a complex orthography, where multiple letters and groups of letters can represent a certain sound or sounds (Ramirez, Chen, Geva, & Kiefer, 2010).

The other major challenge relates to the nature of language acquisition itself. A widely used framework for evaluating and communicating the level of a student's English language acquisition was developed by the WIDA consortium, which stands for World-class Instructional Design and Assessment (Wisconsin Center for Education Research, 2018).

WIDA levels are based on both strands and function of language usage. The five strands of language development are:

- social and instructional,
- English language arts,
- mathematics,
- science,
- social studies.

Across these domains, the framework then considers the individual's language usage across the functions of listening, speaking, reading, and writing. The levels are a continuum that can be used to describe students' language proficiency. The continuum ranges from "entering," the most basic level of language competency where student English skills are just beginning, to "reaching" where students' abilities have reached English language proficiency (Wisconsin Center for Education Research, 2018). See Table 1.1 for a description of all of the WIDA levels.

Table 1.1 WIDA English Language

Level	Description
Level 1 Entering	Knows and uses a small amount of social language and a small amount of academic language with visual supports
Level 2 Beginning	Knows and uses some social English and general academic language with visual supports
Level 3 Developing	Knows and uses social English and some specific academic language with visual supports
Level 4 Expanding	Knows and uses social English and some technical academic language
Level 5 Bridging	Knows and uses social English and academic language with grade level materials
Level 6 Reaching	Knows and uses social and academic English at the highest level measured

Adapted from: Wisconsin Center for Education Research. https://wida.wisc.edu/

When a person is acquiring a second language, some common phenomena are likely to occur. Sometimes educators mistakenly identify these phenomena as indicators of a language disorder, when these phenomena are actually typical during second language development and are not indicative of a disability. These common phenomena related to normal language acquisition are illustrated in Table 1.2.

Language is used to communicate in both informal social situations as well as formal academic settings; however, the skills needed in these contexts are not the same. Cognitive demands related to the process of acquiring knowledge and understanding information influence the amount of stress a language task places on a person. Concrete language use about objects and activities in the immediate environment is less cognitively demanding, while abstract language use about complex processes not immediately visible is more cognitively demanding. The cognitive demands of language can be classified as **basic interpersonal communication skills**, or BICS, and **cognitive academic language proficiency**, or CALP. BICS are low demand language tasks needed for everyday language use in social conversations. For instance, a low demand language task might involve asking for food,

Table 1.2 Normal Language Acquisition Phenomena

Phenomenon	Definition	Example
Interference	**Interference**, also called transfer, means that the English learner may make an error in English because they "transfer" an aspect of their first language (LI) to their second language (English).	For example, in Spanish, "Puede recomendar unos buenos alimentos?" means "Can you recommend some good food?" However, a literal translation would be "Can you recommend ones good food?" A Spanish-speaking child who said "Can you recommend ones good foods?" would be manifesting transfer from Spanish to English with the slightly different article use from Spanish.
Silent Period	The **silent period** is when an English learner is first exposed to a second language and speaks very little because they are focusing on listening and understanding English.	A young student may be in the silent period for a year or more, while an older student may be in the silent period for only a few weeks or months.
Code-switching	**Code-switching** is when an English learner "switches" back and forth between their first and second languages among sentences and phrases.	For example, a Spanish speaker might say, "I'm going on vacation soon. Estoy emocionado!" (I'm going on vacation soon. I'm excited!") Or, a Chinese speaker might say, "I like blue. It is my zuì xǐ huan de yán sè [favorite color] of all!"
Language Loss	**Language loss**, also called subtractive bilingualism, occurs when some English learners lose skills and fluency in their first language if it is not reinforced and maintained while the student is learning English.	Language loss can impede a child's learning as well as be detrimental to his/her family life, particularly if the parents speak only the first language. It is better for students when additive bilingualism occurs—where students learn English while their first language and culture are maintained and reinforced.

Adapted from: The American Speech-Language-Hearing. https://www.asha.org/public/speech/development/easl/

asking to use the bathroom, or talking about preferred toys. CALP refers to high demand language tasks needed for the academic language of school, which includes reading and writing in addition to conversation.

High demand language tasks might include being asked to tell the main idea of a story, complete a mathematics operation, or explain a historical event.

Like culture, these concepts are often conveyed through the metaphor of an iceberg (see Figure 1.3). BICS communication skills develop and are "visible" much more quickly than CALP skills with deficiencies being difficult to "see." Considering that BICS develops within two years of learning a new language while CALP requires a minimum of five to seven years, an English learner's level of language proficiency could easily be misidentified. For example, a teacher may notice a student easily conversing in English with friends in the cafeteria and mistakenly assume that the student is able to understand the oral lectures and readings in academic classes.

BICS and CALP are not the only considerations related to language difficulty; language is also contextual. Contextual cues include non-verbal and visual cues that support

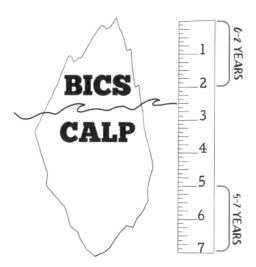

Figure 1.3 BICS and CALP iceberg

understanding and attempts to communicate. This might include face-to-face conversations where facial expressions and gestures support communication or hands–on classroom activities that support attempts to understand and use academic language. Similarly,
a lack of contextual cues can impede understanding and attempts to communicate. This
might include difficulty following oral directions or comprehending information read in
a textbook. **Cummins' quadrant** (Cummins, 1984) illustrates this relationship between
content difficulty and context using school-based examples (see Figure 1.4).

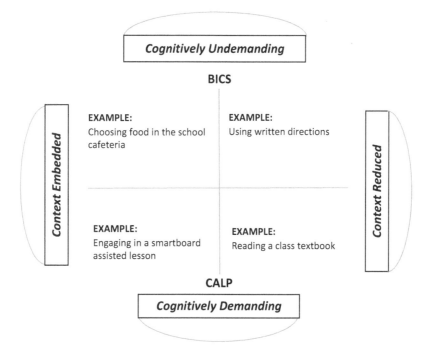

Figure 1.4 Cummins' quadrant
Inspired by: Baker, C. (2001). *Foundations of Bilingual Education and Bilingualism*. Clevedon, England:
Multilingual Matters Ltd.

Knowing and understanding the different aspects of English language acquisition, as well as the WIDA English language proficiency framework can help teachers support the reading development of students who are learning English as a second language.

Language-based Disabilities

Many students in today's classrooms are identified with a disability and receive special education services that follow an individualized education program. There are 13 categories of students that can receive special education services (see Figure 1.5). Several of these disability categories include underlying language deficits that have direct implications for reading development, including autism, emotional/behavioral disorder, attention deficit/hyperactivity disorder, speech–language disorder, and learning disability.

Reading is a particular area of difficulty for students with learning disabilities with 80–90% of these students struggling in the area of reading (Pullen, Lane, Ashworth, & Lovelace, 2011). Students with language related disabilities that affect reading are likely to have other challenges related to learning as well, including attention and motivation (Swanson & Hoskyn, 2001). Processes most related to reading disabilities include issues with language development, especially phonology, and memory (Griffiths & Snowling, 2002).

Phonology and syntax are aspects of language that are important to becoming a proficient reader. Phonology involves the awareness and manipulation of individual sounds in words.

Disability Category	Prevalence
Specific learning disability	2,339,866
Speech or language impairment	1,018,462
Other health impairment	970,002
Autism	616,234
Intellectual disability	418,395
Emotional disturbance	344,977
Developmental delay	159,531
Multiple disabilities	122,442
Hearing impairment	64,812
Orthopedic impairment	34,859
Traumatic brain injury	25,323
Visual impairment	24,428
Deaf-blindness	1,306

Students with these disabilities tend to have language and attention problems that impede their reading and writing development.

Figure 1.5 Disability categories covered under special education
Data source: https://www2.ed.gov/programs/osepidea/618-data/static-tables/index.html

Syntax involves the grammatical structure of sentences. It is well documented that students with learning disabilities have difficulties in these areas of language that significantly affect their reading and writing development. You will learn more about this is Chapters 6, 9, 12, and 14.

Memory also plays an important role in reading. According to Information Processing Theory (Slavin, 2003), there are three types of memory that work together when a person processes and stores information gained through the senses: short-term memory, working memory, and long-term memory. **Short–term memory** holds information for only a short period of time while the brain decides whether to process or discard it. Students with learning disabilities have been found to have deficits in short-term memory, particularly for auditory information (Kibby, Marks, Morgan, & Long, 2004). This means that these students may forget what they have heard almost immediately.

Working memory is "the ability to retain information in short–term memory while processing incoming information" (Siegel & Mazabel, 2013, p. 201). This is an important aspect of cognition, because at this stage, information can either be effectively processed or discarded. In reading, working memory is important because this allows information that was read to be remembered while new words and phrases are being decoded and identified. Figure 1.6 depicts the ways in which information might be effectively or ineffectively processed in working memory.

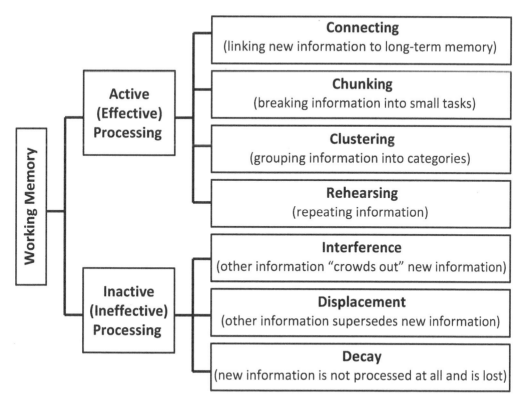

Figure 1.6 Working memory processing

Adapted from: Hallahan, D. P., Lloyd, J. W., Kauffman, J. M., Weiss, M. P., & Martinez, E. A. (2005). *Learning disabilities: Foundations, characteristics, and effective teaching* (3rd ed.). Boston, MA: Pearson.

An important part of working memory is **executive functioning**—self-managing of one's self and resources to achieve a goal. According to Hallahan and colleagues (2005), effective executive functioning necessitates that students believe:

- in their own ability to accomplish a task (called self-efficacy),
- that outcomes are within their control (called internal locus of control), and
- that positive outcomes are a result of their effort, including effort to utilize strategies (called effort attributions).

Problems in the executive system of students with learning disabilities include difficulties with attention and shifting and updating information in working memory (Swanson & Sáez, 2003; Swanson, Harris, & Graham, 2013).

Long-term memory is where information is held over a long period of time and includes episodic memory, semantic memory, and procedural memory (Slavin, 2003). **Episodic memory** is the storage of memories organized by space and time. A student with challenges with episodic memory may have difficulties sequentially retelling events heard or read. **Semantic memory** is the organization of information we know—also referred to as schema. A student with challenges involving semantic memory may have difficulties making connections between related terms and concepts. **Procedural memory** is the storage of memories related to how to do things. A student with challenges involving semantic memory may have difficulties learning and applying learning strategies consistently. Students with learning disabilities are especially inefficient at storing and extracting information from long-term memory (Kame'enui et al., 2002).

A Focus on Accommodations and Modifications

In addition to specialized instruction, students with language-based disabilities may need accommodations and/or modifications in order to benefit from instruction.

- **Accommodations** are "changes to the education program that do not substantially alter the instructional level, the content of the curriculum, or the assessment criteria" (Cohen & Spenciner, 2003, p. 9).
- **Modifications**, sometimes referred to as adaptations, are "changes in content or standards" that change the nature of the task and the content being taught (Polloway, Patton, & Serna, 2008, p. 6).

The committee that puts together the individualized education plan (IEP) for a student receiving special education services determines whether a student needs accommodations or modifications to make sufficient progress in the curriculum or toward IEP goals. If an accommodation or modification is warranted, then it is provided both in instructional and testing settings.

The Nature of Schools

For most students, learning to read occurs primarily within the context of schools. As such, teachers need to understand the school context where this learning occurs and the general progression of skill development within the general education curriculum so that they can recognize when students are developing skills adequately and when they are not. While many school buildings in use today are still the actual physical structures of 50 years ago, the instruction that takes place within them is quite different.

Today's Classrooms

Today's classrooms are also incredibly diverse. The nation's public school population is over 50 million students (NCES, 2013). Within this student population, approximately 42% are a racial/ethnic minority. Students learning English as a second language make up around 6% of the total school population. At the same time, learners with disabilities served under *IDEA* are 8% of the nation's learners, with the majority of those students labeled as having a learning disability (NCES, 2013; IDEA, 2004). An additional 6% of learners are considered gifted and talented (National Association for Gifted Children, 2018). With these different learning needs, demands on teachers are ever increasing. To meet the varied learning needs of students, teachers work collaboratively with other educators and specialists within their school setting. Specialists common to today's schools are listed in Table 1.3.

Table 1.3 Specialist Roles

Specialist	Expertise
Special Education Teacher	Special education teachers work with students who qualify for special education services for learning, mental, emotional, or physical disabilities. These specialists have expertise in administering educational assessments and providing specialized instruction, behavioral supports, and accommodations and modifications to the general curriculum.
English Language Learner Teacher	English language learner (ELL) or English as a second language (ESL) teachers work with students who are learning English as a second language. These specialists have the expertise needed to evaluate students' English proficiency and to provide specialized instruction and supports for second language learners.
Reading Specialists	Reading specialists work with students who are at-risk in the area of reading development, particularly in the elementary grades. These specialists have expertise in reading assessment and instruction.
Librarians	School librarians work with all of the students and teachers in a school. These specialists are an important resource for locating texts and other media that supports student learning.
Technology Specialists	Technology specialists work with teachers to provide technology support, including software that supports student learning in classrooms.
Speech–Language Clinicians	Speech–language clinicians work with students with speech–language disorders or other language-based disabilities. These specialists have expertise in typical and atypical language development, assessment, and instruction.
Occupational Therapists	Occupational therapists work with students with disabilities that impact their fine motor development. These specialists have expertise that can support the handwriting development of students.

Elementary school students have one teacher for all of their core content instruction. In the primary grades, instruction focuses on basic reading skills needed to identify sounds and words automatically and read connected text fluently (Joseph & Schisler, 2009). As students progress to upper elementary grades, the focus will shift to fluently reading longer amounts of connected text, and understanding the words and overall meaning of what is being read. Students across the elementary grades will typically have a 60- to 90-minute block of time dedicated to reading and writing. This reading instruction can involve small group work with the teacher, and reinforcement in centers or through peer-learning activities. Around 4th grade, the focus of reading instruction shifts from teaching students "how to read" to teaching students how to "read to learn" (Chall, 1983).

As students enter middle school, the nature of instruction shifts due to changes in the structure of the school day and the focus of the curriculum. At the middle school level, more specific content area information is being introduced, so individual subjects each have their own 45- to 90-minute class block. Within language arts classes, some time is still being spent as a whole class on oral language, reading, and writing skills through reading short stories and longer novels prescribed by the curriculum, but not typically on individualized reading skills needed by students. Practice with writing conventions occurs through student writing of five paragraph essays and short stories, and oral language skills are further developed through oral presentations on readings and other information. In content area classes, reading and writing instruction is not a core focus and is not explicit, but rather, it is a means to learn content information, including learning content area vocabulary. Similarly, oral language skills are addressed primarily through talking and sharing information aloud on the content area topic.

External Influences on School Performance

Some of the changes that have occurred in today's schools are driven by external influences intended to improve school performance. For example, the federal law *No Child Left Behind* (2001) mandated assessments to ensure progress of learners who have historically not had access to high-quality reading instruction, including students from low SES families, minority students, English learners, and students with disabilities. Results from these assessments are used to determine whether schools have made "adequate yearly progress" which drives school funding and resource decisions. These laws have also been instrumental in requiring schools to meet the reading needs of all students through the use of evidence-based practices in reading instruction.

Even more recently, based on the educational climate of "access for all students," there has been an effort to standardize what is taught and learned by students through national and state standards. For instance, the Common Core State Standards (CCSS; 2019) were developed to use across states to ensure that all students will gain a certain set of academic skills, including core reading abilities, after the completion of each grade so that by graduation all students will possess an overall collection of skills that would make them employable. Another example is the Next Generation Science Standards (NGSS Lead States, 2013), which are science standards across K–12 grade levels, that are focused on developing student science-related skills that include reading skills used to access and understand science content.

A Focus on Influential Reports on Literacy

In order to meet the rising demand to provide evidence-based instruction, several key reviews related to reading instruction were conducted and widely disseminated. Over the last two decades, these reviews have greatly influenced how reading instruction is provided in the classroom as well as how educators communicate about reading instruction.

Put Reading First

The following five areas of reading were identified as effective for helping students in grades K through 3 learn to read: (1) phonemic awareness instruction; (2) systematic and explicit phonics instruction; (3) repeated and monitored oral reading fluency instruction; (4) indirect and direct vocabulary instruction; and (5) specific reading comprehension strategy instruction (Armbruster, Lehr, & Osborn, 2001).

Reading Next

The following 15 elements of literacy instruction practices were identified as effective for helping students acquire literacy skills in middle school and high school: (1) direct, explicit comprehension instruction; (2) effective instructional principles embedded in content; (3) motivation and self-directed learning; (4) text-based collaborative learning; (5) strategic tutoring; (6) diverse texts; (7) intensive writing; (8) technology components; (9) ongoing formative assessment of students; (10) extended time for literacy; (11) professional development; (12) ongoing summative assessment of students and programs; (13) teacher teams; (14) leadership; and (15) comprehensive and coordinated literacy programs (Biancarosa & Snow, 2006).

Writing Next

The following 11 elements of current writing instruction practices were identified as effective for helping adolescent students learn to write: (1) writing strategies; (2) summarization; (3) collaborative writing; (4) specific product goals; (5) word processing; (6) sentence combining; (7) prewriting; (8) inquiry activities; (9) process writing approach; (10) study of models; and (11) writing for content learning (Graham & Perin, 2007).

Response to Intervention

As you have learned in this chapter, today's schools include a wide range of learners, many of whom will struggle to learn at some point in their schooling. While solid instruction in core general education courses is crucial, it is not sufficient for all learners, including most students with learning disabilities and many students who are learning English as a second language. To address the needs of all students, a plethora of initiatives exist within U.S. schools. Perhaps the most common contemporary initiative is responsiveness to intervention (RTI). Teachers need to understand the function of these initiatives and how to apply their knowledge of reading assessments and interventions within these frameworks.

Response to Intervention, or RTI, is a framework used to systematically identify and address the learning needs of a wide range of students, and especially those that are at-risk for falling behind in reading. RTI and other multi-tiered systems of support (MTSS) models vary throughout the country (Berkeley, Bender, Peaster, & Saunders, 2009; Berkeley, Sutton, & Sacco, 2018), but generally, tiered models contain the following elements:

1. screening to identify students who may need additional assistance,
2. progressively intensive tiers of intervention that use evidence-based instruction and ongoing progress monitoring,
3. data-based decision making within and between tiers.

Most RTI models contain three tiers. As shown in Figure 1.7, most students (~80%) benefit from instruction in Tier 1, some students (~15%) need Tier 2 interventions to make sufficient progress, and a few students (~5%) require intensive Tier 3 reading interventions.

Tier 1 refers to quality general education instruction. General screening to identify students who may need additional assistance occurs at this tier as well. When a student is flagged in a screening or is not making sufficient progress in the general education curriculum, the student will progress to Tier 2.

Tier 2 instruction is intended for students who need more instructional time, increased intensity of instruction in small groups, and more repetitions or "doses" of instruction (e.g., daily vs. every other day) (Stahl & McKenna, 2013). Student progress will be formally monitored to evaluate how the student is responding to the intervention. If the student is making the desired progress, he or she will return to Tier 1 upon completion of the intervention. If the student is not making sufficient progress, then adjustments may be made to the instructional plan. If this change still does not result in sufficient progress, the student may progress to Tier 3.

Tier 3 instruction is intended for students who do not respond to Tier 2 interventions or who have significant reading problems. Often students in Tier 3 have severe reading disabilities that are difficult to remediate. In this tier the most intensive interventions are provided and progress is monitored daily. You will learn more about intensive reading interventions in Chapter 8.

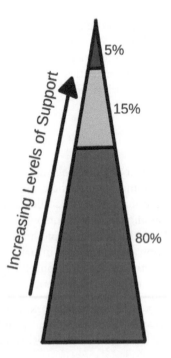

Figure 1.7 Response to intervention tiers

Whether a school's tiered system of support is called RTI, multi-tiered systems of support (MTSS), or some other name, the purpose is to provide systemic support for students, particularly in foundational learning such as reading. While the broad purpose of tiered models is the same, the specifics of implementation can vary across and within states. For this reason, training related to specific procedures for implementing the model, including specification of who is responsible for each aspect of the process, is provided by the individual school.

Organization of the Book

Literacy development is a highly integrated process. While there is a developmental progression of reading skills, numerous reading skills develop simultaneously and in a reciprocal way that supports further development. This integrated and reciprocal relationship exists with language and writing as well. Keep this in mind as you continue reading. Chapters in this textbook have been delineated by skill areas solely for the purpose of clarity for the reader. The actual process of learning to read is much more complicated. Indeed, as Moats titled her 1999 paper, "*Teaching Reading* IS *Rocket Science.*"

References

Adams, M. J. (1994). *Beginning to read: Thinking and learning about print*. Cambridge, MA: MIT Press.

American Psychological Association (APA). (2019). *Education and socioeconomic status*. Retrieved March 30, 2019 from https://www.apa.org/pi/ses/resources/publications/education.aspx

Armbruster, B., Lehr, F., & Osborn, J. (2001). *Put reading first: The research building blocks for teaching children to read*. Washington, DC: National Institute for Literacy.

Baker, C. (2001). *Foundations of Bilingual Education and Bilingualism*. Clevedon, England: Multilingual Matters Ltd.

Baumert, J., Nagy, G., & Lehmann, R. (2012). Cumulative advantages and the emergence of social and ethnic inequality: Matthew effects in reading and mathematics development within elementary schools? *Child Development, 83*, 1347–1367.

Biancarosa, C., & Snow, C. E. (2006). *Reading next—A vision for action and research in middle and high school literacy: A report to Carnegie Corporation of New York* (2nd ed.). Washington, DC: Alliance for Excellent Education.

Berkeley, S., Bender, W. N., Peaster, L. G., & Saunders, L. (2009). A snapshot of progress toward implementation of responsiveness to intervention (RTI) throughout the United States. *Journal of Learning Disabilities, 42*, 85–95.

Berkeley, S., Sutton, J., & Sacco, D. (2018, February). *A snapshot of RTI implementation a decade later: New picture, same story?* Presented at the annual meeting of the Council for Exceptional Children, Tampa, FL.

Chall, J. S. (1983). *Stages of reading development*. New York, NY: McGraw-Hill.

Cohen, L.G., & Spenciner, L.J. (2003). *Assessment of children and youth with special needs*. Boston, MA: Allyn & Bacon.

Common Core State Standards Initiative. (2019). *English language arts standards*. Retrieved February 2, 2019 from http://www.corestandards.org/ELA-Literacy/introduction/key-design-consideration/

Coulmas, F. (2003). *Writing systems: An introduction to their linguistic analysis*. Cambridge, MA: Cambridge University Press.

Cummins, J. (1984). *Bilingualism and special education: Issues in assessment and pedagogy*. San Francisco, CA: College-Hill Press.

Graham, S., & Perin, D. (2007). *Writing next: Effective strategies to improve writing of adolescents in middle and high schools—A report to Carnegie Corporation of New York*. Washington, DC: Alliance for Excellent Education.

Griffiths, Y. M., & Snowling, M. J. (2002). Predictors of exception word and nonword reading in dyslexic children: The severity hypothesis. *Journal of Educational Psychology, 94*, 34–43.

Hallahan, D. P., Lloyd, J. W., Kauffman, J. M., Weiss, M. P., & Martinez, E. A. (2005). *Learning disabilities: Foundations, characteristics, and effective teaching* (3rd ed.). Boston, MA: Pearson.

Individuals with Disabilities Education Act, 20 U.S.C. § 1400. (2004).

Joseph, L. M., & Schisler, R. (2009). Should adolescents go back to the basics? A review of teaching word reading skills to middle and high school students. *Remedial & Special Education, 30,* 131–147.

Kame'enui, E. J., Carnine, D. W., Dixon, R. C., Simmons, D. C., & Coyne, M. D. (2002). *Effective teaching strategies that accommodate diverse learners* (2nd ed.). Upper Saddle River, NJ: Merrill Prentice-Hall.

Kibby, M., Marks, W., Morgan, S., & Long, C. (2004). Specific impairments in developmental reading disabilities: A working memory approach. *Journal of Learning Disabilities, 37,* 349–363.

McLaughlin, K. A., & Sheridan, M. A. (2016). Beyond cumulative risk: A dimensional approach to childhood adversity. *Current Directions in Psychological Science, 25,* 239–245.

Moats, L. C. (1999). *Teaching reading is rocket science: What expert teachers of reading should know and be able to do.* Paper prepared for the American Federation of Teachers. Retrieved March 30, 2019 from: https://www.aft.org/sites/default/files/reading_rocketscience_2004.pdf

National Association for Gifted Children. (2018). *Gifted education in the U.S.* Retrieved February 9, 2019 from https://www.nagc.org/resources-publications/resources/gifted-education-us

National Center for Education Statistics (NCES). (2013). *The nation's report card: A first look: 2013 mathematics and reading (NCES 2014–451).* Washington, DC: Institute of Education Sciences, U.S. Department of Education.

Neuman, S. B., & Celano, D. (2012). *Giving our children a fighting chance: Poverty, literacy, and the development of information capital.* New York, NY: Teachers College Press.

NGSS Lead States. (2013). *Next generation science standards: For states, by states.* Washington, DC: The National Academies Press.

No Child Left Behind Act of 2001, P.L. 107–110, 20 U.S.C. § 6319. (2002).

Paris, S. G., Lipson, M. Y., & Wixson, K. K. (1983). Becoming a strategic reader. *Contemporary Educational Psychology, 8,* 293–316.

Polloway, E. A., Patton, J. R., & Serna, L. (2008). *Strategies for teaching learners with special needs* (9th ed.). Upper Saddle River, NJ: Pearson.

Pressley, M., & Fingeret, L. (2006). Fluency. In M. Pressley (Ed.), *Reading instruction that works: The case for balanced teaching* (3rd ed., pp. 219–247). New York, NY: Guilford.

Pullen, P. C., Lane, H. B., Ashworth, K. A., & Lovelace, S. P. (2011). Specific learning disabilities. In J. M. Kauffman & D. P. Hallahan (Eds.), *Handbook of special education* (pp. 286–299). New York, NY: Routledge.

Ramirez, G., Chen, X., Geva, E., & Kiefer, H. (2010). Morphological awareness in Spanish-speaking English language learners: Within and cross-language effects on word reading. *Reading and Writing, 23,* 337–358.

Reardon, S. F., Valentino, R. A., Kalogrides, D., Shores, K. A., & Greenberg, E. H. (2013). *Patterns and trends in racial academic achievement gaps among states, 1999–2011.* Retrieved from https://cepa.stanford.edu/content/patterns-and-trends-racial-academic-achievement-gaps-among-states-1999-2011

Reutzel, D. R., & Cooter Jr., R. B. (2019). *Teaching children to read: The teacher makes the difference* (8th ed.). New York, NY: Pearson.

Siegel, L. S., & Mazabel, S. (2013). Cognitive processes and reading disabilities. In H. L. Swanson, K. R. Harris, & S. Graham (Eds.), *Handbook of learning disabilities* (pp. 186–213). New York, NY: Guilford Press.

Slavin, R. E. (2003). *Educational psychology: Theory and practice* (7th ed.). Boston, MA: Allyn & Bacon.

Stahl, K. A. D., & McKenna, M. C. (2013). *Reading assessment in an RTI framework.* New York, NY: Guilford Press.

Stanovich, K. E. (1986). Matthew effects in reading: Some consequences of individual differences in the acquisition of literacy. *Reading Research Quarterly, 21,* 360–407.

Swanson, H. L., Harris, K. R., & Graham, S. (Eds.). (2013). *Handbook of learning disabilities.* New York, NY: Guilford Press.

Swanson, H. L., & Hoskyn, M. (2001). Instructing adolescents with learning disabilities: A component and composite analysis. *Learning Disabilities Research & Practice, 16,* 109–119.

Swanson, H. L., & Sáez, L. (2003). Memory difficulties in children and adults with learning disabilities. In H. L. Swanson, K. R. Harris, & S. Graham (Eds.), *Handbook of learning disabilities* (pp. 182–198). New York, NY: Guilford Press.

Wisconsin Center for Education Research. (2018). *WIDA.* Retrieved January 30, 2019 from https://wida.wisc.edu/

Chapter 2

Assessment of Reading

Fundamentals of Assessment

Assessment is a necessary aspect of good instruction. When selecting an assessment, an educator will need to consider the purpose of the assessment in order to determine what type of assessment will be most appropriate. In some cases, assessments are used to formally evaluate student outcomes or to identify serious learning problems. Assessment information drives instructional decisions, both prior to instruction and in evaluating whether instruction has been effective. Regardless of the type of assessment, it is important to consider information about the student, called background information, that can help contextualize assessment results.

Background Information

It is important for teachers to consider the child holistically when interpreting assessment information and designing instruction. To do this, a teacher gathers background information about the student. Background information includes areas other than instruction that might explain a student's struggles with reading. For example, environmental factors or educational history might contribute to the student's performance. Finally, background information includes information about student motivation that can be used to design instruction that is engaging for the student.

Exclusionary Information

In some cases, background information can be used to rule out other factors that might be causing or contributing to difficulties the student is having—referred to as **exclusionary**

A Focus on Exclusionary Criteria for Special Education Eligibility

Additional exclusionary criteria are necessary when the purpose of an assessment is to determine whether a student is eligible for special education services according to the Individuals with Disabilities Education Act (IDEA)—the federal law providing protections to students with disabilities and their families. For example, according to IDEA (2004), "specific learning disability does not include learning problems that are primarily the result of visual, hearing, or motor disabilities, of mental retardation, of emotional disturbance, or of environmental, cultural, or economic disadvantage." In other words, if any of the items on this list are the primary reason that the student is under-performing, then the student cannot qualify for special education services for a specific learning disability. It should be noted that environmental factors include instruction, and so a student could not be found eligible for special education if it is determined that the primary reason for the student's performance is a lack of adequate instruction in the area of concern.

factors. For example, if the student is in need of reading glasses, it would affect the student's ability to read words fluently. This vision issue would need to be corrected before it could be determined whether the student also has difficulties with reading. Similarly, if the student has problems with his hearing, this must be ruled out before determining whether the student is actually having difficulty distinguishing sounds in words. Therefore, it is necessary for a child that is struggling in school to have a current vision and hearing exam.

Environmental Factors

It is also important for teachers to consider how a child's environment can influence academic performance. **Environmental factors** might include the student's living situation, economic status, and cultural background (see Chapter 1 for more information). Housing is a basic human need, and therefore, students who are homeless or who split time between multiple residences due to divorce or other factors may struggle in school. Students who are homeless or who do not have one permanent place to live may not be able to focus on learning in school because they are concerned about where they will sleep that night or whether they will have food to eat. Some students are not homeless, but are living in a household that is experiencing severe economic hardship or poverty. Learners in these challenging economic circumstances may not have the home resources and supports for reading from which other students benefit.

Along similar lines, some students are from cultural backgrounds that value reading and education differently than school districts. Students from different cultural backgrounds may have parents with differing abilities to read themselves, as well as varying cultural perceptions about the importance of reading. All of these environmental factors can play a role in student reading struggles because they may influence the time, resources, and supports available for reading at home.

Educational History

Information contained in a student's formal school records is referred to as the student's **educational history**. A student's educational history can help a teacher understand the instructional approaches that have been previously tried and the effectiveness of those efforts. This can help determine whether lack of reading instruction is at least part of the reason that reading difficulties are occurring. Formal school records also contain results from assessments that give an indication of how the student is performing compared to peers.

Because language plays such a significant role in academic learning, information about the individual's language development is also an important component of a student's educational history—particularly if the student has displayed atypical language development or is acquiring English as a second language. For example, if a student is struggling with orally producing particular phonemes when talking, that learner will typically have the same articulation difficulties when reading aloud. If a child is just learning to speak English, then learning to read English adds an additional layer of difficulty.

Observed Testing Behavior

Behavior that the student displays during testing situations can give teachers important insights into the individual student. If a student easily engages in conversation with whomever is conducting the reading assessment and is engaged and focused during the evaluation, then it is likely she feels comfortable with reading tasks and does not experience difficulties with attention during reading. If a student seems uneasy and fidgety during the reading assessment, especially when being asked to complete particular reading tasks, then it is likely the student experiences difficulties when reading or does not feel comfortable in completing challenging reading assignments. A student who has difficulties attending during a reading evaluation may have attention difficulties generally or struggle with reading tasks specifically. Similarly, if a student seems anxious during a reading evaluation, this may be an indicator of anxiety about reading specifically or academics/school in general. These and other behaviors that students display when undergoing reading assessment are documented because exhibited behaviors can help explain the student's reading experience and performance on reading assessments.

Language is an observable specific student behavior that is likely to have a direct effect on reading performance. When assessing students, teachers note specific language usage as this helps them determine student strengths or areas of concern. If a teacher observes that a second language learner is having difficulty expressing himself in English, it may be indicative of difficulties with acquisition of academic language. Difficulties in pronouncing or articulating words may be signs of underlying speech difficulties. Trouble selecting or choosing words for language use during the assessment may be indicative of a form of language disorder. Any concerns noted with language development or acquisition would be discussed with the speech–language clinician or ELL teacher in the school.

Student Motivation

Students are more likely to be motivated to read when they are presented with engaging material that will capture and hold their interest (Guthrie & Wigfield, 2000). Students who are presented with materials that are simply not of interest are less likely to read them, so many valuable practice opportunities are lost for these readers. It is only through practicing reading that a student's reading abilities will continue to evolve and make progress. Therefore, it is important to learn what types of topics and genres students enjoy reading. Further, learning about things that students enjoy in general can provide a window of opportunity for selecting topics that a student might enjoy reading about.

Student attitudes toward reading, either positive or negative, can also influence the amount of effort students dedicate to learning to read, and conversely, student reading abilities influence their attitudes about reading (Kush & Watkins, 1996). Students who approach reading with a positive attitude are likely to read more and take risks with new reading tasks. Students who approach reading with a negative attitude are less likely to read. Understanding past student experiences can help teachers make instructional decisions that foster positive student attitudes about reading or change negative ones.

Student experiences can help shed light on why a student is motivated or demotivated to read. If a student has had positive experiences with reading, they are more likely to see themselves as good readers and to want to read. Positive experiences can include successes with reading in school as well as positive reading memories, such as alone time reading with a parent or other important family member. If a student has had negative experiences with reading, they are more likely to see themselves as poor readers and to want to avoid reading. Negative experiences can include struggling or failing at reading tasks, particularly if these failures occur in front of peers.

Although student motivation plays an important role in students' willingness to attempt reading tasks, it is an internal construct, meaning that it cannot be readily observed. As such, intentional steps will need to be taken to gather this information directly from the student. One common way to do this is through a reading interest inventory. **Reading interest inventories** are general surveys of a wide range of topics related to reading including student interests, attitudes, and experiences. Interest inventories take a variety of forms including oral interviews and conversations with the teacher, open-ended or Likert type surveys that students fill out independently, and interest inventories that are a combination of these two approaches where the teacher reads prompts aloud and the student provides a written response. Use of these different types of interest inventories vary based on grade level administration options (group or individual), and ability level of the student. See Table 2.1 for sample interest inventory items.

Table 2.1 Interest Inventory Examples

Motivational Component	Sample Interest Inventory Item
Interests	• What do you like to read about? • Check the things that you like to read about (history, sports, cars, science fiction, westerns, mysteries) • Do you have a hobby? • Most of all I would like to have _____ • Reading is one of my favorite things to do at home (always describes me, sometimes describes me, never describes me)
Attitudes	• Do you like to read? • Do you think of yourself as a good reader? • Reading is important because _____ • One thing I don't like about school is _____ • I don't like to read aloud (always describes me, sometimes describes me, never describes me)
Experiences	• Does someone read books to you? • Tell me about one good experience you have had with reading. • When you were small, were there a lot of books in your home? (yes or no) • I get ashamed when _____ • My friends help me with my reading (always describes me, sometimes describes me, never describes me)

Formal Assessments

Formal assessments are standardized and norm-referenced tests used to measure academic achievement and to diagnose learning problems (Gillet, Temple, Temple, & Crawford, 2017). Persons who administer formal assessments need to be sufficiently trained to administer, score, and interpret the assessment. Often, school personnel who administer formal assessments are school psychologists or other specialists.

The best formal assessments have gone through careful evaluation to determine whether they are reliable and valid. The **reliability** of an assessment involves three assumptions:

1. The same results would be obtained from similar, but different test questions— called **internal consistency**,
2. The same result would be obtained if the test was administered on a different day or time—called **stability**,
3. The same result would be obtained if administered by a different tester—called **interrater reliability** (Salvia, Ysseldyke, & Witmer, 2012).

Validity, on the other hand, relates to the extent to which the test items measure the intended construct, such as vocabulary knowledge or reading comprehension. Validity includes an evaluation of whether the test adequately represents the construct being tested, whether the test provides similar results to other trusted tests of the same content, and the extent to which the test measures what it says it does (Gillet et al., 2017). A test that has strong reliability and validity provides confidence in trusting the test results. For this reason, the reliability and validity of an assessment is considered when deciding to use it for educational decisions, particularly if those decisions are high stakes—such as identifying a student as having a disability.

Characteristics of Formal Assessments

Standardized assessments have strict guidelines for how they are administered and scored to ensure that results are trustworthy. These standardized procedures ensure that the test is consistently given following the same steps every time, no matter who is administering the exam, where and when it is administered, and to whom it is administered. When administering a formal reading assessment, it is necessary for procedures laid out by the test publisher to be strictly followed.

The term **norm-referenced** indicates that result can be compared to the performance of other students of the same age, referred to as "referencing the norming group." The norming process involves the selection of a few thousand students across the country at each age and/or grade level of the test to establish "typical" age or grade level performance. In order to make comparisons to norming data, there are a variety of scores produced by norm-referenced tests that need to be understood.

The first type of score is the correct number of items on the assessment, called the **raw score**. This score has limited value until it is converted into a **standard score** that can be compared to the scores of students of the same age or grade in the test's norming group. The scores from the norming group are located in published norming tables and fall within a **normal distribution** between 0 and 160. Figure 2.1 displays the normal distribution. Notice that a standard score of 100 is the mean, and scores are in the average range if they are within one standard deviation of that mean—in other words between 85 and 115. Scores that are two standard deviations from the mean, between 70 and 84 or between 115 and 130, are in the below average or above average range respectively.

Standard scores can also be converted to a **percentile rank** that represents the percentage of scores in a frequency distribution that are equal to or lower than a given score. For example, a student who obtains a standard score of 100 would rank at the 50th percentile, which means she performed better than 50% of her peers on that assessment. Standard scores and percentile ranks are the most accurate and clear way for educators to communicate about

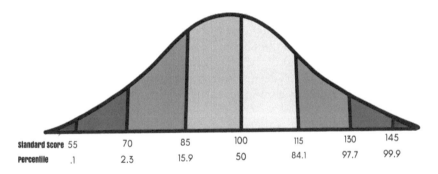

Standard score	55	70	85	100	115	130	145
Percentile	.1	2.3	15.9	50	84.1	97.7	99.9

Figure 2.1 Normal distribution

a student's standardized test performance. Because percentile ranks are easily understood, they are particularly helpful when sharing results with parents.

Many standardized tests also allow age and grade equivalents for students to be determined. **Age equivalents** show the approximate age level at which a student is performing, and a **grade equivalent** is an estimate of the grade level at which he is performing. Because age and grade equivalents are estimates of student ability, parents and educators should use caution when interpreting student performance based on them. These scores are especially limited in utility for interpreting performance of students who are far below expected age or grade level.

Purposes of Formal Assessments of Reading

Formal assessments tend to be **summative**, meaning that they are given after instruction has ended to evaluate how much was learned. Information from formal assessments is used to determine how well students are achieving compared to their same age peers in various aspects of reading. The National Assessment of Educational Progress (NAEP; National Center for Education Statistics, 2009), the Iowa Test of Basic Skills (The University of Iowa, 2014), and the Stanford Achievement Test (SAT; Pearson, 2018) are examples of national tests that include items related to reading performance of students.

Other common formal assessments include end of year state tests of reading performance that are used to evaluate the progress of the individual student and the performance of the school overall—called **adequate yearly progress (AYP)**. Because these assessments are generally given to all students in the school, they are administered in group settings. Traditionally, these tests involve a test booklet and scantron, but increasingly these tests are administered on the computer to allow for faster scoring. Although formal assessments are generally used for assessing how well students have achieved after a period of learning, in some cases, they are used to screen for students that are not achieving as expected so that additional assessments and needed intervention can be provided early.

Formal assessments are also used for diagnostic purposes. Unlike achievement tests that are group administered, diagnostic assessments are typically (but not always) administered individually and data are used in the eligibility process for determining whether a student qualifies for special education services. Examples of diagnostic assessments of achievement, including reading, are the Wide Range Achievement Test-5 (WRAT-5; Wilkinson & Robertson, 2017), the Wechsler Individual Achievement Test-III (WIAT-III; Pearson, 2009), the Kaufman Test of Educational Achievement-3 (K-TEA-3; Kaufman & Kaufman, 2014), and the Woodcock-Johnson Tests of Achievement-IV (WJ-IV; Schrank, Mather, & McGrew, 2014).

Informal Assessments

Informal assessments are any assessments that are not standardized and norm-referenced (Kritikos, 2010). Informal assessments tend to be narrower in scope than formal assessments with more items related to the targeted domain. Because informal assessments are closely related to the content or skills being targeted for instruction, informal assessments are primarily used for instructional decisions. Less extensive training is needed for informal assessments and teachers typically administer them.

Characteristics of Informal Assessments

Informal assessments fall along a continuum from observation of naturally occurring events to structured semi-standardized assessments that are not norm-referenced. For example,

authentic assessments are conducted to capture real world demonstrations of a skill (Johnston & Costello, 2005). This type of assessment is often used in the early grades through observation or student work products that enable evaluation of valued skills that students use on an everyday basis. **Performance-based assessments** are used to evaluate student products for demonstration of academic knowledge, skills or behavior (Cohen & Spenciner, 2003). Performance-based assessments might include portfolios or projects. Both of these types of assessments are generally evaluated using some sort of rubric or checklist.

Other informal assessments commonly used in schools are **criterion-referenced assessments**. As the name implies, criterion-referenced assessments evaluate student performance compared to a predetermined criterion. A teacher-made test or quiz with forced choice and/or essay items is an example. At times, grade level assessments will not be appropriate for a particular student based on his or her skills and abilities. In this case, it is important that the learner be evaluated using developmentally appropriate materials that can accurately assess the student's current level of functioning in addition to how they are progressing with grade level curriculum.

Purposes of Informal Assessments of Reading

Informal assessments tend to be formative, meaning that they are ongoing and assess learning as it occurs. While informal reading assessments can be used for different specific purposes, the overall end goal of these assessments is effective instruction that results in student progress in reading. Informal assessments provide critical information to teachers in real time, allowing them to modify instruction to help students succeed with reading tasks more immediately. Informal assessments are a means to screen for larger issues, to gather data to inform instruction, or to monitor student progress.

Figure 2.2 displays how instruction is informed by data from screening instruments, supplemental assessments, and progress monitoring measures. Notice that regardless of the assessment given, results should always be used to inform instruction. This concept is referred to as "using data to drive instruction" or "data-driven instruction."

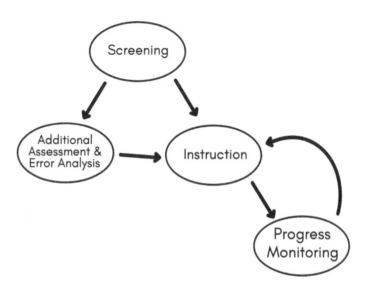

Figure 2.2 Data-driven instruction

A **screening** is an informal assessment instrument used to gauge students' skill levels in a particular reading area or several areas. Screenings are often done at specific junctures to flag students who do not have prerequisite reading skills. Screenings are short in length and easy to administer making it an efficient way to quickly identify the strengths and weaknesses of many students. Data from this assessment will inform the instruction that the teacher provides. However, poor student performance on a screening may indicate that further evaluation is needed (Overton, 2016).

Additional assessment could be comprehensive or skill specific, and it is likely to include an analysis of the types of errors that students consistently make while reading. In the next chapter, you will learn more about one of the most common comprehensive assessments— the informal reading inventory. The final chapters of each of the remaining sections of the book contain more information about skill specific reading assessments.

After instruction, informal assessments can be used to systematically track student progress on a set schedule, called **progress monitoring** (Johnson, Mellard, Fuchs, & McKnight, 2006). For most students, formal progress monitoring in specific reading skills is not needed, but for some students, a regular schedule of tracking progress in specific skill weakness areas is important. Two approaches commonly used for progress monitoring are curriculum-based assessment and curriculum-based measurement (Berkeley & Riccomini, 2017). See Table 2.2 for a comparison of the characteristics of these approaches.

Table 2.2 Curriculum-based Assessment versus Curriculum-based Measurement

Curriculum-based Assessment	*Curriculum-based Measurement*
• Ongoing over time • Items created directly from instruction program to assess mastery of content • Include teacher-made tests of a selected curriculum domain	• Ongoing over time • Items address a wide range of skills sampled from an entire school year • Include standardized procedures for administration, scoring and interpretation

Assessment Application

While reading assessments have unique characteristics, there is a commonality to the flow of activities in the assessment process. When preparing to assess a student's reading, teachers actively think through the steps in the assessment process for each learner they are hoping to evaluate. Specifically, four core areas of the assessment process are considered: selection, administration, scoring, and interpretation. Figure 2.3 highlights guiding questions an educator asks while moving through this assessment process. Note that the steps are sequential with one question needing to be considered and acted upon before proceeding to the next. Additionally, thoughtfulness is needed at every step in the process in order for the most accurate reading data to be collected on a student.

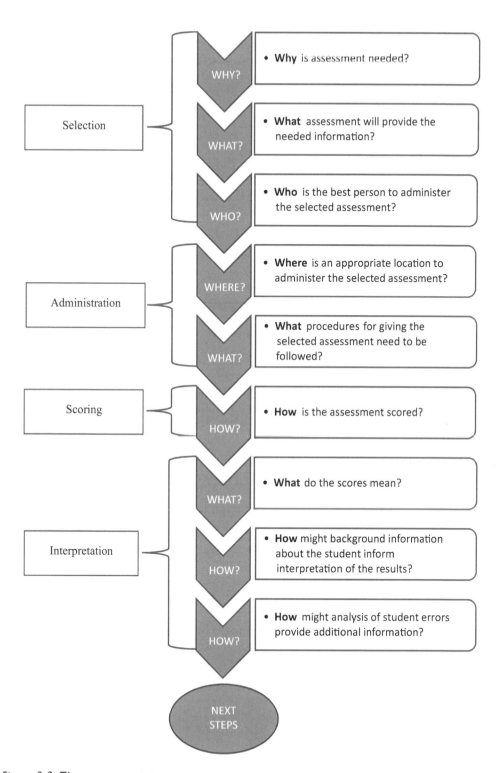

Selection

- **Why** is assessment needed?
- **What** assessment will provide the needed information?
- **Who** is the best person to administer the selected assessment?

Administration

- **Where** is an appropriate location to administer the selected assessment?
- **What** procedures for giving the selected assessment need to be followed?

Scoring

- **How** is the assessment scored?

Interpretation

- **What** do the scores mean?
- **How** might background information about the student inform interpretation of the results?
- **How** might analysis of student errors provide additional information?

WHY?

WHAT?

WHO?

WHERE?

WHAT?

HOW?

WHAT?

HOW?

HOW?

NEXT STEPS

Figure 2.3 The assessment process

Selection

The first part of the assessment process is to select an appropriate assessment instrument. Specifically, it needs to be determined *why* an assessment is needed, *what* assessment will provide the needed information, and *who* is qualified to administer the assessment. When considering why an assessment is needed, it is important to be very clear about what the purpose of giving a particular assessment to a child would be. Is it to assess what words a student recognizes? Is it to assess his understanding of text? Thinking through why the assessment is needed helps the teacher to best identify which assessment to give.

In addition to considering what assessment will provide the needed information, it also needs to be determined whether a formal or informal assessment would be more appropriate. As you have learned in this chapter, formal and informal assessments have different purposes and result in information that is distinct in nature.

Additionally, it must be decided who will administer the assessment. This requires making a determination about the person or persons who are capable of administering the particular assessment to a student in terms of training and qualifications. Informal assessments are typically administered by a general education classroom teacher or another specialist (such as a reading specialist or a special education teacher), depending on the level of expertise needed for the specific reading assessment. Formal assessments require specialized training and are generally administered by a school psychologist or specially trained special education teacher.

Administration

The next step in the process is to administer the assessment. In this step, it will need to be determined *where* the assessment will be administered as well as *what* procedures need to be followed. For individual reading assessments, a quiet one-on-one environment is often needed. It is important to carefully think about what space will be most suitable based on this need, including when the space will be free from distractions. For instance, when other students are engaged in center-based learning in other parts of the classroom, a one-on-one informal reading assessment in the general education classroom may be possible.

A Focus on Preparing Testing Materials

In order to minimize impact on instructional time and keep students engaged, it is important for the assessment process to be as efficient as possible. This means that it is critical for the tester to ensure that all needed testing materials are located and organized before sitting down to test a student. This would include:

- Making all needed copies of word lists, passages and test protocols. It is best to have all possible levels available in case a student performs better or worse than anticipated.
- Having ready writing utensils (and backups) and a writing surface, such as a clipboard.
- Having a timer ready (including extra batteries).
- Organizing needed materials so that the tester can quickly access anything needed for the assessment. A student should never be left waiting during an assessment!

Next, the test administrator reviews what procedures are required when giving the assessment. This requires being thoughtful about all the details needed for using the reading evaluation with the student, from the materials, to the timing, to the selection of the items to be given within a specific measure. For example, the teacher might decide to break up the assessment administration into developmentally appropriate lengths of time over a number of test sessions. When administering the assessment, any administration rules are carefully followed and the tester is careful to document any behaviors the student displays that would be pertinent to interpreting the test results. These behaviors were discussed in the "Background Information" section of this chapter.

Scoring

The next step in the process requires understanding *how* to score the assessment. How a reading measure is scored is based on the items the student answered correctly or incorrectly. Formal assessments tend to have strict scoring rules based on a student's age or grade, while informal assessments are often more flexible and can be individualized based on a student's needs.

Interpretation

The next step in the process is the interpretation of the results to determine *what* the results mean. This includes considering *how* student background information and consistent student errors help explain student performance. With formal assessments, interpretation involves comparing the student's results to norms of students of the same age or grade level. With informal assessments, a student's abilities may be interpreted based on curriculum or skills taught and the student's level of mastery of these skills. In addition, student responses are analyzed carefully to look for error patterns that can help to inform instruction. Finally, background information about the student is considered as part of the interpretation process, because this information allows the test results to be contextualized.

Next Steps

In some cases, the initial assessment selected may not provide all of the information that is needed and a supplemental assessment may need to be administered and/or an analysis of student errors may need to be conducted to provide more information about where the student is struggling. In this situation, the next step is additional assessment.

After assessment, the next step should always include using information gained to inform instruction. Assessment results provide important information about what skills to teach and how intensively. Assessment results also provide information to help with making decisions about what materials and texts to use in instruction. You will learn about the different skill areas where assessment might need to be provided throughout this book. Another consideration for instruction is decision making about what ongoing assessments will be given to students to assess their skill progression on a continual basis and determine the effectiveness of instruction that has been provided.

A final next step is to consider how collective results will be shared with relevant stakeholders such as the parent, reading specialist, special educator, ELL specialist, or speech–language clinician. Parents always need to be kept abreast of findings from any assessment that is given to their child. School-based stakeholders also need to be informed, especially when a student may require instruction by multiple specialists within the school. If all stakeholders cannot physically get together, it would be important to write up the results in an informal reading report that explains the results and next steps.

Application Vignette: A New Student in Mrs. Jones' 4th Grade Classroom

During the second quarter of the school year, a new student named Kevin moves into the area and is placed in Mrs. Jones' 4th grade classroom. As is often the case, few records have accompanied Kevin to the school and little is known about his specific academic skills. At this time of the year, the teacher has already assigned her students to groups for reading and writing, and she would like to determine the most appropriate group placement for Kevin. She knows the first step will be to assess, so she asks herself a series of questions to help herself work through the assessment process.

Why is Assessment Needed?

Mrs. Jones needs to obtain a comprehensive picture of Kevin's reading strengths and weaknesses to effectively teach in the areas where skill development is needed. Obtaining a comprehensive picture of Kevin's reading, which addresses both the major areas of word identification and comprehension, warrants some form of reading assessment.

What Assessment Will Give Me the Needed Information?

The next step will be for Mrs. Jones to determine what type of assessment should be administered to get the comprehensive information needed for reading instruction. Mrs. Jones will first need to consider whether a formal or informal measure would best give the full picture of the student's reading. Since Mrs. Jones is not trying to understand how the student performs relative to peers, but rather, is interested in information that can inform instruction, Mrs. Jones decides to use an informal reading assessment versus a formal one. An informal reading assessment will be more likely to clearly identify the student's specific reading strengths and weaknesses and best aid the teacher in pinpointing the appropriate areas of reading that should be the focus of instruction.

After deciding on an informal measure generally, Mrs. Jones needs to select a specific type of reading evaluation to gather this comprehensive picture of the student's reading. She decides to administer an informal reading inventory (IRI). The IRI is a reading assessment that is used to identify a student's reading level to assist in the selection of appropriately leveled instructional materials and the pedagogical approach to instruction. While it is not a diagnostic measure used to determine a reading disability, an IRI helps figure out what types of reading instruction will meet students' needs because it evaluates word identification, fluency, and comprehension abilities.

Who is the Best Person to Administer the Selected Assessment?

Many teachers in the school, including the reading specialist and the special education teacher who co-teaches with Mrs. Jones, are qualified to administer the IRI. However, because Mrs. Jones is also qualified to administer this assessment, she elects to administer it herself.

Where is the Appropriate Location to Administer the Selected Assessment?

Ideally, an IRI would be administered in a separate space outside the classroom, but since it is an informal assessment, this is not required. It is not feasible for Mrs. Jones to administer the IRI in a separate space outside the classroom, so she decides to administer the assessment in a quiet space in the room while the other students are completing independent seatwork. Because the length of the assessment will be determined by the student's performance, she knows that this may take several days to complete.

How is the Assessment Administered and Scored?

Although Mrs. Jones has attended a training provided in her school district about how to administer and score an IRI, she reviews the testing guidelines to refresh her memory of the nuances of the test. She knows that oral reading assessments are very similar in how they are administered and scored and it would be easy to mix up procedures with another assessment. She also uses this time to gather all of the testing materials that will be needed. (You will learn more about administration and scoring procedures for IRIs in the next chapter, Chapter 3.)

How is the Selected Assessment Interpreted?

Mrs. Jones knows that interpreting the results of the IRI will be a multi-step process. First, she considers Kevin's performance level with decoding and comprehension. She sees from the assessment results that the student is decoding at an instructional level with 2nd, 3rd, and 4th grade text, and he is at an independent level with 1st grade text. The IRI results also indicate that his comprehension is at an instructional level with grade level text and he is independent with material a year below grade level.

Mrs. Jones knows that students tend to make consistent errors and so her next step is to do a careful analysis of the errors that Kevin makes while reading. She notices that Kevin misses many phonetically regular words read in isolation that he reads correctly when reading connected text. This suggests to her that he is using context clues when reading passages to help him figure out unknown words, but he does not appear to have strong phonics strategies. She also notices that he tends to leave endings off words both when reading words in isolation and in connected text. This tells her that he may not be attending to important aspects of morphology and syntax, which is likely to hinder his reading and writing development.

What are Next Steps?

First, Mrs. Jones will use the assessment results to select the level of text she should use in instruction and assign for homework. Results from the decoding portion of the assessment tell her that the student has some gaps in word identification skills that she will need to address in instruction, perhaps including Tier 2 intervention if he does not make progress quickly in the core curriculum (Tier 1). Based on the error analysis, Mrs. Jones will use a phonics-based approach for both reading and spelling with special attention to word endings.

Mrs. Jones also plans to administer a supplemental phonological awareness assessment to determine whether the problems that Kevin is having with decoding are stemming from an underlying issue with phonology. If the supplemental assessment confirms that this is also an area of need, Mrs. Jones will incorporate phonemic awareness activities into her instruction as well. The decoding results also tell her that homework practice to improve fluent reading should be with 1st grade text. Mrs.

Jones knows that she will need to monitor Kevin's performance carefully to ensure that he is making sufficient progress.

Kevin's relatively stronger performance on the comprehension portion of the assessment tells her that the student has cognitive strengths that are helping him compensate for problems with accurately identifying all the words in text. She will focus instruction for comprehension on grade level strategies that the student will then be able to practice with text that he can decode at an independent level—initially this will be first grade text.

Mrs. Jones considers whether there may be others with whom she should share the findings. Kevin is not significantly behind expected reading performance for his grade, so she does not think that it is necessary to pull in other specialists in the school at this time. However, she plans to share Kevin's assessment results with his parents at the first parent–teacher conference and give them strategies for supporting his reading practice at home.

References

Berkeley, S., & Riccomini, P. J. (2017). Academic progress monitoring. In J. M. Kauffman, D. P. Hallahan, & P. C. Pullen (Eds.), *Handbook of special education* (2nd ed., pp. 334–347). New York, NY: Routledge.

Cohen, L. G., & Spenciner, L. J. (2003). *Assessment of children and youth with special needs.* Boston, MA: Allyn & Bacon.

Gillet, J. W., Temple, C. A., Temple, C. N., & Crawford, A. N. (2017). *Understanding reading problems* (9th ed.). Boston, MA: Pearson.

Guthrie, J., & Wigfield, A. (2000). Engagement and motivation in reading. In M. Kamil, P. Mosenthal, D. Pearson, & R. Barr (Eds.), *Handbook of reading research* (pp. 518–533). Mahwah, NJ: Earlbaum.

Individuals with Disabilities Education Act, 20 U.S.C. § 1400. (2004).

Johnson, E., Mellard, D. F., Fuchs, D., & McKnight, M. A. (2006). *Responsiveness to intervention (RTI): How to do it* [RTI manual]. Lawrence, KS: National Research Center on Learning Disabilities.

Johnston, P., & Costello, P. (2005). Principles of literacy assessment. *Reading Research Quarterly, 40,* 256–267.

Kaufman, A. S., & Kaufman, N. L. (2014). *Kaufman Test of Educational Achievement* (3rd ed.). San Antonio, TX: Pearson.

Kritikos, E. P. (2010). *Special education assessment: Issues and strategies affecting today's classrooms.* Upper Saddle River, NJ: Merrill.

Kush, J. C., & Watkins, M. W. (1996). Long-term stability of children's attitudes toward reading. *The Journal of Educational Research, 89,* 315–319.

National Center for Education Statistics. (2009). *National Assessment of Educational Progress: An overview of NAEP.* Washington, DC: National Center for Education Statistics, Institute of Education Sciences, U.S. Dept. of Education.

Overton, T. (2016). *Assessing learners with special needs: An applied approach.* London: Pearson.

Pearson. (2009). *Wechsler Individual Achievement Test* (3rd ed.). San Antonio, TX: Pearson.

Pearson. (2018). *Stanford Achievement Test series* (10th ed.). San Antonio, TX: Pearson.

Salvia, J., Ysseldyke, J., & Witmer, S. (2012). *Assessment: In special and inclusive education.* Belmont, CA: Cengage Learning.

Schrank, F., Mather, N., & McGrew, K. S. (2014). *Woodcock-Johnson Tests of Achievement* (4th ed.). Orlando, FL: Houghton Mifflin Harcourt.

The University of Iowa. (2014). *Iowa assessments.* Orlando, FL: Houghton Mifflin Harcourt.

Wilkinson, G. S., & Robertson, G. J. (2017). *Wide Reading Achievement Test* (5th ed.). San Antonio, TX: Pearson.

Chapter 3

Informal Reading Inventories

Fundamentals of Informal Reading Inventories

The term **informal reading inventory (IRI)** is the general term for all comprehensive informal assessments. While teachers can create their own IRI, the process can be time consuming and there are many free and published IRIs available on the market today. There are strengths and weaknesses to each of these IRIs that teachers need to consider if they are selecting an assessment, although in many cases the assessment will be pre-selected by their school district. Table 3.1 below highlights some of the most commonly used IRIs. Regardless of the specific IRI selected, all IRIs provide important information about a student's reading skills that can be used to inform instruction.

Reading Skills Assessed

All IRIs provide information about a student's proficiency in word identification, fluency, and reading comprehension. However, additional information about other important reading skills can be obtained from an IRI as well, including information about the student's language development, background knowledge, and motivation for reading. Each of these areas of reading are described next.

Table 3.1 Informal Reading Inventory Descriptions

IRI	Publisher	Website for Test Description
Analytical Reading Inventory	Pearson	https://www.pearson.com/us
Basic Reading Inventory	Kendall Hunt	https://he.kendallhunt.com
Burns/Roe Informal Reading Inventory	Cengage Learning	https://www.cengage.co.uk
Classroom Reading Inventory	McGraw-Hill	https://www.mheducation.com
Developmental Reading Assessment (DRA)	Pearson	https://www.pearsonassessments.com
Ekwall/Shanker Reading Inventory	Pearson	http://ptgmedia.pearsoncmg.com
Jennings Informal Reading Assessment	Unknown publisher	http://wps.ablongman.com/wps/media/objects/2688/2753469/Richek_AppD.pdf
Morris Informal Reading Inventory	The Guilford Press	https://www.guilford.com
Qualitative Reading Inventory (QRI)	Pearson	https://www.pearson.com

Word Identification

Word identification refers to a student's ability to identify phonetically regular words both through using knowledge of letters and corresponding sounds to decode words and through automatic recognition of words by sight. A student's word identification is assessed by evaluating the words that a student reads incorrectly when reading aloud—called **miscues**. Students tend to be consistent in the types of errors that they make giving important clues to teachers as to where instruction is most needed. Therefore, in addition to the number of words that a student reads incorrectly, teachers carefully analyze the types of errors that are made. In order to conduct an analysis of student miscues, special notations are used to note the specific types of errors. Figure 3.1 shows standard miscue notations as well as notations for items that are not miscues, meaning they are not counted as errors for scoring purposes, but are noted, nonetheless.

MISCUES	NOT MISCUES (but should be recorded)
Omission: Circle a word that is not read. I saw a ⬭black⬭ cat.	**Repetition:** Draw a line below the repeated word. I saw a <u>black</u> cat.
Insertion: Insert an added word with a caret notation. big I saw a ∧ black cat.	**Hesitation of correctly pronounced word:** Write an 'H' over the hesitated word. H I saw a black cat.
Substitution/mispronunciation: Write the misread word above the word. was I saw a black cat.	**Omitted punctuation:** Circle ignored punctuation. I saw a black cat⬭
Reversal: Use notation below to indicate that words were read out of order (counts as two errors). I saw a black cat.	**Student correction:** Write an 'SC' over the initial error. was SC I saw a black cat.

Figure 3.1 Standard miscue notations

In addition to common miscues, there are additional errors that may occur during an assessment that the test administrator should know how to address. These include:

- omissions of an entire line or phrase,
- repeated mispronunciations,
- mispronunciations of proper names, and
- mispronunciations due to accent or dialect.

When a student omits an entire line or phrase, it is counted as only one error. The reasoning behind this is that the student has lost his place only one time, and therefore, it counts as a single error. Note that it is acceptable to allow students to use a mask, such as a plain bookmark, to help themselves keep their place while reading when administering an IRI.

When a student repeatedly mispronounces the same word in different places in the passage, it is scored incorrectly each time. This is why it is critically important not to pronounce any words for a student during an assessment as this has the potential to artificially inflate the student's reading level. Instead, if a student is stuck for longer than three seconds, the tester will prompt the student to "keep going."

Scoring rules vary for proper names. If a student mispronounces a name the same way each time, it only counts as an error one time—pronouncing *Magellan* as "Magullun," for example. If a student mispronounces a name changing the gender of the character, it is a miscue each time the error occurs—pronouncing "Michelle" for *Michael*, for example. If a student mispronounces a name differently each time, it is counted as an error in each instance—for example, one time saying "Mary," the next time saying "Maria," and the next time "Marie." These same principles apply to proper names of places as well.

When administering IRIs, students are never penalized for mispronunciations of words due to their accent or dialect. Students are also not penalized for mispronunciations of words due to speech–language disorders. If the tester is not certain whether the pronunciation is because of a speech issue or a reading issue, the tester can query further *after* the passage has been read and all questions have been asked and answered. Specifically, the tester might say aloud one of the missed words suspected to be a mispronunciation due to a speech problem and ask the student to repeat it aloud. If the student is not able to pronounce the word (the student says "sip" instead of "ship" or "cat" instead of "cats," for example), then the error was likely due to a speech issue. If the student is able to repeat the word enunciating all the sounds in the word (the student says "ship" for "ship"), then the mispronunciation in text was likely a true reading miscue.

Reading Fluency

Reading fluency is how quickly and accurately a student reads and it is necessary for adequate comprehension. Speed is determined by how quickly a student reads. Accuracy is determined through the number of miscues that a student makes while reading. Combined, speed and accuracy are referred to as the student's **reading rate**. Number of correct words read in one minute is the most frequently used measure of fluency.

Reading Comprehension

Reading comprehension refers to a student's understanding of what they have read. To evaluate comprehension, IRIs include comprehension questions that students answer after reading a passage. Most commercial IRIs label each question asked after the student reads to reflect the cognitive demands required of the student. There are many ways to classify demands of questions on a reader; however, IRIs tend to focus on explicit questions and implicit questions. **Explicit questions** require a student to recall information that was stated directly in the passage. **Implicit questions** require a student to infer information based on information provided in text or using information in the text along with the reader's existing knowledge and experiences. Additionally, in lower grade level passages, published IRIs generally include a retell option that can give additional insights into a student's ability to recall, sequence, and articulate information—all indicators of comprehension.

Other Skills

IRIs provide insights into other skills related to reading as well. Oral language is foundational to word identification and reading comprehension. Through the process of administering an IRI, anecdotal observations reveal a lot about a student's oral language development. For example, the tester will observe and note the complexity of sentences and the vocabulary that the student uses in conversation with the tester and in responding to questions. The tester will also note any suspected speech–language problems or English language acquisition issues that might be interfering with a student's performance.

Information from an IRI also provides insights into what the student already knows about the topics of the passages read—called **background knowledge**. Background knowledge can include student knowledge of words, or **vocabulary**. Vocabulary plays an important role in reading comprehension, so information gained from paying close attention to the words a student uses to express ideas can be revealing. This background knowledge can also include a student's existing knowledge of **reading strategies** for reading and understanding text. As you learned in Chapter 1, proficient readers approach text strategically, while struggling readers do not.

Student attitudes toward reading can be revealed through student behavior and affect during the assessment. For example, one student may prattle on about favorite books, past experiences, and people in their life that they share reading experiences with even when not directly asked. Conversely, another student may display a flat affect, attempt to avoid the reading tasks of the assessment, or give minimal responses to questions posed by the tester. These sorts of behaviors give clues to the motivation each student may have for reading. This information is important for a teacher to be aware of because motivation can support or impede student efforts to learn to read.

Reading Levels

In education, the term "level" is used to refer to both the difficulty of text and the degree of student proficiency in reading text. Although these concepts can be interdependent, they represent distinct concepts.

Text Level

Text level refers to the difficulty of text, which is based on complexity of writing and difficulty of concepts and vocabulary. Two of the most commonly used levels are grade levels and lexiles. A comparison of these two leveling systems is presented in Table 3.2. IRIs include passages that are leveled by grade. Leveled passages available in an IRI typically range from primer or pre-primer to 8th grade, although some IRIs also include high school level text. Lexiles reflect a range of text difficulty as well and are commonly used to assist in the selection of appropriate independent reading material for students.

Table 3.2 Grade and Lexile Levels

Grade	Lexile Levels	Grade	Lexile Levels
K (primer)	BR40L–230L	6	855L–1165L
1	BR120L–295L	7	925L–1235L
2	170L–545L	8	985L–1295L
3	415L–760L	9	1040L–1350L
4	635L–950L	10	1085L–1400L
5	770L–1080L	11 and 12	1130L–1440L

Source: Lexile data obtained from MetaMetrics, Creator of The Lexile Framework for Reading. https://lexile.com/parents-students/measuring-growth-lexile-measures/evaluating-performance-by-grade/

Some IRIs contain both narrative and expository passages at each grade level. Even though a narrative and an expository passage may represent the same grade level where respective texts are used, teachers should keep in mind that expository texts tend to be more challenging for students. Administering both a narrative passage and an expository passage at the student's grade level can help reveal any difficulties that the student might have with specific text structures. (For students reading below grade level, evaluating both narrative and expository of text at the level where instruction is provided would be more appropriate.) This is particularly important in the upper grades where expository texts, such as textbooks, are more prominently used in content area classrooms.

Student Reading Level

"Level" can also refer to how well a student reads a particular text, called a student's **reading level**. Although typically referred to as a singular level, a student's reading level actually represents both a student's word identification and comprehension performance. Further, an IRI yields three types of student performance levels:

- independent level,
- frustrational level,
- instructional level.

A student's **independent level** is the level of text that is easy for the student—with the student having strong word recognition and comprehension and needing very little assistance, if any. Independent level text is appropriate for independent reading without assistance, such as homework. **Frustrational level** text is too difficult for a student—with the student making many errors in word identification and showing limited comprehension. Frustrational text should be avoided. A student's **instructional level** is the level of text that is "just right"—meaning that it is challenging for the reader, yet still comfortable (Gillet, Temple, & Crawford, 2004). At this level, word recognition and comprehension are good, but some assistance with word identification may be needed, particularly for new skills and strategies. Instructional level text should be used for instruction. Thus, when deciding what text to use with students, it is helpful to follow the "Goldilocks principle": independent level text is easy, frustrational level text is too hard, and instructional level text is just right for teaching (see Figure 3.2). You will learn more about student levels of performance later in this chapter.

Figure 3.2 The Goldilocks principle

Assessment Application

As you learned in the last chapter (Chapter 2), there is a multi-step process that educators go through when assessing a student: selection, administration, scoring, and interpretation.

Selection

IRIs are criterion-referenced assessments. As you will recall from the last chapter, this means that the scores obtained are compared to a criterion. In the case of an IRI, the criterion is the student's level of performance (instructional, independent, frustrational) on reading passages that are leveled by grade. The IRI is an excellent choice when comprehensive information about a student's reading is desired as a mechanism to make instructional decisions.

Purpose and Information Obtained from an IRI

IRIs are widely used in schools because of the wealth of information that can be gained from them. IRIs can be used to determine the severity of a student's reading problems in the areas of word identification and comprehension relative to grade level expectations. This information is then used to select appropriate text for instruction (the student's instructional level) and for independent practice (the student's independent level). In addition, IRIs can be used to determine student strengths and weaknesses in word identification and comprehension. This provides teachers with information about specific skills that should be targeted for instruction. Additional information about a student's fluency, language development, background knowledge, and attitudes toward reading can also be obtained.

In addition, results from an IRI can be used to document student growth. Periodic administration of the IRI (generally at the beginning and end of the school year) can help determine changes in a student's reading skills, over time. When using an IRI to evaluate student growth, it is important to ensure that the same types of passages are being compared. Expository text tends to be more difficult than narrative text (Saenz & Fuchs, 2002), so comparing one to the other can result in an over- or under-estimation of a student's growth.

Qualifications to Administer an IRI

When first learning how to administer an IRI, teachers will find attending a training to be helpful. However, teachers with a foundation in reading or experience giving other reading assessments may feel prepared to administer the assessment after reading the testing manual. The person selected to administer the IRI can vary based on the purpose of the assessment. When an IRI is administered to an entire class to assess student performance with grade level material, the general education teacher would typically administer the IRI. In cases where there is a concern about an individual student and a complete IRI and error analysis is needed, the assessment is more likely to be administered by a specialist in the building, such as a reading specialist or a special education teacher. If a student is in the early stages of learning English, an English as a second language teacher, or other teacher who speaks the student's first language, might be a good choice to administer the assessment. These specialists are also more likely to be involved in administration of an

IRI in the upper grades where individual assessments of students' oral reading occur less often as part of general education practice.

Administration

Assessment procedures for an IRI can vary depending on whether the purpose is to assess a student's ability to read grade level text or whether the purpose is to determine the level of text where the student reads instructionally, which may or may not be grade level text. Administration procedures will also vary between teacher-developed IRIs created using curriculum materials (e.g., Carnine, Silbert, Kame'enui, Slocum, & Travers, 2017) and published IRIs. Even within published IRIs, there can be variation in administration procedures, such as the timing for administering word list retell and silent passage options (e.g., Gillet et al., 2004). This chapter will present one common way to administer an IRI to develop a complete profile of the student's reading ability. This approach is most helpful for obtaining the comprehensive information needed to identify and support struggling readers.

Regardless of the purpose or approach, an IRI is one of the more structured informal assessments, and as such, there are procedures that need to be followed in order for the results to be meaningful. However, teachers have some flexibility when administering the assessment; for example, teachers need to give the directions specified for the assessment, but they can use their own words rather than reading from a script. Teachers also have a bit of latitude with scoring and interpretation because there are judgement calls that need to be made during administration as well as scoring. Because there is a certain amount of "gray area" with this type of assessment, it is especially important for teachers to understand which procedures cannot be altered without interfering with the accuracy of the results. These considerations are highlighted throughout this section.

The Test Setting

Although a separate room would be ideal for administering any assessment, if a separate room is not feasible, teachers will structure the testing situation so that it facilitates enough quiet and privacy to successfully administer a one-on-one assessment. This situation could be arranged in the classroom when other students are engaged in centers-based learning or independent work time. The entire administration could be done over several days, as long as questions about a passage are asked during the same testing session in which the passage is read. While it is not required for the IRI to be conducted in a separate space, it is important for teachers to consider potential reasons that a student would not demonstrate his or her true ability in the planned testing environment. For example, administering an IRI to students one at a time in the back of an early elementary classroom would not be a problem because reading with students individually is part of the typical instruction and students are not likely to feel uncomfortable. However, administering an IRI to a 9th grader who is struggling with reading at the back of a biology classroom would be hugely problematic. Being asked to read aloud and answer questions aloud within hearing range of peers would likely embarrass the student causing him not do his best and making any resulting information untrustworthy. In this latter scenario, a separate testing space would be required.

General Assessment Procedures

In this chapter, guidelines commonly found across IRIs are described. However, because there are variations among specific IRIs, it is extremely important that test administrators review the administration directions for the specific assessment that is selected. The general steps for administering an IRI are to:

1. Administer word lists by having the student read lists of words aloud while the teacher records any errors.
2. Administer reading passages. First, the student reads aloud while the teacher records any errors. Then, the student is asked questions to determine what he or she understands about the passages.

In order to determine the independent, instructional, and frustrational levels for a student in the areas of word identification and comprehension, multiple passages need to be administered.

In other words, to determine a student's level of performance for word identification, the student's independent, instructional, and frustrational levels must be determined. For most students, the level of performance for word identification and comprehension will be the same. However, for a relatively small number of students, level of performance for word identification and comprehension will be different. Because this sort of atypical development is characteristic of students who have or are at-risk for serious reading problems, it is important to monitor students with these profiles carefully.

Once all needed passages have been administered, the student's level of performance is determined and an error analysis is conducted to identify additional information that can inform instruction. Depending on the IRI used, additional supplemental information can also be obtained.

Procedures for Administering Word Lists

The primary purpose of administering the word lists is to determine the starting point for passage reading. Information obtained from student performance reading words in isolation can also be helpful when conducting an error analysis after the assessment is complete. Error analysis will be described in more detail later in this chapter.

The following steps are followed when administering word lists:

1. Begin by choosing a word list that is two to three grade levels below the child's chronological grade placement.
2. Administer the first word list by asking the student to read the words in the list one at a time and recording student responses as accurate or inaccurate.
3. Count the total number of errors and compare this total to test guidelines to determine whether the list is at the student's independent, instructional or frustration level.

    *   If the student scores at the independent level, *move up* one grade level and administer this list.
    *   If the student scores at the instructional or frustrational level, *move down* one grade level and administer this list.

4. Continue until you have found the student's independent, instructional, and frustrational levels.
5. Determine the word list that was at the student's highest instructional level. This is the passage where you should begin passage administration.

Administration of word lists might be skipped if the IRI is being used solely to determine students' performance level with grade level text. For example, if a 5th grade teacher is using the IRI to assess an entire class's level of performance with 5th grade text only, administering the word lists is not necessary.

Procedures for Administering Passages

When administering a complete IRI, the tester should begin with the passage that corresponds to the grade level of the word list that was the student's highest instructional level.

Next, the passage administration steps are followed:

1. Ask the student the background knowledge questions and record the student responses on the test protocol.
2. Place the passage in front of the student and ask the student to read the passage aloud. While the student is reading, record miscues on the test protocol. During this step, the tester may use a one-minute timer to notate the last word read after one minute (for later use in calculating fluency). Note that the student should not stop reading when the timer goes off, but should read the entire passage while the tester records miscues.
3. Remove the passage from the student and ask the student the comprehension questions after the passage. Record student responses on the test protocol.
4. Score the assessment to determine next steps.

A rationale for each of these steps is provided in Table 3.3. These steps should be repeated until the student's instructional, independent, and frustrational grade levels are determined for both word identification and comprehension.

Scoring Passages

A student's level of performance is obtained for both word recognition (student ability to accurately identify words in the passages) and comprehension (student ability to understand content presented in the passages). It is important to consider word identification and comprehension separately because they do not develop at the same rate for all students.

Developmental differences between these skill areas can give important clues to where a student is struggling. They can also give an indication of where modifications and accommodations may need to be provided.

The degree of student accuracy required to be at the independent, instructional, or frustrational level is presented in Table 3.3. These criteria are used in the following scoring procedures:

1. Score the word identification, fluency and comprehension portions of the assessment:

    *   Word identification—Count the total number of miscues made by the student while reading the passage aloud. Then, compare this number to test guidelines to determine whether the passage is at the student's independent, instructional or frustrational level.
    *   Fluency—Count the number of words read in one minute. Then, subtract the number of errors that occurred within that minute to determine the student's oral reading rate, or fluency.
    *   Comprehension—Count the number of comprehension questions about the passage that the student answers correctly. Then, compare this number to the test guidelines to determine whether the student's comprehension is at an independent, instructional or frustrational level.

Table 3.3 Informal Reading Inventory Levels

	Independent	Instructional	Frustrational
Word Recognition	≥ 95%	≥ 90%	< 90%
Comprehension	≥ 95%	≥ 70%	< 70%

2. After scoring, the tester needs to decide what passage should be administered next. Specifically:

   • If the student scores at an independent level, the tester should *move up* one grade level and administer this passage.
   • If the student scores at an instructional or frustrational level, the tester should *move down* one grade level and administer this passage.

3. Continue until you have found the student's independent, instructional, and frustrational levels.

A Focus on Advanced Administration Tips

We never want to over-assess students, and as such, there are some advanced administration tips to prevent this concern. Consider the following scenarios that might occur during testing:

Scenario #1

A student scores at a frustrational level for comprehension, but he scores at an instructional or independent level for decoding. Moving to a higher grade level is necessary to determine the student's highest instructional level for decoding, but the comprehension questions for the passage will almost certainly be too difficult for the student. What should the tester do?

Advanced administration tip:

Administer the next highest grade level, but only score oral reading (decoding errors) and fluency. Do not ask the comprehension questions.

Scenario #2

A student scores at a frustrational level for decoding, but she scores at an instructional or independent level for comprehension. Moving to a higher level is necessary to determine the student's highest instructional level for comprehension, but decoding the passage aloud will almost certainly be cumbersome and potentially embarrassing for the student. What should the tester do?

Advanced administration tip:

Administer the next highest grade level, but if you think you have learned all you can about decoding, allow the student to read the passage silently instead of aloud.

It is important to be cautious when referring to a student's independent, instructional, and frustrational levels because student performance can be influenced (positively or negatively) by background knowledge, text structure (narrative vs. expository), and whether the passage was read orally versus silently. Occasionally, a student may have an outlier level where a judgement call needs to be made. For example, a student has the following comprehension levels:

- 2nd grade independent,
- 3rd grade frustrational,
- 4th grade instructional.

On its face, these levels may seem like an error. However, if the student knew a tremendous amount about the topic and vocabulary within the 4th grade passage, that might explain the unusually strong understanding of the passage. Conversely, if the student knew a great deal about the 2nd and 4th grade passages, but nothing at all about the 3rd grade passage, it might explain why the student did not understand as much as expected from the 3rd grade passage.

Application Vignette: Administering an IRI from Beginning to End

In the last chapter, a scenario was presented about Mrs. Jones who has a new student, Kevin, in her 4th grade class. Few records accompanied him to his new school and Mrs. Jones worked through the full assessment process to learn more about Kevin's reading performance. This vignette will illustrate the steps she took to administer a complete IRI.

Word Lists

From the IRI training that Mrs. Jones attended, she knows that she will need to administer the word lists first. To begin, Mrs. Jones decides to start with the 1st grade word list because it is three years below Kevin's grade level. She knows this will increase the likelihood that Kevin will do well on his first attempt, which will be important if testing indicates that Kevin has a serious reading problem.

While Kevin reads the lists of words aloud, Mrs. Jones marks words as correct or incorrect, making sure to make a notation next to every word. She knows that if she only makes a notation for misread words this may make Kevin nervous, or worse, inadvertently cue Kevin to his errors, prompting him to try to correct them. Because Mrs. Jones needs to obtain as much information about Kevin as possible, she uses timed/untimed scoring procedures. This means she scores any word as incorrect when Kevin does not read it automatically (within three seconds); however, she also notes words that Kevin can read more slowly by sounding them out. She knows this will help her to determine skills where Kevin has gaps or needs more practice.

When Kevin finishes reading the first list of words, Mrs. Jones uses the scoring guidelines for the assessment to determine whether his reading is at an independent, instructional or frustrational level. She then continues administering additional word lists until she has identified his independent, instructional, and frustrational levels for reading words in isolation.

Passages

Once Mrs. Jones has finished administering all appropriate word lists, she moves on to administering the reading passages, where Kevin will read passages aloud and then answer comprehension questions. To begin, Mrs. Jones selects one of the graded passages that corresponds to the highest grade level word list for which Kevin read at an instructional level.

Background Knowledge

Before asking Kevin to read the passage, Mrs. Jones asks him a few of the background knowledge questions related to the passage and jots down his responses on the test protocol. She knows this will be helpful for interpreting any outlier comprehension scores. Students tend to understand more of what they read when they have background knowledge and vocabulary about the subject matter, and they tend to understand less of what they read when they do not have background knowledge and vocabulary about the subject matter.

Mrs. Jones knows that asking a few questions before asking the student to read aloud breaks the ice a bit when students are nervous about reading. Further, how a student responds, including non-verbal body language, generally gives Mrs. Jones a feel for student attitudes about reading as well as a general indication about the student's oral language abilities.

Word Identification

After asking the background knowledge questions, Mrs. Jones puts a copy of the story in front of Kevin to read and she puts the test protocol of the same passage on her clipboard. She tells Kevin that she is going to make notes on her paper to help her remember what happens while he is reading and that he should do his best reading. She also mentions that she will be using a timer to help her remember when to make some notes and that he should just ignore it.

When Kevin begins reading, Mrs. Jones uses miscue notations to indicate mistakes that he makes while reading. She continues recording errors throughout the entire passage, including noting in the passage when the timer goes off at a one-minute mark. When Kevin finishes reading, Mrs. Jones uses the scoring guidelines for the assessment to determine whether his reading is at an independent, instructional or frustrational level. After she asks the comprehension questions for this passage, she will use this information to make decisions about additional passages that will need to be administered. Regardless of how Kevin does on the comprehension items, Mrs. Jones will continue passage administration until she has identified his independent, instructional, and frustrational levels for reading words in context.

Fluency

The IRI that Mrs. Jones is using has a formula for computing fluency (correct words read over time) for the entire passage. However, Mrs. Jones finds it more user friendly to compute fluency for the first minute of reading instead. Later, Mrs. Jones will compare Kevin's fluency rate to norming tables for the expected reading rate for his grade. This will tell her how Kevin's fluency rate compares to his grade level peers. If Kevin is not reading on grade level, she will also compare his reading rate at his highest instructional level to typical student performance at that grade level. For instance, if Kevin is at an instructional level with 2nd grade text, Mrs. Jones will compare his reading rate to the norms of typical 2nd grade students. This will help Mrs. Jones set realistic short-term fluency goals.

Comprehension

As soon as Kevin has finished reading the passage (and even before Mrs. Jones tallies his miscues and calculates his fluency), Mrs. Jones will take the passage away from him and ask him the comprehension questions on her protocol. These questions are a combination of explicit and implicit questions. Mrs. Jones knows that she may need to make judgement calls about whether answers are correct or not, and so she has made sure to refresh her memory by rereading the passage before the testing session began. Relying on the student's oral reading of the passage would not be helpful because she knows her full attention will be on listening for miscues and recording them.

When all of the comprehension questions have been asked and answered, she will total the number of errors and use the scoring guidelines to determine whether Kevin's comprehension is at the independent, instructional, or frustrational level. She will use this information to make decisions about what additional passages are needed. Regardless of how Kevin does with word identification, Mrs. Jones will continue passage administration until she has identified his independent, instructional, and frustrational levels for reading comprehension.

Error Analysis

Students tend to be consistent in the types of errors that they make while reading. Some students may have trouble with specific vowel patterns or leave endings off of words. Others might struggle with decoding multisyllable words or automatically recognizing sight words. Therefore, it is important for teachers to look carefully at the types of errors that students make while reading as this can help them customize instruction to address specific needs of students. (You will learn more about error analysis of word identification miscues in Chapter 9.) Some examples of error patterns that can be discerned from an IRI are presented next.

An advanced administration option for most IRIs is to delineate student errors on word lists as identified within three seconds ("timed") or identified but taking longer than three seconds ("untimed"). This distinction gives teachers insights into a student's automaticity with word identification, which is an important aspect of skill mastery. In both administrations, the overall number of "errors" would be exactly the same and would result in the same interpretation of the student's independent, instructional, or frustrational level. However, noting words that students are able to identify more slowly by sounding them out gives an indication of the student's emerging skills.

Look at the word lists in Figure 3.3. Notice that both would be scored exactly the same with the following words scored as incorrect: *capture, ankles, saltwater,* and *gently*. However, by noting student responses after three seconds, additional information is obtained about a student that has emerging skills. In this example, the word *ankles* was read inaccurately immediately, and the word *gently* was read incorrectly even with additional time. However, the student was able to decode accurately the words *capture* and *saltwater* with more time to sound the word out. An error analysis reveals to the teacher that the student has knowledge of phonetic strategies and is working toward automaticity. The instructional approach used with this student is likely to be different than for a student that has not yet acquired any phonetic skills to decode unknown words.

Word	Timed
beach	C
capture	I
surface	C
footprints	C
ankles	I
saltwater	I
gently	I
tradition	C

Errors = 4

Word	Timed	Untimed
beach	C	
capture		C
surface	C	
footprints	C	
ankles	I	
saltwater		C
gently		I
tradition	C	

Errors = 4

Figure 3.3 IRI word lists

Another error analysis strategy that lends particularly well to an IRI is a comparison of words that are read incorrectly in word lists versus passages. Words within word lists appear in isolation. Those same words also appear in the passages, but are surrounded by other words that serve as hints to the types of words that would make sense within sentences, called context cues. These context cues can be related to the meanings of the words and/or the part of speech needed to make the sentence grammatically correct—the syntax of the sentence.

Look at the example in Figure 3.4. Notice that the student is not able to identify the word *capture* in either the word list or the passage, and he identifies *gently* on the word list, but he skips the word altogether when reading the passage. The student also misses the word *saltwater* both in isolation and in context; however, his approximation *seawater* makes sense in the sentence suggesting that he may be paying attention to the meaning of the sentence. Similarly, he reads *ankles* incorrectly in isolation, but with context, he decodes it accurately. This shows that context supports this student's word reading, but only when it is a word known to the student. This suggests that additional phonics skills are needed so that the student is better able to learn new words while reading rather than being bound by his existing vocabulary.

Word	Timed
beach	C
capture	I
surface	C
footprints	C
ankles	I
saltwater	I
gently	I
tradition	C
thought	C
equal	C

Our Family Vacation

In the distance, ships floated on the surface of the water.

The sun shone down brightly. Waves lapped gently upon the

shore. My sister and I decided to have a competition and race to

the pier just like we do every year. It has become a family

tradition.

My mother held our beach bags while our father got out

his camera to capture the big event. "Your mark. Get set. Go!"

my mother shouted. We took off like a shot. Our bare feet

splashed saltwater and sand around our ankles. We left a trail

of footprints in our wake. We raced neck and neck past

sunbathers and children building castles. Two dogs decided to

join the fun.

Figure 3.4 IRI decoding error analysis

Items noted that are not miscues can give anecdotal information to the tester about what is happening with the student's reading as well. For example, if a student repeats words or phrases numerous times throughout the reading or fails to attend to punctuation, it is an indication that the student is having trouble with an important aspect of fluency called prosody that can impede comprehension. By collecting this information, a teacher can compare test protocols at different points in time to help evaluate whether interventions to address these areas are working for the student.

Error analysis can also be used to try to gain insight into a student's underlying problems with comprehension. Most IRIs contain both explicit and implicit questions. You will remember from the beginning of this chapter that answers to explicit questions can generally be found directly in the text in a single sentence, while answers to implicit questions need to be inferred from a variety of sources within the text and sometimes include the student's existing knowledge about the topic. When conducting an error analysis, teachers begin by looking for a "split" in correct responses to comprehension questions—where a student gets most or all of the explicit questions correct but only a few or no implicit questions correct (or vice versa). This will help inform instruction because the strategies used for remembering explicitly stated information are different than strategies used for making inferences.

Look at the example student responses in Figure 3.5. You will notice that the student consistently misses implicit questions which suggests that this student is having difficulty making connections between concepts he reads about in text as well as connections between the text and his own knowledge about the topic. In addition, the student gets one of the explicit questions correct and the other incorrect. In some cases, factors such as the student's word identification skills, background knowledge, and/or vocabulary can impede comprehension. For question number 1, this appears to be the case. While reading the passage, the student could not correctly decode the word *pier* and did not correct his reading error with the help of context from the other words in the sentence—this suggests that he may not know what the word *pier* means. In addition, when answering the background knowledge question *"Does your family have any traditions?"* he says, *"I don't know"* (see Figure 3.6). This suggests he may not know what the word *tradition* means either. Because question number 1 required an understanding of both the word *pier* and *tradition*, it is not surprising that a student without an understanding of these two words would not know the answer to the question even though it was stated explicitly in text.

Passages in the lower grades often contain a "retell" feature where students are asked to restate information that they remember from the passage. This feature can give insight into student strengths and weaknesses with cognition and memory. Conversely, passages in the upper grades sometimes have additional questions that can give an indication of strategy use. In addition, after all comprehension items have been asked, answered, and scored, some testers allow students to "look back" to the main passage for answers to missed items to determine how efficiently they are able to skim and scan for information. Although revised student responses would not change the student's comprehension score, it does provide important anecdotal information for the teacher when determining which reading strategies to teach.

Comprehension Questions

I
1. Why was racing to the pier a family tradition? (answer: they do it every year) [*explicit question*]
   I don't know?

C
2. What were people doing on the beach (answer: sunbathing; building sandcastles) [*explicit question*]
   building castles

I
3. At the start of the race, who was winning? (answer: neither of them; they were tied) [*implicit question*]
   the brother

I
4. Who raced with the siblings? (answer: two dogs) [*implicit question*]
   their mom and dad

Figure 3.5 IRI comprehension error analysis

Background Knowledge

1. Have you ever been to the beach?
   Yes! My grandparents live by the beach and my family goes to visit them in the summer.

2. What kinds of things happen at the beach?
   People swim.

3. Does your family have any traditions?
   I don't know.

Figure 3.6 IRI background knowledge questions

Interpretation

An important first step in interpretation is to make a decision about whether the student is performing as well as expected with grade level material. In instances where this is not the case, then a judgement needs to be made about the seriousness of the reading problem. For example, a different decision about severity would be made about a middle school student who is only behind by a year or two compared to a student who is three or more years below grade level. The former might receive supplemental instruction within the bounds of the regular classroom—Tier 2 in an RTI model—while the latter would need intensive intervention—Tier 3 in an RTI model—and would likely be referred for special education evaluation if not already identified. These judgement calls will vary based on the age of the student and other contextual information, for example, if the student was an English learner in the early stages of second language acquisition.

A next step is to evaluate whether the student has an even or uneven learning profile. The word identification and comprehension of most students typically develops evenly. For example, for a 3rd grader, levels for both word identification and comprehension might look like this:

- 2nd grade text would be independent,
- 3rd grade text would be instructional,
- 4th grade text would be frustrational.

However, students who are struggling readers, and particularly students with disabilities, are likely to display uneven learning profiles (Carnine et al., 2017). See Table 3.4 for a description of reading profiles of students who display significant reading problems. In addition, these students may display a wide range of grade levels that are instructional for them. For example, a student might demonstrate word identification at an instructional level with 2nd, 3rd, and 4th grade text. This type of profile is an indicator of students who have gaps in their learning that need to be addressed.

Table 3.4 Skill Profile Explanations

Skill Profile	Explanation
On or close to grade level with word identification, but below grade level with comprehension	This student will need direct instruction in comprehension strategies to assist with understanding of text.
On or close to grade level with comprehension, but below grade level with word identification	This student will need systematic, explicit instruction in phonics and word identification strategies. See Chapter 8 for more information about intensive reading instruction.
Far below grade level in both decoding and comprehension	This student will need instruction in word identification and comprehension. Initially, teaching should focus on systematic explicit instruction in phonics as improvement in the student's ability to access text effectively may naturally support better comprehension of text. See Chapter 8 for more information about intensive reading instruction.
On grade level in both decoding and comprehension, but with fluency at a significantly slower rate than grade level peers	This student will need additional fluency practice and accommodations to support the student's ability to keep up with the volume of reading expected while working to increase reading rate.

As you learned in Chapter 2, interpretation also involves determining whether additional skill specific assessments are needed, using data to inform instruction, and sharing relevant information with stakeholders. The remainder of the chapters in this book focus on these areas as well as how to make instruction beneficial to a wide range of learners.

References

Carnine, D. W., Silbert, J., Kame'enui, E. J., Slocum, T. A., & Travers, P. (2017). *Direct instruction reading* (6th ed.). Boston, MA: Pearson.

Gillet, J. W., Temple, C., & Crawford, A. N. (2004). *Understanding reading problems: Assessment and instruction* (6th ed.). Boston, MA: Allyn & Bacon.

Saenz, L. M., & Fuchs, L. S. (2002). Examining the reading difficulty of secondary students with learning disabilities: Expository versus narrative text. *Remedial & Special Education, 23*, 31–41.

SECTION I: APPLICATION ACTIVITIES

Show What You Know!

In this section, you learned that student perspectives about their reading are important to understand as part of an overall assessment of a student's reading. This information can be critical for planning instruction and interpreting test results. Can you spot this type of information in a reading interest inventory? Take the quiz below to find out.

Directions:

Review the following sample items from a variety of reading interest inventories. Indicate whether each item would help you better understand a student's attitudes, interests, or motivation for reading. Then, check your answers with the key.

1. I love to read (always describes me, sometimes describes me, never describes me)
2. What is your favorite TV show?
3. How do you feel about reading for fun at home?
4. Circle all of the things that you love: animals, sports, art, cooking, science, movies, school, music
5. How much time do you spend reading?
6. Do you check out books from the school library?
7. When I come to a word I don't know, I can ______ (almost always figure it out, sometimes figure it out, almost never figure it out, never figure it out)
8. Knowing how to read well is ______ (not very important, sort of important, important, very important)
9. List activities you enjoy doing
10. Most books are too long and boring (yes, no)
11. Does anyone read with you at home? Who?
12. I like reading about sports (yes, no)

Answer Key: Interests—items 2, 4, 9, 12
Attitudes—items 1, 3, 8, 10
Experiences—items 5, 6, 7, 11

Partner Activity/Discussion

In **Appendix A**, you will find the profiles of four 5th grade students. Review each student's IRI results. Then, discuss the strengths and weaknesses of each student along with how these data can inform instructional decisions.

Learn More: Multimedia Activity

In this section you learned about students who are at-risk for reading problems. For this activity, you will go deeper in your learning by exploring the Misunderstood Minds website. This site houses a wealth of resources about students with learning problems, including profiles of students and interactive activities (in attention, reading, writing, and math) that allow visitors to experience firsthand what it might feel like to struggle with learning. Have fun learning!

Directions:

1. **Before**

   In the first text box below, list key ideas you know (K) after reading this section of the textbook. In the next text box, write questions about what you want to learn (W) from completing this multi-media activity.

K (Know)	What do you already know about this topic? 1. 2. 3. 4.
W (Want to learn)	What do YOU want to learn more about? 1. 2. 3. 4.

2. **During**

   Explore the Misunderstood Minds website at https://www.pbs.org/wgbh/misunderstoodminds/index.html. Use the information you find here to answer your questions!

3. **After**

   After you have finished reading about the areas you wanted to learn more about, look back at what you indicated you knew before starting (K) and wanted to learn (W). Can you now answer the questions? How does this new information connect with what you knew before starting? Write the answers to your questions in the text box below. Be sure to add any additional unexpected information that you learned (L) as well!

L (Learned)	What did you learn? 1. 2. 3. 4.

Section II

Foundations of Early Reading and Writing

Section II: Overview

Proficiency in oral language and early reading skills serves as the foundation for later success in reading and writing. Although language continues to develop throughout the lifespan, there is an emphasis on oral language development from the time children are born and into the early grades. This is because oral language develops alongside beginning reading. Both language and reading are developmental in nature and there is a reciprocal relationship between them. In other words, oral language development fosters the development of early reading skills and vice versa. The first two chapters in this section focus on instructional approaches that help students develop oral language and other early reading skills. The final chapter in this section presents the characteristics of students who enter school without meaningful early language or reading experiences and describes how to use assessment data to inform instructional choices for these students.

- Chapter 4: Oral Language Development
- Chapter 5: Early Reading
- Chapter 6: Supporting All Students in Early Reading Development

Guiding Questions

As you are reading, consider the following questions:

- How does receptive and expressive language relate to later reading and writing development?
- What are the "building blocks" of language and why are they important for later reading and writing development?
- What instructional approaches are used to foster oral language development?
- What skills are foundational for early reading development?
- How do early reading skills support later reading development?
- What instructional approaches are used to foster acquisition of early reading skills?
- What challenges do at-risk students have with language development and acquisition of early reading skills?
- What assessments are used to informally assess a student's early reading skills?
- What additional instructional supports are needed for readers who struggle to acquire early reading skills?

Chapter 4

Oral Language Development

Fundamentals of Language Development

Oral language development begins in infancy and continues to advance throughout a person's lifespan (Polloway, Miller, & Smith, 2012). Language enables people to communicate. Because oral language is the foundation that supports later reading and writing development, it is important for teachers to have a firm understanding of the core elements of communication and language.

Communication

Communication is the ability of a person to take in environmental information, analyze and synthesize this information, and then produce some form of verbal and/or nonverbal response (Kovecses, 2006). Babies' first cries are the rudimentary start to oral language development and communication. As children grow, they will develop the ability to communicate through written language as well (Reutzel & Cooter, 2019). Communication is essential to human existence, and the effective use of communication is key to student academic progress.

Core communication skills are generally categorized as receptive and expressive language. **Receptive language** is the ability to hear and understand language messages, while **expressive language** is the ability to process others' language messages and then to make a language response (Reutzel & Cooter, 2019). As shown in Figure 4.1, receptive language includes both understanding oral speech messages as well as written messages (reading). Expressive language includes both conveying messages through oral speech and through writing.

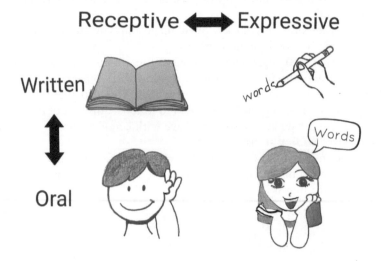

Figure 4.1 Receptive and expressive language

Listening, speaking, reading and writing play reciprocal roles in language development. Receptive and expressive oral language contributes to a child's later academic development in reading and writing, and in turn, reading and writing fosters continued language development (Mercer & Mercer, 2005). In addition, increases in receptive language skills foster increases in expressive language skills, and vice versa. Similarly, improvements in reading skills foster improvements in writing skills, and vice versa. Because language proficiency develops in this way, it is critical that teachers address receptive and expressive oral language development throughout the school years in addition to the development of reading and writing.

Language

The three core elements of language are form, content, and use. These core elements comprise oral communication (listening and speaking) and support more advanced written communication (reading and writing). For this reason, they are often referred to as the "building blocks" of language (Polloway et al., 2012). See Figure 4.2.

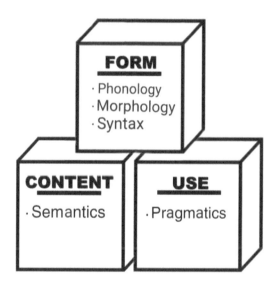

Figure 4.2 The building blocks of language

Form

Form is how words and sentences are structured within language (Kuder, 2018). Form encompasses three specific aspects of language: phonology, morphology, and syntax.

Phonology is the study of speech sounds and how they are used within a language. A **phoneme** is the smallest unit of sound within a language. In English, there are a total of 44 phonemes (Polloway et al., 2012). Individual phonemes are essential to language because phonemes are used to construct words (Mercer & Mercer, 2005). Phonemes are the individual sounds of speech, such as /t/, /p/, and /s/. These phonemes can be combined for more complicated sound constructions. For instance, when babies begin to produce sounds orally, they combine long strings of single phonemes, such as repeated /m/-/m/-/m/, /b/-/b/-/b/, and /d/-/d/-/d/. These single phoneme strands are then eventually combined into strings of varied sounds like / bŭ bŭ/, /wŭ-tŭ/, and /yă-yð/. An important distinction to note is that phonology involves the sounds of a language, but not the written letters.

Morphology is the study of the forms of words—how a word changes both to make new meanings and to follow the rules of sentence structure. A **morpheme** is the smallest unit of a word that conveys meaning (Athans & Devine, 2010). There are two types of morphemes, free morphemes and bound morphemes (Reutzel & Cooter, 2019). **Free morphemes** can stand alone as words that have meaning on their own. **Bound morphemes** are meaningful parts of words, but only when connected to free morphemes. For example, in the word *dogs*, the free morpheme "dog" represents a person's four-legged pet, and the bound morpheme "-s" indicates that there is more than one four-legged pet. In another example, the free morpheme in the word *laughed* is "laugh" indicating a good chuckle, and the bound morpheme is "-ed" indicating that the chuckle happened sometime in the past. **Morphological awareness**, or the ability to understand and manipulate morphemes, is important for reading because it enables students to understand the meanings of increasingly complex words (Carlisle, 2004).

Syntax is the set of rules that govern the arrangement of words and phrases to create structurally sound sentences that convey meaning in a language (Owens, 1994). This includes how sentences are combined, how clauses are used, and the usage rules for the various parts of speech: nouns, verbs, adjectives, adverbs, articles, prepositions, and conjunctions. For example, the most basic sentence in English requires that a sentence contain a subject (noun) and a predicate (containing a verb related to the subject). As such, the sentence "*Girl bike school.*" does not use appropriate syntax because it does not contain a verb. Rather, a syntactically correct sentence would be "*The girl rode her bike to school.*" In this second sentence, "the girl" is the subject, and "rode her bike to school" is the predicate that indicates what the girl did. Together, syntax and morphology comprise **grammar**.

Content

Content involves the higher order language skill of **semantics**—the study of the meanings of words used in language (Kintsch & Kintsch, 2005). Initial meaning making in oral language is the beginning of vocabulary development. A student's **vocabulary** encompasses the words a student can understand and use (Mercer & Mercer, 2005). Children learn their first spoken words from the objects, people, and activities in their immediate environment (Polloway et al., 2012). These first words are ones that are useful to the child in their environment, such as their name, *mom*, *dad*, and basic survival words like *food* and *bathroom*. These words also include words that they will use often. This might include words that label things that interest them and activities they do regularly, such as going to school or playing at the park. As semantics develop, word knowledge becomes more complex. As children develop their meaning making abilities, they will also learn that some words can have multiple meanings and that they will need to differentiate between these subtleties in definitions. Further, multiple meaning words are often more abstract and complex in nature (National Reading Panel, 2000). You will learn more about instructional practices to improve students' vocabularies in Chapter 11.

As students develop their semantic abilities, they are better able to understand and communicate meaningful ideas using oral language vocabulary. This also helps students to make sense of and use written vocabulary within reading and writing tasks (Mercer & Mercer, 2005). Students' semantic abilities encompass both knowledge of individual words and also comprehension of those words in connected text (Polloway et al., 2012). Students' abilities to use these semantic skills with written vocabulary words is discussed further in Chapter 11.

Use

Use refers to the social conventions of communication, called pragmatics. **Pragmatics** "describes how people get things done through their language by using an informal conversational 'code' of conduct" (Polloway, Patton, & Serna, 2008, p. 124). These social conventions are the rules people follow when using and altering their language based on specific situations, social contexts, and audiences (Bryant, 2009). Social conventions of language include an array of areas related to *what* content is conveyed and *how* that content is conveyed. For example, when communicating, it is expected that someone will tell the truth, only ask for information really wanted, offer only information that is relevant, give the listener neither too much nor too little background information, and clearly present ideas (Polloway et al., 2008). Conventions for how this information is communicated include rules for conversation such as taking turns, making eye contact, standing a socially appropriate distance away from the listener, and not interrupting the speaker. This language area also incorporates the idea of **inflection**, which is the vocal intonation that helps convey meaning beyond that of actual word meaning. For instance, a speaker typically raises the intonation of his voice at the end of a question, while statements are typically kept at a uniform tone (Polloway et al., 2012). Pragmatics also incorporates the idea of nonverbal cues, such as body language and facial expressions, that help to convey a person's intended message during verbal interactions (Wharton, 2009; Wiig & Semel, 1984).

Listening Comprehension

While oral language skills are foundational to the many underlying processes of early reading and writing, one particularly pivotal skill is **listening comprehension**. Students have the most accurate listening comprehension when they can understand the format of the message that is being communicated (using their knowledge of phonology, morphology, and syntax), and then break down that message into understandable pieces that they can think through and act upon (using their knowledge of semantics and pragmatic skills). Learners use their semantics skills to derive meaning from spoken messages and their pragmatics skills to help sift through a speaker's message to notice implied subtleties in meaning. Listening comprehension skills help young learners to understand the directions given by teachers as well as to obtain key literacy and other academic content in the classroom. Additionally, the listening comprehension skills of pre-readers serve as a bridge to the comprehension skills needed for comprehension of printed text (Polloway et al., 2012).

Once a student engages in a listening comprehension task, there is usually some sort of response expected, whether it be following through on teacher directions, making a verbal response, or completing an academic task. As a result, the students' responses require a firm grasp on expressive language skills as well. Developing students' listening comprehension skills is an important area of language development.

Stages of Language Development

When children develop language skills, most of them progress roughly at the same rate through what are called the **developmental stages of language** (Paul, 2001). At each stage, specific oral language and communication skills are cultivated that support academic learning. Teachers who understand these developmental stages are better equipped to support students.

Prelinguistic Stage

The first stage of language development is called the **prelinguistic stage**. This stage typically spans from birth to 12 months old. Within this stage, babies progress from making reflexive sounds like burping and crying to more intentional communication. Babies' language development begins with unintentional crying, which then changes to differentiated crying where their cries sound different depending on whether they are hungry, tired, or uncomfortable. From that point, babies' nonverbal communication progresses from smiling, to tracking their parent or caregiver with their eye gaze, and then establishing joint attention with their parent or caregiver on an object in the immediate environment. Eventually, little children will begin to point to and reach for different objects within the environment as well. Babies also progress verbally by first cooing, then babbling repeated consonant and vowel strings, and finally using intonation with sounds to approximate real words.

Emerging Language Stage

There can be some overlap between language development stages, especially as children begin to bridge from one stage to another. This is true between the prelinguistic and the emerging language stages. The **emerging language stage** typically spans between 12 to 18 months and 26 months. This stage begins as young children are beginning to say single words that have meaning. Many of these words will begin as approximations, where adults can detect what word a child is trying to say and help them to more clearly articulate the word through use of repetition. By the end of this stage, many children will have more than 50 words within their oral vocabulary. Thus, over time, oral communication becomes the most dominant form of communication in this stage.

The words that children begin speaking in this stage are personally meaningful to them because they typically identify objects and activities in the child's environment. Besides simply uttering words, children will also begin to understand the meanings of an increasing number of words. In fact, children usually understand more words than they can actually say themselves in this stage. For example, they understand simple statements and questions posed by parents and caregivers before they can speak these words themselves. In terms of pragmatics, children begin having the ability to use simple one-word utterances as different types of expressions through varying inflection. For instance, a child may really enjoy playing with balls, so the word *ball* might become one of the first words in his oral vocabulary. With that word, the child may be able to make the statement, "*Ball.*" when he is showing his parent or a friend a ball in his hand. He may be able to ask, "*Ball?*" when he is questioning someone about rolling or tossing him a ball. He may also exclaim, "*Ball!*" to show his sheer joy at seeing a new ball for the first time. When children are at the end of the emerging language stage, they are beginning to form up to two-word utterances. This is the beginning of syntax, which enables learners to convey thoughts that are even more complex as they enter the next language stage.

Developing Language Stage

During the **developing language stage**, children's language has a developmental explosion. This stage typically spans from a little over two years old until almost four years old. When using words, children's articulation of phonemes is becoming progressively more accurate, resulting in the majority of children's spoken words being intelligible by the end of this stage. The volume of known words increases exponentially as well with the child leaving this stage being able to say 200 or more words. Morphological development advances during this period too, with children able to convey more complex ideas with their words, including plurals and beginning verb tense. Additionally, students will develop the ability to speak in entire syntactically correct sentences and even tell beginning stories using multiple sentences. When speaking, these early learners are also able to use different sentence forms and language conventions to convey a larger breadth of thought, sometimes with these thoughts spreading beyond a child's immediate environment.

Language for Learning Stage

The next stage is referred to as the **language for learning stage**, which occurs as students enter school and includes language learned as a part of educational experiences. This stage spans from ages five to ten years. Students begin to develop more sophisticated vocabularies with greater depth of understanding and expression of word meanings. Their use of sentences also begins to become more complex, incorporating noun and verb phrases, passive speech, a wider range of conjunctions, and adjectives and adverbs. They also grow in their understanding of more subtle components of pragmatics such as making indirect requests and repairing conversation that has broken down by clarifying meaning. Students begin to display an emerging and increasing proficiency with the structures of narrative and expository discourse as well. Finally, students begin to develop metalinguistic awareness, or an awareness of language and language components. This includes increasing proficiency with phonological awareness and a developing awareness of figurative language.

Adolescent/Advanced Language Stage

As students enter adolescence, they enter the **adolescent/advanced language stage**. This stage typically begins around age 11 and continues through adulthood. In this stage, students continue to develop more sophisticated vocabularies that include inferring meanings of words from root structures, understanding derivations of words, synonyms and antonyms of words, and homonyms. Similarly, student understanding and use of appropriate syntax becomes more advanced with increasing sentence length and use of subordinate, superordinate, and coordinate clauses. Further, student development in pragmatics allows them to more effectively communicate and includes the skills needed to persuade, negotiate, and navigate a variety of social contexts. These skills also become more advanced in students' understanding and expression of language through print.

Instructional Approaches

While there are dueling theories of language development, it is generally agreed that young children learn language skills through social interactions, essentially observing others' language and participating in conversations themselves (Kuhl, 2004). While children reach many developmental language milestones before kindergarten, schools and teachers can foster lifelong language development through both authentic language interactions that happen as part of the social learning process in schools, as well as through structured academic learning tasks that incorporate oral language elements.

Early Learning Experiences

By the time students enter kindergarten, their oral language skills have been developing since the time they were born. A child's oral language skills develop naturally from birth as a means to communicate needs and wants. For the typical learner, specific oral language instruction is not needed before entering school; simply providing as many opportunities as possible for that child to engage in receptive and expressive oral language situations is beneficial. While homes can be busy places, having families build in time for child-centered discussions and book reading in their daily routine can be key in developing children's oral language skills.

Opportunities to foster language development can include the child's verbal interactions with siblings and other playmates as well as everyday conversations with parents or caregivers. It can even include the language used in imaginary play when the student is talking aloud to him or herself. All of these opportunities provide a space for the child to practice listening and expressing ideas, but they also provide practice with the social conventions of language, called pragmatics. For example, conversational turn taking is based off the child's understanding of semantic information shared within a social language situation, and then using their knowledge of pragmatic cues to engage in ongoing conversations. Within these conversations, the goal is for students to engage multiple times as both the speaker and then the listener. The more times the learner is able to go back and forth in these language situations, the more developed their conversational turn taking becomes.

Typical interactions at home also lend to student practice in following oral directions given by a parent or caregiver. In the beginning, a child can be given an oral direction to complete one task at a time, such as *"Make your bed"* or *"Clean up your toys."* Over time, as the child builds proficiency in listening and then completing tasks, these oral directions can be expanded incrementally to multi-step directions with two or three steps. For instance, a child that successfully completes a requested direction like *"Empty the trash"* would be able to progress to two-step directions of *"Empty the trash and then set the table."* As they progress even further, a parent or caregiver may go as far as three-step directions with *"Empty the trash, set the table, and fill the water glasses."* A child's ability to follow oral directions is the beginning of listening comprehension.

When parents and caregivers engage in storytelling and read aloud to children at home, they become an integral part of the child's first experiences with listening comprehension. When children hear parents and caregivers tell stories or listen to stories being read aloud, they are being exposed to story structure that has a beginning, middle, and end. This early exposure will prime students for comprehension of more complex story structures they will encounter in school. Listening comprehension, storytelling and retelling skills can be stimulated in young children by parents and caregivers by:

- telling children about their own daily experiences,
- explaining to children about a particularly important part of their day,
- asking the child to tell about their day from beginning to end,
- asking the child to explain about the best or most important part of their day.

In Photo 4.1, the father is telling a story and using a lion puppet to help with conveying what is happening in the story. The child is engaged with what is happening with the father's story as can be seen through their joint attention on the puppet and their dialogue.

Photo 4.1

FATHER: The lion says to his friends that he is sad.

CHILD: Why Daddy? Why is the lion sad?

FATHER: He is sad because no one will share their special things with the lion. Each of his friends has something special. The zebra has grass he likes to eat. The hippo has some special mud she likes to roll in. The tiger has a special snack he likes to eat. But, none of them will share with the lion.

CHILD: Aww, poor lion! I'd share my blankey with him.

FATHER: That gives the lion an idea! Maybe the lion should share one of his own special things with his friends first. Maybe the lion could share his special bone. Would you like it if the lion shared his special bone with you?

CHILD: That would be nice! But silly Daddy, I don't eat bones!

Listening experiences are also fostered by shared reading experiences. Reading to a child can be a powerful learning experience that not only supports language and early reading development, but also creates positive memories that the child will associate with reading. Ideally, a parent or caregiver will read to a child every day. Tips for reading include:

- Read books on a wide variety of topics that span both fiction and nonfiction.
- Pause during book reading to ask questions about book content.
- Pause during book reading to ask children to make predictions about what will happen next in the book.

As mentioned above, shared book reading can be a positive bonding experience between child and parent or caregiver, especially when it is done each day and is a time the child looks forward to. Additionally, these experiences serve as a model of fluent reading and support development of listening comprehension. In addition, positive experiences with reading as a young child create positive attitudes about reading as an enjoyable activity. Photo 4.2 depicts the authors' early reading experiences that set them on the path to becoming lifelong readers.

In today's society, many students are exposed to structured learning environments through daycare or preschool experiences. Many of these learning environments are similar

Photo 4.2

to those they will encounter in school. These experiences typically enhance children's language development and might include:

- listening to a teacher's language use during circle time,
- listening comprehension opportunities when the teacher reads aloud or tells a structured story and asks questions,
- following structured multi-step oral directions for tasks and project completion,
- exposure to new and more complex vocabulary through exploratory learning activities,
- field trips and special guests that expose students to new vocabulary and related semantic learning,
- turn taking through large and small group structured learning arrangements where students are asked to share ideas aloud.

Development of language will continue when students enter school and throughout the child's lifespan!

Fostering Language Development in K–12 Classrooms

By the time students enter kindergarten, most students will have developed significantly across all areas of language. Phonologically, students at this age should be able to articulate most sounds, with some still experiencing some difficulties with /r/, /s/, /z/, and voiced and un-voiced /th/ (Peña-Brooks & Hegde, 2000). Morphologically, students should be appropriately using word endings indicating plurals and basic verb tense. With syntax, students should be speaking in five- to six-word sentences and using varied sentence types. For semantic develop-ment, students should have a grasp of at least 2,000 words in their vocabulary. Pragmatically, students should understand conversational turn taking and be able to take upwards of five to six language turns with conversation partners. They also understand rules of politeness and conversational repairs where the speaker corrects language when it has been used incorrectly. Listening comprehension skills, which encompasses a student's ability to hear and understand read-aloud stories and oral directions, is in its infancy awaiting further development.

Students enter the K–12 setting with a variety of oral language experiences and abilities, but all need to develop a firm base of academically focused oral language skills that support beginning reading and writing skill development. When teachers observe student language difficulties in naturally occurring school language situations, they can then provide targeted and specific instruction based on students' needs. It is students' understanding of the sounds, words, and sentences they have heard as part of their oral language development that helps them start recognizing and understanding language in written form. Overall, oral language abilities serve as a foundation for language arts skills, which are used across content areas as students progress in school.

Language development continues naturally in the classroom environment. This language development is founded in communication for socialization, basic needs, and sharing of information. The more opportunities a child has to engage in language situations, the greater oral language development is possible for that child. Fostering continued development of oral language skills is a key job for educators. This development can be cultivated by ensuring that the classroom and learning environment is a language-rich environment. This naturally stimulates further language development through the authentic language interactions that occur. Students' language skills are also cultivated by the daily tasks they are asked to participate in. This includes learning across academic areas as well as the socialization opportunities that are an integral part of their learning experience. Natural language opportunities that are embedded in the classroom environment include:

- academic and language usage modeled by teachers in classroom instruction,
- exposure to content information across the subject areas that fosters learning of oral academic vocabulary,
- social situations where students learn the differences between what appropriate language use is in academic versus social settings (e.g., classroom versus playground),
- teacher–student academic and non-academic conversations,
- student–student academic and non-academic conversations,
- activities that require students to listen and complete tasks following multi-step teacher directions.

These natural classroom language opportunities help students develop oral language skills through authentic language usage. Students may be fine-tuning articulation of a few sounds that may be developing through age eight or nine. Multiple opportunities for practicing these sounds enhances articulation (Peña-Brooks & Hegde, 2000). Adult and peer language models promote growth in student use of complex morphological constructions of words as well as more complex sentence structures. Semantic and pragmatic skills develop further as students experience interactions that use both academic and non-academic vocabulary as they progress in school and participate in an ever-growing variety of social situations in the classroom, on the playground, and in the cafeteria. The more language experiences a student has, the more developed a student's semantic and pragmatic abilities become, which are important in enhancing listening comprehension skills.

Further instruction in conversational turn taking can be employed in the classroom through a teachers' use of different peer groupings to facilitate learning. Teachers can use peer groups for discussions and experiential learning. Within these groups, students have the opportunity to use their conversational abilities to build knowledge, clarify misunderstandings, and interpret contextual information. Students in these groupings should have heterogeneous abilities spanning from children who excel in their oral language abilities to those who may have minimal ability in expressing their thoughts aloud. These group experiences will help students negotiate learning outcomes while incorporating all language abilities in the process.

While many language skills evolve through natural language opportunities throughout the school day, there are times when students will benefit from explicit instruction in oral language. Many school systems are now recognizing and using this connectivity between oral language, reading, and writing in language arts. As a result, schools directly teach needed oral language skills throughout K–12 learning. This skills instruction begins in the early grades with establishing a shared base of oral language skills across young learners. Instruction continues in the upper grades with a focus on fostering oral language skills through discussion and formal oral presentations, where students use information they have read about and/or expressed in writing.

Fostering Listening Comprehension

Actively developing the effective listening comprehension skills of pre-readers supports their later proficiency with comprehension of printed text (Polloway et al., 2012). Additionally, hearing and understanding the vocabulary used by parents and caregivers in their speech exposes students to words that they will eventually encounter while reading. This oral vocabulary exposure is important because it is the first time learners will hear many of the useful, important, and difficult words that they will eventually need to understand in printed text. As students continue to build their reading skills throughout their years in school, teachers can continue to use oral language opportunities to help students support, strengthen, and share their understanding of what they have read.

Listening comprehension skills help young learners to understand the directions given by teachers in the classroom. The more experiences students have with following directions, the better they will be able to complete directions as instructed. Teachers can provide these practice opportunities, by giving students oral directions with increasing steps and complexity. When students struggle with direction following, teachers can provide visual and auditory cues as needed. Teachers can track student proficiency in following directions by using checklists to track how many directional steps students can follow successfully as well as the number and types of prompts needed. These oral direction-following skills can support later understanding of nonfiction text that involves written directions or steps in a process.

Listening comprehension instruction involving narrative stories typically begins in classrooms with our youngest learners. This development is supported through instruction where teachers read books aloud to students, because these learners typically are not yet reading themselves or are just beginning to read. Through this instruction, students have an oral reading model to which they can listen. Before reading, the teacher can engage in discussion about different aspects of the target book including the title, cover image, or pictures throughout the book. In this phase of instruction, the teacher is attempting to stimulate active student engagement with the book's content. The teacher also might guide discussions about what students already know about the topic of the book to help them make connections with their existing knowledge about the topic.

As teachers read the book aloud, they will pause to ask students oral questions at different points to gauge students' understanding. They can also pause at key places to ask students to predict what they think will happen next. By encouraging students' active engagement in the listening process and cultivating development of students' existing knowledge and vocabulary, teachers are stimulating and developing student skills for understanding book content they hear. In Photo 4.3 below, a teacher shares a colorful story via a big book with high-interest pictures.

Photo 4.3

The teacher pauses at pre-marked places in the book indicated with sticky tabs used throughout the book. At these places, the teacher asks students specific questions about what is happening in the story and asks them to make predictions about what will happen next. Further, she is constantly monitoring their engagement and understanding of the story events shared.

During these early read-aloud experiences, students also learn about the basic elements of story structure. Teachers can begin instruction in this area by teaching students that stories have a beginning, middle, and end. Additionally, teachers can also informally assess students' abilities to sequence events in a story as a gauge of student understanding of story structure. Oftentimes, teachers will use structured story retell checklists to monitor if students grasped story elements and included key events in the retell. Story retell is a skill that students will continue to develop and utilize as they begin to read about books on their own and then discuss or write about these experiences.

When teachers are working on listening comprehension, they use high-interest children's books rich with pictures for younger students. In developing students' ability to understand content through listening comprehension, it is important that teachers expose students to both fiction and nonfiction or informational texts. Students who are exposed to a wide variety of books from an early age have more opportunities to develop conceptual knowledge on diverse topics (Roberts & Duke, 2009). This exposure helps students develop their conceptual knowledge, setting the stage for later reading skills (Calkins, Ehrenworth, & Lehman, 2012; Smolkin & Donovan, 2001). Developing students' listening comprehension skills at an early age helps prepare them with tools for building vocabulary and facilitating comprehension that are needed for later texts they read by themselves, which will be discussed further in Chapters 10 and 11.

A Focus on How a Student's L1 Can Support Development of Their L2

Students who are English language learners have the difficult task of learning English as their second language (L2) while simultaneously learning academic content. However, knowledge that students have from their first language (L1) can help students learn an L2. The more extensive the knowledge and skills these learners have within their L1, the more help it can provide them in learning English.

For students learning a second language, it is a different task than learning their native language. When students initially are learning receptive and expressive skills in their first language, they have no knowledge of how language functions in terms of the elements of form, use, and content. However, in learning an L2, students have this language foundation from their L1 from which to build. Teachers can focus on making connections between the language elements in their L1 and how they function in English as their L2.

Orthography

Older students who have developed reading and writing skills in their L1 will have their understanding of their L1's letter/sound system to build from in developing similar skills in English as their L2. Teachers can further bridge learning between a student's L1 and English when they have the same or similar orthography. When students are reading and writing in English, teachers can make explicit connections with how word constructions in English have similar characteristics to their native language. With L1s that have different orthographies than English, teachers can work to compare and contrast the sound/symbol relationships of the two writing systems to facilitate student understanding for decoding and encoding words in English.

Language Development and Use

As you learned in Chapter 1, English language learners acquire basic interpersonal communication skills (BICS) before cognitive academic language proficiency (CALP). BICS refers to the social, contextualized language that develops within the first year or two of second language acquisition. CALP is the decontextualized, academic language that can take up to seven years for students to acquire. During this time, teachers must keep in mind that while students are developing their L2 skills in English they may already possess fully developed language skills in their L1. These L1 abilities can be used as a resource for building semantic and pragmatic language skills in English to develop students' vocabulary knowledge and comprehension skills across speaking, listening, reading, and writing in English.

Just as students who are native speakers of English can have varying levels of competency in their speaking, listening, reading, and writing skills, competencies of ELL students will fall along a similar continuum in their L1. Where teachers see strengths in students' use of their L1, they can student L1 language skills are used to build proficiency in English. For instance, when teaching vocabulary, teachers are able to show or demonstrate specific words they are trying to teach ELL students for more concrete English vocabulary. However, for higher level and more abstract vocabulary, teachers will want to tap into students' vocabulary base in their L1. In some cases, students will already have existing knowledge about a topic already in their L1, and teachers will need to find a way to activate this knowledge for learning the same vocabulary in English. In other cases, students will not have any existing knowledge on a topic, even in their L1, and the teacher's task will then be to start fresh in English.

Similarly, teachers can call on students' knowledge of and experiences with social language usage from their L1. This knowledge can help facilitate ELL students' understanding of similar social situations using English, as well as help in supporting comprehension of implied ideas and concepts within text. Using ELL students' overall language abilities in their L1 is critical to support the most effective growth in these students' English language skills.

References

Athans, S. K., & Devine, D. (2010). *Fun-tastic activities for differentiating comprehension instruction, grades 2–6*. Newark, DE: International Reading Association.

Bryant, J. (2009). Language in social contexts: Communicative competence in the preschool years. In J. B. Gleason (Ed.), *The development of language* (7th ed., pp. 192–226). Boston, MA: Pearson.

Calkins, L., Ehrenworth, M., & Lehman, C. (2012). *Pathways to the common core: Accelerating achievement*. Portsmouth, NH: Heinemann.

Carlisle, J. F. (2004). Morphological processes that influence learning to read. In C. A. Stone, E. R. Silliman, B. J. Ehren, & K. Apel (Eds.), *Handbook of language and literacy: Development and disorders* (pp. 218–339). New York, NY: Guilford Press.

Kintsch, W., & Kintsch, E. (2005). Comprehension. In S. G. Paris & S. A. Stahl (Eds.), *Children's reading comprehension and assessment* (pp. 71–92). Mahwah, NJ: Lawrence Erlbaum.

Kovecses, Z. (2006). *Language, mind, and culture: A practical introduction.* Oxford, UK: Oxford University Press.

Kuder, S. J. (2018). *Teaching students with language and communication disabilities* (5th ed.). Boston, MA: Pearson.

Kuhl, P. K. (2004). Early language acquisition: Cracking the speech code. *Nature Reviews Neuroscience, 5*, 831.

Mercer, C. D., & Mercer, A. R. (2005). *Teaching students with learning problems* (7th ed.). Upper Saddle River, NJ: Pearson/Merrill Prentice Hall.

National Reading Panel. (2000). *Report of the national reading panel: Teaching children to read: An evidence-based assessment of the scientific research literature on reading and its implications for reading instruction: Reports of the subgroups.* National Institute of Child Health and Human Development, National Institutes of Health.

Owens Jr., R. E. (1994). Development of communication, language, and speech. In G. H. Shames, E. H. Wiig, & W. A. Secord (Eds.), *Human communication disorders: An introduction* (4th ed., pp. 36–81). Boston: Allyn & Bacon.

Paul, R. (2001). *Language disorders from infancy through adolescence.* St. Louis, MO: Mosby.

Peña-Brooks, A., & Hegde, M. N. (2000). *Assessment and treatment of articulation and phonological disorders in children.* Austin, TX: PRO-ED.

Polloway, E., Miller, L., & Smith, T. (2012). *Language instruction for students with disabilities* (4th ed.). Denver, CO: Love Publishing.

Polloway, E. A., Patton, J. R., & Serna, L. (2008). *Strategies for teaching learners with special needs* (9th ed.). Upper Saddle River, NJ: Pearson.

Reutzel, D. R., & Cooter Jr., R. B. (2019). *Teaching children to read: The teacher makes the difference* (8th ed.). New York, NY: Pearson.

Roberts, K. L., & Duke, N. K. (2009). Comprehension in the elementary grades: The research base. In K. Ganske, & D. Fisher (Eds.), *Comprehension across the curriculum: Perspectives and practices K–12* (23–45). New York: Guilford Press.

Smolkin, L. B., & Donovan, C. A. (2001). The contexts of comprehension: The information book read aloud, comprehension acquisition, and comprehension instruction in a first-grade classroom. *The Elementary School Journal, 102*, 97–122.

Wharton, T. (2009). *Pragmatics and non-verbal communication.* Cambridge, UK: Cambridge University Press.

Wiig, E. H., & Semel, E. M. (1984). *Language assessment and intervention for the learning disabled* (2nd ed.). Boston, MA: Allyn & Bacon.

Chapter 5

Early Reading

Fundamentals of Early Reading

When walking into a preschool or kindergarten classroom, it will likely appear that students are doing a lot of playing. This would be an accurate perception. Play is how the learning of young children happens! As such, teachers in these classrooms should be very purposeful in setting up instructional environments to promote important pre-skills that will serve as a foundation for students as they begin to read and write (National Association for the Education of Young Children, 2009). To accomplish this, teachers need to understand important early literacy concepts, including concepts of print, phonological awareness, alphabetic knowledge, listening comprehension, and early writing.

Concepts of Print

It is important for young children to understand the nature of print, referred to as **concepts of print**, because this is predictive of later reading proficiency (National Early Literacy Panel, 2008; Scarborough, 2009). Concepts of print include an understanding that print is comprised of individual words separated by white spaces, that words are read in a certain order, and that words convey the meaning rather than the pictures (Justice & Pullen, 2004). Concepts of print also include knowing that:

- A book has a front and a back and a cover.
- We read the words in a book, not the pictures.
- Print goes from left to right and from top to bottom.
- Language is made out of words.
- Words are made out of sounds.
- Sounds can be matched with letters.
- There is a limited set of letters.
- The letters have names.
- Other parts of print have names, such as *sentence, word, letter, beginning*, and *end*.
  (Gillet, Temple, & Crawford, 2004, p. 15)

However, all children do not enter school with this understanding of how books work, and they will need overt learning experiences to acquire this understanding (Neuman, 2013).

Phonological Awareness

Phonological awareness involves hearing and orally manipulating words and parts of words (Reutzel & Cooter, 2019; Snow, Burns, & Griffin, 1998). Phonological awareness is not synonymous with phonics, although they are often confused. Phonics is the association of a letter or group of letters with a corresponding sound. You will learn more about phonics in Chapter 7. Phonological awareness does not involve printed letters, but rather the manipulation of the sounds themselves. This sensitivity to the sound structure of words is important for learning to read (Armbruster, Lehr, & Osborn, 2001). Most children develop phonemic awareness naturally through emergent literacy experiences at home and at school, but for those students who do not, explicit instruction is needed (Vukelich, Christie, Enz, & Roskos, 2016).

Phonological awareness is often confused with phonemic awareness as well. Phonological awareness refers to all activities that involve orally manipulating words and parts of words. Thus, phonemic awareness falls under the broader category of phonological awareness. **Phonemic awareness** refers more specifically to the manipulation of phonemes, or sounds, within words and is most closely related to the skills needed for reading. A phoneme does not always correspond to the sound of an individual letter, but rather can represent sounds comprised of combinations of letters as well. For example, /c/, /t/, and /m/ are phonemes, but so are /ch/, /ea/, and /or/. Further, an individual letter can represent multiple phonemes. For example, the letter "x" comprises the sounds /k/ and /s/. As illustrated in Figure 5.1, phonological awareness is developmental in nature progressing from awareness of words, to parts of words (such as syllables), and finally to individual phonemes within words (Moats & Tolman, 2009).

The development of both phonological awareness and phonemic awareness can be promoted through explicit instruction and appropriate play-based learning experiences at school. There are an array of skills that fall within the category of phonemic awareness, including phoneme isolation, identification, categorization, blending, segmenting, segmentation, and

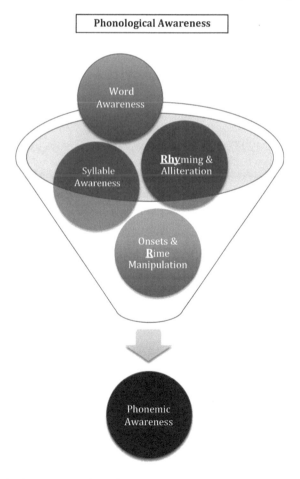

Figure 5.1 Phonological awareness funnel

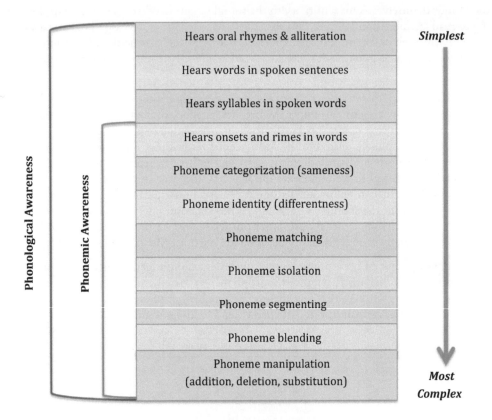

Phonological Awareness

Phonemic Awareness

Hears oral rhymes & alliteration	*Simplest*
Hears words in spoken sentences	
Hears syllables in spoken words	
Hears onsets and rimes in words	
Phoneme categorization (sameness)	
Phoneme identity (differentness)	
Phoneme matching	
Phoneme isolation	
Phoneme segmenting	
Phoneme blending	
Phoneme manipulation (addition, deletion, substitution)	*Most Complex*

Figure 5.2 Phonological awareness continuum

deletion (Edelen-Smith, 1997). Phonological awareness develops from the simplest concepts (awareness of individual words in spoken language) to the most complex (ability to manipulate individual phonemes within words) (Adams, 2001). This developmental progression of skills is presented in Figure 5.2. **Segmenting** and **blending** of oral sounds are the most critical phonemic awareness skills as they provide a solid foundation for later segmenting and blending of printed words, which is necessary for decoding (Reutzel & Cooter, 2019). Students who are proficient with foundational phonological skills, such as identifying sounds at the beginning, middle, and end of a word, are more likely to be successful with activities focused on the more advanced skills of segmenting and blending sounds.

It is important to note that sensitivity to words, word parts, and sounds can also be fostered through exposure to print that is read aloud to students—particularly texts that rhyme or have alliteration—words that begin with the same sound, such as *ball*, *bear*, and *box*. In addition, seeing adults write down their speech as well as attempting to write words on their own can help students to acquire awareness of phonemes (Gillet et al., 2004).

Alphabetic Knowledge

Knowledge of letters and their corresponding sounds, called **sound/symbol relationships**, is predictive of later reading proficiency (Catts, Fey, Zhang, & Tomblin, 1999; Huang, Tortorelli, & Invernizzi, 2014). Carnine and colleagues (2017) recommend four guidelines for introducing letters. Following these guidelines helps teachers get the most bang for their instructional buck.

First, only the most common sound for a new letter/sound should be introduced initially. The most common sounds for single letters are presented in Table 5.1 along with a keyword for each sound, tips for pronunciation, and cues that teachers should use when working

Table 5.1 Sound/Symbol Relationships for Single Letters

Letter	Sound	Example Keyword	Check Yourself!		
			Voiced or Unvoiced?	*Stretch or Stop Sound?*	*Teaching Cues for Students*
Aa	/ă/	apple	voiced	stretch	/ăăă-apple/
Aa	/ā/	acorn	voiced	stretch	/āāā-acorn/
Bb	/b/	bee	voiced	stop	/b/-/b/-/b/-/bee/
Cc	/c/	cat	unvoiced	stop	/c/-/c/-/c/-/cat/
Dd	/d/	duck	voiced	stop	/d/-/d/-/d/-/duck/
Ee	/ĕ/	egg	voiced	stretch	/ĕĕĕ-egg/
Ee	/ē/	eat	voiced	stretch	/ēēē-eat/
Ff	/f/	fish	unvoiced	stretch	/fff-fish/
Gg	/g/	goat	voiced	stop	/g/-/g/-/g/-/goat/
Hh	/h/	house	unvoiced	stop	/h/-/h/-/h/-/house/
Ii	/ĭ/	igloo	voiced	stretch	/ĭĭĭ-igloo/
Ii	/ī/	ice	voiced	stretch	/īīī-ice/
Jj	/j/	jelly	voiced	stop	/j/-/j/-/j/-/jelly/
Kk	/k/	key	unvoiced	stop	/k/-/k/-/k/-/key/
Ll	/l/	lion	voiced	stretch	/lll-lion/
Mm	/m/	moon	voiced	stretch	/mmm-moon/
Nn	/n/	nail	voiced	stretch	/nnn-nail/
Oo	/ŏ/	octopus	voiced	stretch	/ŏŏŏ-octopus/
Oo	/ō/	open	voiced	stretch	/ōōō-open/
Pp	/p/	pig	unvoiced	stop	/p/-/p/-/p/-/pig/
Qq	/q/	queen	voiced	stop	/kw/-/kw/-/kw/-/queen/
Rr	/r/	rainbow	voiced	stretch	/rrr-rainbow/
Ss	/s/	sun	unvoiced	stretch	/sss-sun/
Tt	/t/	tree	unvoiced	stop	/t/-/t/-/t/-/tree/
Uu	/ŭ/	umbrella	voiced	stretch	/ŭŭŭ-umbrella/
Uu	/ū/	unicorn	voiced	stretch	/ūūū-unicorn/
Vv	/v/	vase	voiced	stretch	/vvv-vase/
Ww	/w/	wagon	voiced	stretch	/www-watch/
Xx	/x/	x-ray	unvoiced	stop	/ks/-/ks/-/ks/-/x-ray/
Yy	/y/	yarn	voiced	stretch	/yyy-yarn/
Zz	/z/	zebra	voiced	stretch	/zzz-zebra/

Inspired by: Bursuck, W. D., & Damer, M. (2011). *Teaching reading to students who are at risk or have disabilities.* Boston, MA: Pearson.

with students. Notice that letters with continuous sounds—such as /a/, /m/, and /s/, are "stretched out" (/ăăăă/); these sounds are called **stretch sounds**. This increases the time the student has to recognize the sound when listening. **Stop sounds**, such as /b/, /c/, and /d/, are repeated numerous times (/b/.../b/.../b/) to increase the time a student has to recognize the sound when listening. Stop sounds cannot be stretched out without adding an unstressed vowel—called a **schwa**. For example, stretching out the sound for the letter "b" results in /b/ being pronounced as /buh/. This is problematic for students as they attempt to sound out and spell words. Because the development of sound/symbol relationships is critically important to the reading development of children, it is of utmost importance that their teachers correctly pronounce sounds during instruction and when giving feedback.

Do you know how to correctly pronounce all of the sounds? Test yourself! Say each letter, sound, and keyword aloud and then follow the directions in the check yourself columns. You may be surprised to find that there are some letters that you do not enunciate properly or to which you have been adding a schwa without realizing it!

Second, letters that are visually or auditorily similar should not be introduced at the same time. Students can easily confuse these letters. See Table 5.2 below for a listing of these letter pairs.

Table 5.2 Visually and Auditorily Similar Words

Visually Similar Letters		Auditorily Similar Letters	
★ b and d	★ n and m	★ /f/ and /v/	★ /k/ and /g/
★ b and p	★ v and w	★ /t/ and /d/	★ /m/ and /n/
★ p and q	★ n and r	★ /b/ and /d/	★ /ĭ/ and /ĕ/
		★ /b/ and /p/	★ /ŏ/ and /ŭ/

Third, letters that are more useful should be introduced before less useful letters. Some letters are more useful than others because they appear most often in words. For example, because all words in English have at least one vowel, vowels have high utility. Conversely, the consonants *j, q, z, y, x, v,* and *w* have less utility than the other consonants because they are found relatively infrequently in words.

Finally, following this same logic, lower case letters should be introduced before upper case letters. This is because lower case letters appear much more frequently in text.

Listening Comprehension

Listening comprehension is a foundational skill in early reading instruction, but development typically begins far before entering the kindergarten classroom. Parents and caregivers can engage in meaningful oral communication with children that fosters later comprehension of printed text (Nation, 2005). For example, parents or caregivers might engage with very young children in oral communication about objects in the immediate environment that require joint attention (Polloway, Miller, & Smith, 2012). When students enter school, teachers will draw students' attention to oral language within the school environment. This listening comprehension relates to the "language of school"—taking turns speaking and listening, following directions, and learning and using new vocabulary. See Chapter 4 for more information on how to develop these important oral language skills.

Teachers will also use books to foster students' listening comprehension. For example, a teacher might encourage students to identify what happens at the beginning, middle, and end of a story to foster their ability to recall events in sequence. Children's listening abilities then progressively advance to understanding increasingly complex or abstract language within stories (Polloway et al., 2012). All of these areas of development in listening comprehension translate into tools that assist learners as they enter the early reading stage (Bishop, 1997). Further, students with stronger and more well-developed foundations in listening comprehension are better equipped for initial reading comprehension tasks.

Early Writing

Early writing experiences are important for literacy development because they help students to recognize the relationship between phonemes and letters, called sound/symbol relationships, which fosters both reading and writing (Gillet et al., 2004). A student's early attempts at writing provide insight into a student's proficiency with sound/symbol relationships. Additionally, early writing attempts foster further development of sound/symbol relationships as well as an understanding of how written words work.

Spelling is developmental in nature and students' spelling abilities progress in stages. The **precommunicative spelling stage**, also referred to as pre-literacy, involves a student's first attempts to communicate through writing (Bear, Invernizzi, Templeton, & Johnston, 2016). This includes drawings and scribbles, but in this stage, students do not yet display an understanding of sound/symbol relationships or concepts of print. Photo 5.1 shows two examples of student writing in the precommunicative stage. The first example is from early in this stage where the student has drawn an undiscernible picture of what he calls a "beep-beep" (car) and has written incomplete forms of two letters he has attempted. The second example is from the end of this stage where the student has drawn a field of flowers and has formed a string of letters with his name. Notice that the letter string shows no letter/sound correspondence with what he states he has written "see the pretty flowers."

Photo 5.1a "Beep, beep"

Photo 5.1b I can "see the pretty flowers"

As a student begins to acquire an awareness of the relationship between sounds and the letters that represent them, these sound/symbol relationships begin to appear in the student's writing. This is referred to as **semi-phonetic spelling**, early letter name, or letter name-alphabetic stage (Bear et al., 2016). In this stage, students represent words predominantly with first and then last consonants. This semi-phonetic representation of words, often referred to as invented spelling, reinforces a student's emerging phonemic and phonetic awareness in addition to spelling. Photo 5.2 shows the writing of a student in the semi-phonetic spelling stage. You will learn about more advanced spelling stages in Chapter 13.

Photo 5.2 "I like apples and pizza"

Instructional Approaches

There are a variety of instructional approaches for teaching early reading and writing. These include setting the stage for learning, modeling proficient reading and writing, developmentally appropriate explicit instruction, and practicing through play.

Set the Stage for Learning

Effective early childhood teachers know that children are able to learn a great deal about print from their environment (Sulzby & Teale, 2003). These teachers set the stage for learning through an intentional arrangement of the learning space and the materials within them. This includes fostering language and literacy development through **print-rich classrooms**. To create a print-rich classroom, a teacher considers how print is displayed and used within instructional routines. For example, labeling objects in the classroom is a great way to expose students to words that represent vocabulary they interact with on a regular basis. Additional examples of print commonly found displayed in early childhood classrooms include:

- alphabet friezes,
- word walls and other word displays,
- student writing,
- word family charts.

Classrooms can also be structured to make text and print accessible for students to interact with. In Photo 5.3, the student is interacting with the words in the morning routine, by adding a word to complete the sentence, "*Yesterday was Sunday.*"

Photo 5.3

Other examples of print students might interact with include:

- big books from shared reading,
- classroom library and reading area books,
- reading folder activities and games,
- writing center prompts and activities,
- computer software games and activities,
- printed materials in play/science centers.

Environmental print is most effective when it is an integrated part of the classroom routine rather than merely decoration. The physical environment of the classroom is an important aspect of motivating students to learn and it includes "flooding" the classroom with books and filling each day with great reading experiences (Pressley et al., 2003).

Modeling, Modeling, and More Modeling

Modeling good reading and writing is an important part of early literacy development. In the youngest grades, this typically happens during a group activity called **circle time**, where students sit on the floor around the teacher who is modeling the targeted skills using oversized materials. This modeling is sometimes referred to as shared reading or shared writing. A more detailed description of each follows.

Shared Reading

Shared reading is used to foster a wide range of early reading skills. During **shared reading**, a teacher reads a book aloud while children look at the book and listen. In order to ensure that all students are able to view the skill being modeled, teachers will often use an oversized book—called a **big book**, as shown in the picture below. Notice in Photo 5.4 that the student is pointing to a word in the book. In this lesson, the teacher is fostering and informally assessing the student's concepts of print, because students learn concepts of print best when immersed in text with support from an adult (Reutzel, Oda, & Moore, 1989).

Photo 5.4

Shared reading can also be used to help students improve their listening comprehension. It is helpful to select **predictable books**—books with repeated patterns that allow for obvious predictions (Searfoss, Readence, & Mallette, 2001). It is also beneficial to read children's favorite books repeatedly; not only is this enjoyable for the students, but increasing their familiarity with the text helps to foster their reading comprehension (Vukelich et al., 2016). In addition to predictability and repetition, visuals support student understanding when they are first learning to read. Illustrations in picture books provide a visual prompt when students are learning to recall key events to retell the story. In Photo 5.5, students are retelling a story that the teacher read aloud to the class by pasting events from the story in the correct chronological sequence.

Photo 5.5

Shared reading using an interactive format supports dialogue between the teacher and students and provides many opportunities for questions, comments, and sharing of ideas (Pappas, Varelas, Barry, & Rife, 2004). Interactive read-alouds have been shown to enhance oral language and vocabulary development in young children, including those at-risk for reading difficulties (Mol, Bus, & de Jong, 2009). When reading aloud to young children in an interactive shared reading approach, the teacher purposefully pauses throughout the text and facilitates discussions about the content via whole group conversations or peer dialogues (Santoro, Chard, Howard, & Baker, 2008).

One approach for promoting active student interaction with a text is called dialogic reading. **Dialogic reading** is an interactive reading technique in which the teacher reads a book to a child or group of children but also becomes the listener and facilitator of discussions about the text. During dialogic reading, the teacher pauses at least once on each page and poses a question or prompt to the students. The PEER sequence can be used to guide interactions (Whitehurst & Lonigan, 2002):

- **P**rompt students to talk about the text,
- **E**valuate the responses,
- **E**xpand the responses by rephrasing or adding more information,
- **R**epeat the prompt to ensure students have learned from the expansion.

To encourage peer discussion, the teacher may ask students to "turn and talk" to the person next to him/her and discuss the prompt for a brief time (e.g., 30 seconds) before facilitating a class discussion (Kurz, 2018). The teacher may also intentionally use a variety of prompts and questions during shared reading using CROWD strategies (Whitehurst & Lonigan, 2002):

- *Completion*—while reading, leave a blank at the end of a sentence for students to fill in.
- *Recall*—ask questions that focus on the content of the book or what happens in the story.
- *Open-ended*—give a prompt that allows for multiple perspectives, such as *"Tell me what is happening in this picture,"* or *"What do you think will happen next?"*
- *Wh*—Ask *who, what, when, where, why,* and *how* questions.
- *Distancing*—Ask questions that require students to make connections to another story, topic, or life event, such as *"Think about when we went on a walk to look for signs of spring. What did you see?"*

Often these discussions will occur during circle time with students sitting in a semi-circle around the teacher (see Photo 5.6).

Photo 5.6

Shared Writing

Shared writing, also called interactive writing**,** is similar to shared reading in that it gives students an overt model of the writing process. Often a teacher will use chart paper to display writing while thinking aloud. A teacher might also use a **language experience approach** that involves co-construction of writing based on a shared experience (Vukelich et al., 2016). For example, the students might help narrate a story about an event that happened in the school with guided support from the teacher while the teacher models writing the sentences on chart paper. Then, students practice reading the story that they collectively wrote aloud. In Photo 5.7, a language experience approach is being used to create an explanation of how someone brushes his or her teeth. This approach fosters the development of language and concepts, including helping students build vocabulary. It also serves as a powerful example of the writing process. You will learn more about approaches to teach writing in Chapter 13.

Photo 5.7

Developmentally Appropriate Explicit Instruction

While teacher modeling and shared reading and writing experiences can definitely set the stage for student awareness of core reading and writing ideas, explicit instruction is also needed. Explicit instruction is when a teacher directly teaches students desired skills that she wants them to learn. The best format is usually with a smaller group of five to six students versus the whole class. While the teacher works with students, he or she is intentionally providing instruction on targeted skills rather than relying on students to acquire skills simply from exposure. Instruction in early reading skills should occur in kindergarten and first grades through short lessons that are 5–7 minutes long (Reutzel & Cooter, 2019). Core content that lends to explicit instruction includes phonological and phonemic awareness, alphabet knowledge, listening comprehension, and spelling/writing.

Phonological Awareness Activities

Phonological awareness activities occur as structured language play. Generally, a teacher will facilitate this play in small groups through game-like activities where students manipulate sounds in language. Because phonemic awareness is especially important for later reading development, these skills are targeted through instruction. It is very important when targeting phonemic awareness to use the phoneme sounds and not the letter names! Table 5.3 displays important phonemic awareness skills in the order of developmental difficulty. When studying this table, pay attention to the examples as well as the definition of each skill because the examples illustrate how a teacher might teach and informally assess each skill.

Phoneme blending and phoneme segmenting are the most critical of the phonemic awareness skills as these are foundation skills for segmenting and blending letters in words when students begin to learn how to decode print. Although these skills are important, because phonemic awareness is developmental, this is not where instruction would begin. Rather, students develop proficiency in developmentally easier skills and then progress to segmenting and blending. Similarly, instruction does not stop with segmenting and blending because more advanced manipulation of phonemes helps students recognize sound/symbol relationships that will be important for later spelling development.

Table 5.3 Phonemic Awareness Skills

Skill	Definition	Example
Phoneme Isolation	Children recognize individual sounds in a word.	*Teacher:* "What is the first sound in **van?**" *Children:* "The first sound in **van** is /v/."
Phoneme Identity	Children recognize the same sounds in different words.	*Teacher:* "What sound is the same in **fix, fall,** and **fun?**" *Children:* "The first sound, /f/, is the same."
Phoneme Categorization	Children recognize the word in a set of three or four words that has the "odd" sound.	*Teacher:* "Which word doesn't belong? **Bus, bun, rug.**" *Children:* "**Rug** does not belong. It doesn't begin with /b/."
Phoneme Blending	Children listen to a sequence of separately spoken phonemes, then combine the phonemes to form a word.	*Teacher:* "What word is /b/ /i/ /g/?" *Children:* "/b/ /i/ /g/ is **big.**"
Phoneme Segmentation	Children break a word into separate sounds, saying each sound as they tap it.	*Teacher:* "How many sounds are in **grab?**" *Children:* "/g/ /r/ /a/ /b/. Four sounds." ****note:** the important element here is the correct identification of the individual sounds—counting alone is not phoneme segmentation.
Phoneme Deletion	Children recognize the word that remains when a phoneme is removed from another word.	*Teacher:* "What is **smile** without the /s/?" *Children:* "**Smile** without the /s/ is **mile.**"
Phoneme Addition	Children make a new word by adding a phoneme to an existing word.	*Teacher:* "What word do you have if you add /s/ to the beginning of **park?**" *Children:* "**Spark.**"
Phoneme Substitution	Children substitute one phoneme for another to make a new word.	*Teacher:* "The word is **bug.** Change /g/ to /n/. What's the new word?" *Children:* "**Bun.**"

Adapted from: Armbruster, B. B., Lehr, F., & Osborn, J. (2001). *Put reading first: The research building blocks for teaching children to read.* Washington, DC: U.S. Department of Education.

In addition to introducing skills in a developmental sequence, it is important to keep in mind that all tasks are not equally difficult. Identification tasks tend to be easier than production tasks (Edelen-Smith, 1997). **Identification tasks** require students to identify a correct answer from a field of choices, while **production tasks** require students to produce the answer independently. With these definitions in mind, take a look at the following activities. Which ones are identification tasks? Which ones are production tasks?

1. "Listen. Which one doesn't belong? Fish. Frog. Snake."
2. "Listen. 'Dad.' Tell me a word that sounds the same at the end."
3. "Tell me a word that begins with the sound /b/."
4. Show students pictures of a dog, a cat, and a mouse. "Which one begins with /c/?"

If you thought that the first and last prompts are identification tasks and the second and third prompts are production tasks, then you were correct!

Similarly, identification of sounds that comprise words varies in difficulty by the placement of the sound in the word. A sound in the initial position of a word is easiest, followed by a sound in the final position, with a sound in the medial position being most difficult (Edelen-Smith, 1997). Consider the word *cat*. In this word, identification of the /c/ is easiest and students are most likely to be successful with identification of this sound first. Identification of the ending /t/ sound is a bit more difficult and students will most likely be successful with identification of this sound next. Finally, identification of the medial sound /a/ is most challenging and is the skill that students develop last. Some students will have difficulty with auditory discrimination of sounds. Teachers may need to provide these students with additional support by providing teaching cues that you learned about earlier in the chapter to help them "hear" the sounds. Remember that continuous sounds can be stretched out indefinitely, but stop sounds cannot and need to be repeated multiple times taking care to not add a schwa or other vowel sound. Student writing will reflect this developmental progression as well. You will learn more about this later in the chapter.

As students advance, they will work on combining sound sequences. There is a developmental progression of difficulty here as well. A consonant vowel pattern, such as /go/, /me/, and /hi/, would be the easiest combination. A vowel consonant pattern, such as /an/, /up/, and /at/, would be the next easiest combination. Finally, a consonant–vowel–consonant pattern, such as /sit/, /top/, and /pan/, would be a more difficult combination.

Finally, hands-on activities are helpful for many students. For example, **Elkonin boxes** are a tactile approach to helping students learn to manipulate phonemes. When using this method, markers are put in the Elkonin boxes to represent individual phonemes. If a teacher was going to help students practice phoneme manipulation on the initial sound of words ending in "–at," it might look like Figure 5.3.

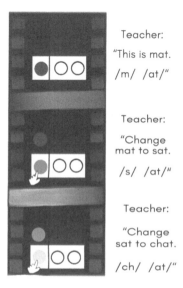

Figure 5.3 Elkonin boxes for phoneme manipulation

Letter/Sound Correspondence Activities

As with phonological awareness activities, activities that foster alphabet knowledge and letter/sound correspondence are most effective when they are play-based activities. This means that teachers working with students at this age take care to make sure that activities are introduced in an engaging way that students find fun. This is important to remember because letter recognition and subsequent pairing of letters to sounds is most effectively accomplished through tasks that allow repeated practice. Some examples include:

- word frieze practice,
- flashcards,
- alphabet books,
- alphabet manipulation,
- letter hunts within books.

The key to the success of learning letter/sound correspondences is multiple exposures and plenty of practice.

Structured Writing Activities

Structured time during the literacy block of early childhood classrooms is needed for writing practice. This practice will not only promote students' writing, but the process of attempting to spell words will reinforce student grasp of the alphabetic principle through their direct application of sound/symbol relationships. Students' early efforts to spell are sometimes referred to as **invented spelling** because words are not spelled conventionally, but rather, words are represented by the letters of the sounds the student hears in those words. These early attempts "motivate children to explore language and to become aware of words, syllables, and phonemes" (Temple, Nathan, & Temple, 2013, p. 103). Therefore, it is important to encourage these efforts and help students to hear the sounds in words when spelling rather than critiquing errors in conventional spelling. Teachers should also incorporate familiar, high-interest materials as the focus of student writing attempts.

Practice through Play

The work of early childhood happens through play. As such, it is important for teachers to create opportunities for students to practice what they have learned in large group circle time and small group lessons through play-based activities (Vukelich et al., 2016). In the early grades, this is generally accomplished through literacy centers that provide opportunities for cooperative learning and student interaction to promote social skills and language development (Morrow, 2002). Diller (2003) explains that literacy centers provide "a time for students to practice reading, writing, speaking, listening, and working with letters and words" (p. 3).

Literacy centers typically occur simultaneously during the guided reading portion of the language arts block of instruction. Students work alone or in small groups at these centers on activities centered on a specific topic or skill (Diller, 2003). Depending on teacher preference, students either attend one center per day or rotate through three to five centers daily while the teacher is conducting targeted small group reading instruction. Literacy center activities provide the teacher with ongoing opportunities to informally assess students on center participation or specific performance tasks.

When planning for literacy centers, the teacher will label each center, have all materials easily accessible and organized, create and post center expectations and model correct behavior and use of each center for the children. A center rotation chart is often displayed with the names of students corresponding to the center they will attend. Following are some of the centers most commonly found.

Big Book and Library/Reading Center

A center focused on big books of familiar stories is a wonderful way for young children to interact with and experience print and illustrations on a large scale. The location of the center should be in an area on the carpet or table that provides plenty of space for each child to spread out and manipulate the big book. This center is equipped with small and large pointers, word windows, and magnifying glasses for students to use while exploring print and reading.

The library or reading corner is typically in a small area or corner of the classroom in which children can enjoy books in a comfortable setting (see Photo 5.8). Pillows or comfortable chairs are often incorporated to create a calm and welcoming environment. The library corner often has a small bookshelf or bins containing a selection of books of high interest. Additionally, audio books may be available for students to listen to using headphones. Reading corner books should be a mix of narrative and informational genres. Books at a variety of reading levels should be represented to support differentiation and the ability for children to read at their independent reading level. Books should also be periodically replaced with new titles and topics to reflect content classroom instruction. Some teachers like to have a theme for their library corner and decorate it accordingly (i.e., a tree that changes with the seasons). Themes can also be reflective units of instruction (i.e., under the sea/ocean life).

Photo 5.8

Literacy Center

A literacy center includes activities related to reading and writing. A literacy center often includes folder games that include content materials that students manipulate in a way that is self-correcting. Folder games allow students to practice, interact with, and reinforce specific skills (i.e., consonant/vowel patterns, vocabulary, narrative story structure) or content across the curriculum (i.e., science concepts). Folder games might include sorting, classifying, matching, sequencing, or word webs. Photo 5.9 depicts a folder game where students will match the name of a letter to the corresponding beginning sound of a picture.

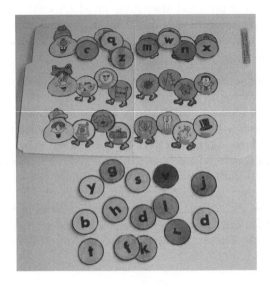

Photo 5.9

The writing center is another potential focus for a literacy center. It is typically located at a small table, equipped with chairs and a variety of paper and writing utensils (i.e., pencils, colored pencils, markers, crayons). Writing supports may consist of a portable word wall (i.e., file folder containing lists of words).

Science Center

The science center reinforces content that is being learned during typical science instruction. Items at the center may include informational books on the topic being studied, a display of related vocabulary words, paper for writing or drawing, and items for students to manipulate. These items provide multiple exposures for students to access text, build vocabulary, and engage in peer discussions surrounding targeted science concepts. Science centers can reinforce science content and support literacy skills simultaneously (Kurz, 2018). Science centers capitalize on children's natural curiosity about science and can promote the connection between science inquiry and literacy skills (Van Meeteren & Escalada, 2010). Photo 5.10 shows a measuring activity in the science center. Notice that important words from instruction are displayed in the center.

Photo 5.10

Dramatic Play Center

The theme of the dramatic play area can also be cross-curricular. For example, when learning about community helpers, props might be provided for students to dress up and act out roles of various professions (i.e., fire fighter, doctor, vet, teacher). The student in Photo 5.11 is pretending to make dinner and set the table. Notice that the placemats have the words *plate*, *cup*, *fork*, *knife*, *spoon*, and *napkin* printed on them to indicate where the utensils go.

Photo 5.11

Blocks and Puzzles Center

The block center contains blocks of various shapes and sizes as well as puzzles. Varying the type of building blocks (i.e., large cardboard blocks, Legos, Duplos, Lincoln Logs) every so often promotes both large and fine motor development. Adding bins of small motor vehicles or figures encourages dramatic play and conversations between peers and fuels the imagination. In Photo 5.12, the girl is working on an alphabet puzzle where she is getting practice learning the shapes of letters through tactile manipulation.

Photo 5.12

Multimedia/Computer Center

The technology center may include hardware such as computers, laptops, or iPads. At the technology center, students interact with educational games and/or websites that reinforce targeted concepts or skills in a content area (i.e., reading, math, science). Some schools have required or recommended software that teachers are expected to incorporate during center time. Notice in Photo 5.13 that the students are interacting with a computer program that is reinforcing letter recognition.

Photo 5.13

Application Vignette: Literacy Integrated with Kindergarten Science (LINKS)

Ms. Harmon is a teacher in an inclusive kindergarten classroom of 24 students. She often finds it challenging to meet increasingly rigorous state-required standards, effectively teach all content areas when a large portion of the school day is devoted to language arts instruction, and differentiate instruction to meet the varying abilities of her students. She recently learned about Literacy Integrated with Kindergarten Science (LINKS), an intervention that purposefully integrates targeted science content into three components of her existing language arts block (e.g., shared reading, literacy centers, and writing). She finds this intervention to be beneficial to her and her students. She is able to meet curriculum requirements and standards in language arts and science simultaneously, and her students are afforded multiple opportunities to learn content from each area concurrently.

Ms. Harmon's typical language arts block begins with reading a story aloud to her class, followed by guided reading groups and literacy centers, and culminating with writing instruction. Ms. Harmon has found LINKS very easy to incorporate into this existing framework and the students really enjoy the science materials and learning opportunities.

The current kindergarten science topic is living things. Ms. Harmon utilizes the LINKS materials for the living things unit during language arts. Three days a week during shared reading, she reads an informational science text such as, *Living or Nonliving?* (Hicks, 2011) using an interactive format as prescribed in LINKS. She begins by discussing the difference between fiction and nonfiction books with her students and taking them on a brief "book walk" to note the features of informational text (i.e., photographs, headings). Before beginning to read, Ms. Harmon also introduces a few key vocabulary words necessary for concept understanding (e.g., living, nonliving, survive). For each keyword, she posts the word and accompanying photo, explains it with a student friendly definition, and facilitates a brief discussion of the word/concept. Now that Ms. Harmon has prepared the students for the book, she reads *Living or Nonliving?* in an interactive format in which she poses a question and facilitates discussion on each page. When she poses a question, she often instructs the students to "turn and talk" to their partner to discuss the question. After 30 seconds or so, Ms. Harmon rings a bell and the students return their attention to their teacher who facilitates a class discussion based on the question posed. At the conclusion of the book, Ms. Harmon reviews the vocabulary and content to ensure student understanding of the concepts.

While Ms. Harmon meets with her guided reading groups of four to six students, the remainder of the students engage in literacy centers. Ms. Harmon incorporates LINKS materials into her centers. At the listening center, the students listen to an audio book about living things. The technology center is set up for the students to engage with the *BrainPOP, Jr.* website to reinforce current science concepts. One of the literacy centers includes file folder games to reinforce science vocabulary words, matching photos of living and nonliving items under each keyword. At the hands-on center students manipulate and sort items into containers labeled *living* and *nonliving*. Children can also view photos and read sentences on the anchor chart at this center (i.e., living things need food). Many of the LINKS literacy centers have accompanying worksheets that can be used for additional practice and to serve as informal assessments. For the students who need differentiation or additional guidance, Ms. Harmon's instructional assistant is available to support students during literacy centers.

During writing instruction, Ms. Harmon incorporates LINKS writing activities twice a week. One day she engages her class in a language experience by posing a prompt such as *What is a living thing?* The students provide responses while Ms. Harmon writes their responses on large chart paper. At the conclusion of the experience, the class and Ms. Harmon read the responses to the prompt. On a subsequent day, the students will complete an individual writing activity about science. Ms. Harmon poses the same prompt as the language experience (e.g., *What is a living thing?*) and the students individually write their responses using invented spelling and drawings. Ms. Harmon encourages students who need extra support to refer to portable word walls or file folders with words and pictures, as they write about science. Ms. Harmon and her assistant are able to differentiate support to her students during individual writing time.

Ms. Harmon has found that by incorporating LINKS into her literacy instruction, her students have a deeper understanding of science concepts and she is able to maximize her instructional time by teaching across the curriculum.

More information about LINKS can be obtained by contacting Dr. Leigh Ann Kurz at rmlak@msn.com.

References

Adams, M. J. (2001). Alphabetic anxiety and explicit, systematic phonics instruction: A cognitive science perspective. In S. B. Neuman & D. K. Dickinson (Eds.), *Handbook of early literacy research* (Vol. 1, pp. 66–80). New York, NY: Guilford.

Armbruster, B. B., Lehr, F., & Osborn, J. (2001). *Put reading first: The research building blocks for teaching children to read.* Washington, DC: U.S. Department of Education.

Bear, D. R., Invernizzi, M., Templeton, S., & Johnston, F. (2016). *Words their way: Word study for phonics, vocabulary, and spelling instruction* (6th ed.). Boston, MA: Pearson.

Bishop, D. V. M. (1997). *Uncommon understanding: Development and disorders of language comprehension in children.* London, UK: Psychology Press.

Bursuck, W. D., & Damer, M. (2011). *Teaching reading to students who are at risk or have disabilities.* Boston, MA: Pearson.

Carnine, D. W., Silbert, J., Kame'enui, E. J., Slocum, T. A., & Travers, P. (2017). *Direct instruction reading* (6th ed.). Boston, MA: Pearson.

Catts, H. W., Fey, M. E., Zhang, X., & Tomblin, J. B. (1999). Language bases of reading and reading disabilities: Evidence from a longitudinal investigation. *Scientific Studies of Reading, 3,* 331–362.

Diller, D. (2003). *Literacy work stations: Making centers work.* Stenhouse Publishers. Retrieved March 30, 2019 from: https://www.birdvilleschools.net/cms/lib/TX01000797/Centricity/Domain/4831/Debbie_Diller_Best_%20Practices.pdf

Edelen-Smith, P. J. (1997). How now brown cow: Phoneme awareness activities for collaborative classrooms. *Intervention in School & Clinic, 33,* 103–111.

Gillet, J. W., Temple, C., & Crawford, A. N. (2004). *Understanding reading problems: Assessment and instruction* (6th ed.). Boston, MA: Allyn & Bacon.

Hicks, K. (2011). *Living or nonliving?* Vero Beach, FL: Rourke Educational Media.

Huang, F. L., Tortorelli, L. S., & Invernizzi, M. A. (2014). An investigation of factors associated with letter-sound knowledge at kindergarten entry. *Early Childhood Research Quarterly, 29,* 182–192.

Justice, L. M., & Pullen, P. C. (2004). Promising interventions for promoting emergent literacy: An overview with practice suggestions. *Topics in Early Childhood Special Education, 23,* 99–113.

Kurz, L. A. (2018). *Literacy integrated with kindergarten science: An investigation of impacts of kindergarten students including those at-risk for learning disabilities.* Doctoral dissertation, George Mason University.

Moats, L., & Tolman, C. (2009). *Language essentials for teachers of reading and spelling (LETRS): The speech sounds of English: Phonetics, phonology, and phoneme awareness (Module 2).* Boston, MA: Sopris West.

Mol, S. E., Bus, A. G., & de Jong, M. T. (2009). Interactive book reading in early education: A tool to stimulate print knowledge as well as oral language. *Review of Educational Research, 79,* 979–1007.

Morrow, L.M. (2002). *The literacy center: Contexts for reading and writing* (2nd ed.). Portland, ME: Stenhouse Publications.

Nation, K. (2005). Children's reading comprehension difficulties. In M. J. Snowling & C. Hulme (Eds.), *The science of reading: A Handbook* (pp. 248–265). Oxford, UK: Blackwell. Malden, MA: Blackwell Publishing.

National Association for the Education of Young Children (NAEYC). (2009). *Developmentally appropriate practice in early childhood programs* (3rd ed.). Washington, DC: Author.

National Early Literacy Panel (NELP). (2008). *Developing early literacy: Report of the national early literacy panel.* Jessup, MD: National Institute for Literacy.

Neuman, S. B. (2013). How we can change the odds for children at risk: Principles for effective leadership in early childhood. In D. R. Reutzel (Ed.), *Handbook of research-based practice in early education* (pp. 3–14). New York, NY: Guilford Press.

Pappas, C., Varelas, M., Barry, A., & Rife, A. (2004). Promoting dialogic inquiry in information book read-alouds: Young children's ways of making sense of science. In E. W. Saul (Ed.), *Crossing borders in literacy and science instruction: Perspectives on theory and practice* (pp. 161–189). Newark, NJ: International Reading Association.

Polloway, E., Miller, L., & Smith, T. (2012). *Language instruction for students with disabilities* (4th ed.). Denver, CO: Love Publishing.

Pressley, M., Dolezal, S. E., Raphael, L. M., Mohan, L., Roehrig, A. D., & Bogner, K. (2003). *Motivating primary-grade students.* New York, NY: Guilford Press.

Reutzel, D. R., & Cooter Jr., R. B. (2019). *Teaching children to read: The teacher makes the difference* (8th ed.). New York, NY: Pearson.

Reutzel, D. R., Oda, L. K., & Moore, B. H. (1989). Developing print awareness: The effect of three instructional approaches on kindergarteners' print awareness, reading readiness, and word reading. *Journal of Reading Behavior, 21,* 197–217.

Santoro, L. E., Chard, D. J., Howard, L., & Baker, S. K. (2008). Making the very most of classroom read-alouds to promote comprehension and vocabulary. *The Reading Teacher, 61,* 396–408.

Scarborough, H. S. (2009). Connecting early language and literacy to later reading (dis) abilities: Evidence, theory, and practice. In F. Fletcher-Campbell, J. Soler, & G. Reid (Eds.), *Approaching difficulties in literacy development: Assessment, pedagogy and programmes* (pp. 23–38). London, UK: Sage.

Searfoss, L. W., Readence, J. E., & Mallette, M. H. (2001). *Helping children learn to read: Creating a classroom literacy environment.* Boston, MA: Allyn & Bacon.

Snow, C. E., Burns, M. N., & Griffin, P. (1998). *Preventing reading difficulties in young children.* Washington, DC: National Academy Press.

Sulzby, E. (1991). The development of the young child and the emergence of literacy. In J. Flood, J. M., Jensen, D. Lapp, & M. R. Squire (Eds.), *Handbook of research on teaching the English language arts* (3rd ed., pp. 273–285). New York, NY: Macmillan.

Temple, C. A., Nathan, R., & Temple, C. (2013). *The beginnings of writing* (4th ed.). Boston, MA: Pearson.

Van Meeteren, B. D., & Escalada, L. T. (2010). Science and literacy centers. *Science and Children, 47,* 74–78.

Vukelich, C., Christie, J., Enz, B. J., & Roskos, K. A. (2016). *Helping young children learn language and literacy: Birth through kindergarten.* Boston, MA: Pearson.

Whitehurst, G. J., & Lonigan, C. J. (2002). Emergent literacy: Development from prereaders to readers. In D. K. Dickinson & S. B. Neuman (Eds.). *Handbook of early literacy research* (Vol. I, pp. 11–29). New York, NY: Guildford Press.

Chapter 6

Supporting All Students in Early Reading Development

Students Who Struggle to Develop Early Reading Skills

As you learned throughout this section, language and early reading skills are critically important for later reading success. However, not all students enter school with meaningful experiences with language or exposure to reading and writing, particularly students from low-income families (Neuman & Celano, 2012). These students are likely to enter school behind their peers and often have difficulty "catching up." In fact, being a poor reader in 1st grade is highly predictive of being a poor reader in 4th grade (Juel, 1988; Scarborough, 2009). This means that students who are struggling to learn language and early reading skills in the younger grades are likely to continue to struggle with accessing print and understanding what they read as they get older. Students who are language learners and students who have language-based disabilities are particularly at-risk to fail to develop early reading skills at the same rate as their typically developing peers.

Challenges Stemming from English Language Development

As you learned in Chapter 1, students who are English language learners are likely to lag behind peers because of differences between the orthography of their first language (L1) and second language (L2), as well as the developmental nature of learning a second language. These students may have difficulty with multiple areas of English language development. A student who is learning English may have difficulty with phonology and acquisition of the alphabetic principle, at least in part, because sounds for letters in the English language may not correspond with sounds in the student's first language. For instance, many German speakers struggle with /th/ in words like *thought* and *thin* because the /th/ sound does not exist in German. As a result, many Germans will pronounce the /th/ as /t/, which can completely change the intended word, such as with *thought* being pronounced *taught* and *thin* as *tin*. Other challenges may stem from differences in the transparency of the orthography of English. For example, Spanish has a transparent orthography where each letter has a consistent letter/sound correspondence; however, English has an opaque orthography, where a letter or letters may make more than one sound or at times make no sound at all. This language difference can make letters like "k" confusing for Spanish speakers when "k" represents /k/ in *kite*, *kangaroo*, and *kind*, but has no sound in *knob*, *knight*, *knife*. These language differences lead to difficulties in speaking and decoding words when reading.

English learners are also likely to have difficulty with morphology. The native languages of these students may or may not have morphemes that function the same way as in English. You learned in Chapter 4 that bound morphemes are meaningful parts of words, but only when attached to a base word (free morpheme), which in English are generally prefixes and suffixes. However, languages such as Tagalog, spoken in the Philippines, can have bound morphemes in the center of the word called infixes. Additionally, English learners may omit affixes in words in a way that is consistent with the speech patterns in their native language. For instance, it is typically easy for Spanish speakers to understand why a plural noun has an *-s* ending in English (for example, *cats*) but not why a singular verb ends in an *-s* (for example, *runs*). These differences between the morphological rules in English and a student's L1 can lead to difficulties in correctly using English morphemes to construct words orally as well as read words with prefixes and suffixes.

Syntax development can be difficult for English learners as well. These students may attempt to use sentence structures in English similar to those of their native language, even when placement of articles and adjectives may be fundamentally different. In many Western European languages, like Spanish, French, Italian, and Portuguese, word order for adjectives and nouns is opposite to English. In these languages, the noun is often followed by the adjective such as *des gâteaux délicieux* in French, which in English is *the delicious cakes*. In East Slavic languages like Russian and Ukrainian, articles are not used, so using the articles *a*, *an*, and *the* in English can be challenging for these learners. Verb tense changes that require changes in the sentence word order can also be confusing for English learners. For instance, it can be challenging for English learners to understand how to change sentences such as *"Where did you go yesterday?"* to *"I went to the park yesterday."* In this sentence, it is difficult for a student to understand why *go* should change to *went* rather than simply saying, *"I go to the park yesterday."* Similarly, irregular language rules in English make understanding the morphology of the language difficult as well.

A Focus on Can Do Descriptors

The Wisconsin Center for Education Research, called WIDA, has developed "Can Do Descriptors" that highlight what English language learners "can do" at various stages of language development in the areas of listening, speaking, reading, and writing. The Can Do Descriptors categorize communication into four different areas they call "key uses": recount, explain, argue, and discuss. A description of each is provided in the table below.

Key Uses	Definition	Example
Recount	To display knowledge or narrate experiences or events.	Example tasks include telling or summarizing stories, producing information reports, and sharing past experiences.
Explain	To clarify the "why" or the "how" of ideas, actions, or phenomena.	Example tasks include describing life cycles, sharing why or how things work, stating causes and effects, and sharing results of experiments.
Argue	To persuade by making claims supported by evidence.	Example tasks include stating preferences or opinions and constructing arguments with evidence.
Discuss	To interact with others to build meaning and share knowledge.	Example tasks include participating in small or large group activities and projects.

Adapted from: Wisconsin Center for Education Research. (2019). *The can do descriptors*. Retrieved from https://wida.wisc.edu/teach/can-do/descriptors

While all students at the early grade levels are in the beginning stages of developing their semantic (vocabulary) and pragmatic skills, English language learners can experience developmental delays. Most young learners are adding to their semantic and pragmatic understandings daily. Each time a word is heard or used, students' meaning making is further developed based on word usage and context. English learners are exposed to an even greater volume of new words than native English speakers, because they are hearing for the first time words that are already familiar to native speakers. While all learners will need multiple exposures to a new word to incorporate it into their vocabulary, English learners may need even more experiences with these words. English learners who enter school at the primary level are at an advantage to English learners who enter school at the secondary level because all primary level students are learning and negotiating the use of social and academic English. In contrast, older students are often expected to keep up with social and academic language at the pace of the school curriculum. While teachers can help students to make connections between English and what they already know in their L1 (see Chapter 4), these students will not acquire new vocabulary and concepts as quickly as their native English-speaking peers.

Challenges Stemming from Disability

Students with language-based disabilities such as learning disabilities (including dyslexia), and language disorders may lag behind their peers in the acquisition of early reading skills and/or display uneven development both within and across the different areas of language. As you learned in Chapter 5, the ability to manipulate phonemes is critically important for later reading proficiency, and therefore, difficulty with discrimination of phonemes directly impedes the reader's ability to acquire alphabetic and phonologically based reading skills (Lovett, Barron, & Benson, 2003). In fact, deficits in phonological awareness are predictive of significant reading difficulties, including learning disabilities in reading (Scarborough, 2009).

Difficulties with phonological development of some students is exacerbated by auditory processing problems (Hallahan, Lloyd, Kauffman, Weiss, & Martinez, 2005). Students who have **auditory processing** problems find it challenging to distinguish sounds in words, particularly medial vowel sounds and sounds that are auditorily similar. Learners with auditory processing problems include students with learning disabilities in reading and language disabilities. For many students with learning disabilities, problems with phonology are compounded by limitations with working memory. As you learned in Chapter, 1, working memory is "the ability to retain information in short-term memory while processing incoming information" (Siegel, 2006, p. 173). Impaired working memory affects student mastery of the alphabetic principle by limiting the ability of students to use phonetic representations to hold letters and words in short-term memory while reading (Mann, 2003).

Students with language-based disabilities also have problems with the other forms of language—morphology and syntax. For example, students might overgeneralize language rules, as evidenced in statements like "*I breaked my pencil*" rather than "*I broke my pencil*" or "*I saw the gooses*" rather than "*I saw the geese.*" Students might also display difficulty with understanding and use of pronouns. While some of these errors are developmental, students with language-based disabilities who have difficulties in these areas are likely to continue to display these types of errors much longer than their typically developing peers. As they get older, students with language-based disabilities may also continue to express themselves using simple sentences and have difficulties understanding more complex sentence constructions (Scott & Windsor, 2000).

Students with language-based disabilities also have difficulties with semantics and pragmatics. It is well documented that the vocabulary knowledge of students with language-based disabilities is usually significantly less developed than their typically developing peers (Baker,

A Focus on Speech–Language Disorders

As the name implies, speech–language disorders involve problems with speech or with language. Speech–language clinicians are specialists in schools that provide services to students who have speech–language disorders, either as a primary or secondary disability or as a related service.

Speech Disorders

Speech disorders involve difficulties with speaking sounds and words. These problems can take a few different forms. Some learners have trouble clearly articulating specific speech sounds, which can impact the clear pronunciation of words. At other times, students may have difficulty with their vocal quality and their speech may sound hoarse. Finally, other students may have disfluent speech that is repeated or has unwarranted pauses and hesitations, which is typically called stuttering (ASHA, 2019).

Language Disorders

Language disorders can impact both receptive and expressive language and interfere directly with student progress in reading and writing. Interventions for language problems may occur in a separate setting or in the classroom where the student receives primary instruction. In addition to the speech–language clinician, the student's general and special education teachers provide supports to help the student develop needed language skills (ASHA, 2019).

Simmons, & Kame'enui, 1998; Bryant, Goodwin, Bryant, & Higgins, 2003). These gaps in vocabulary knowledge begin very early and grow larger over time (Cunningham & Stanovich, 1998). Because pragmatics relates to how language is used in social situations, it may not seem immediately relevant to the development of literacy skills; however, pragmatics skills greatly influence how successful a student is in the academic learning environment, which is inherently social. Students with pragmatics concerns may evidence difficulties by misunderstanding or not appropriately using language in social contexts (Mercer & Mercer, 2005). Students with language-based disabilities can also have difficulty interpreting nonverbal cues such as facial expressions and tone and following conversational rules such as turn taking and not interrupting others who are speaking. These types of skills are necessary in the classroom in order for students to successfully participate in learning experiences with adults and peers.

Assessment of Oral Language and Early Reading Skills

Assessment of oral language and early reading skills is critical for all learners, and especially students who struggle to acquire early reading skills. Assessing these foundational skills will set the stage for as much reading growth as possible for students. Typically, the assessment and monitoring of foundational reading skills occurs in the early elementary grades—kindergarten through 2nd grade. For teachers to appropriately handle monitoring the wide range of early reading skills, multiple data collection methods need to be used. Teachers utilize both early reading screening data as well as anecdotal and structured observation information. They are also likely to have individual skill data sheets for each student to track his or her progress. At times, when a specific skill is being taught to all students, for instance as part of the school's curriculum, a teacher may have class-wide observational data tracking sheets, where all students' progress can be monitored simultaneously. Common early reading assessments are discussed in the rest of this chapter.

Early Reading Screeners

At the beginning of the school year, early reading screeners are used to get a baseline of beginning reading skills typical for early elementary students. **Early reading screeners** are formal assessments that gauge students' beginning reading skills at several different times during the year. Early reading screeners cover multiple beginning reading skills, including:

- concepts of print,
- phonemic awareness,
- letter names and letter/sounds identification,
- letter/sound correspondences (alphabetic principle),
- listening comprehension.

A firm foundation in these basic skills is needed for later decoding of more complicated sound patterns at the word and syllable levels. For this reason, early reading screeners are integral in monitoring student progress and providing data to teachers to use for instruction. As you remember from Chapter 2, the strength of formal assessments is that they measure a breadth of skills and they have been tested and normed using national samples so that comparisons to the performance of same-aged peers are possible.

Some early reading skills are linked to one another. For example, a student's ability or inability to recognize uppercase and lowercase letters is connected to his or her understanding of sound/symbol relationships. If students cannot recognize letters, it would be difficult for them to see a direct connection between specific sounds and letters. At the same time, students who are strong in their ability to identify letters may more easily see the connection between sounds and specific letters. For this reason, screeners are often also administered at a few other key junctures throughout the year to ensure that students are continuing to meet important benchmarks. Repeated screening is intended to catch any concerns as they arise instead of waiting until the student has fallen too far behind to be successfully caught up within the school year. Commonly used formal early reading assessments include the Phonological Awareness Screening Test (PAST; Kilpatrick, 2016), the Phonological Awareness Literacy Screener (PALS; Invernizzi, 2010), the Comprehensive Test of Phonological Processing-2nd edition (CTOPP-2; Wagner, Torgesen, & Rashotte, 1999), and the TPRI Early Reading Assessment (University of Texas, 2019).

Observation/Authentic Assessment

While early reading screeners are indeed helpful, observation of language development and early reading skills as students engage in authentic learning tasks is also prominent in the early grades because observations yield immediate information about how students are progressing. Observations can be anecdotal or guided by checklists of important language and early reading skills. Some of the skills involved in the manipulation of sounds and letters are closely linked to later sounding out of individual words. Assessment of early reading skills should begin with the evaluation of underlying language skills as well, which focus on students' abilities to understand and use oral language that serves as a foundation for written communication.

Observation of Oral Language Development

Classroom teachers primarily assess oral language skills through anecdotal or structured observations. Initial observations are usually in authentic contexts so teachers can see students' everyday language use with peers and adults in their typical environments. See Chapter 4 for more information on language development in the natural environment. Teachers start language observations by simply taking notes on students' abilities to listen and talk, gauging both receptive and expressive language usage within natural social interactions.

Informal observations of language abilities include several important skills. When students engage in discussion with their friends, parents, and other adults, teachers will want to see if students engage in conversational turn taking. Observers look to see whether students provide appropriate verbal and nonverbal responses when listening and then responding during conversations. Another crucial skill is listening comprehension because being able to understand spoken language is closely linked to reading comprehension.

With more structured observations, students engage in oral language situations that are more contrived by the teacher in order to systematically assess and track development. With structured conversational observations, teachers may dictate the conversation topics in which to engage students and then track the students' ability to talk about that topic. The students' abilities to effectively convey their thoughts and stay on topic are key elements for ongoing monitoring. The number of conversational turns they are able to take on a particular topic is important as well, especially if a teacher notices students not being able to take three to four conversational turns at the beginning of kindergarten. Student progress is usually tracked on teacher-made oral language data sheets.

In evaluating listening comprehension in a more structured manner, the teacher could use a shared reading experience with the whole class, small group or individually. The understanding of the story or content of the book read aloud to students would be what is assessed through questioning students to evaluate their listening comprehension. These questions would span the scope of the book read and comprise a range of questioning levels. In cases where a student has a specific listening comprehension weakness in one area, the teacher might handpick and read a selected book that has content targeting only that skill area. For example, to work on evaluating student understanding of difficult words and expressions, a teacher may use an *Amelia Bedelia* book (e.g., Parish, 2009) in which the lead character amusingly misunderstands idioms, multiple meaning words, and other figurative language. In this assessment scenario, a shared reading may still occur within a small group, but it would be limited to students who are struggling with similar listening comprehension skills involving figurative language.

Observation of Early Reading Development

Similar to oral language assessment, early reading skills are typically monitored by observation in both authentic and more structured contexts. These observations are done in an ongoing manner to keep close watch on students' skill development. These early skills are critical because they set the stage for higher-level reading development as students progress in school.

Teachers observe students anecdotally, making notes about what they are seeing and not seeing related to students' reading and writing development. Teachers might observe students during circle time, reading centers, shared reading, and a wide variety of other natural classroom reading situations. Some of the skills teachers want to track are:

- concepts of print,
- phonological and phonemic awareness,
- alphabet identification,
- knowledge of sound/symbol relationships,
- listening comprehension,
- early writing.

For instance, a kindergarten teacher may be circulating around her room during reading centers and notice a student correctly matching letters and sounds while playing a matching game with his peers. She will note this observation. Conversely, if she notices a student who is having difficulties matching letters and sounds, she will immediately give feedback to the student to help him be successful. She will make a note of this as well, so she remembers to reteach or reinforce the skill with that student at a later time.

Oftentimes, teachers will want to observe beginning reading and writing skills in a more structured manner. This might include using more formal observational checklists to collect data by checking off skills as the teacher observes them in the classroom. For instance, teachers can use checklists to monitor students' mastery of concepts of print. For this purpose, teachers can have a comprehensive listing of the multiple skills students need to be familiar with for successful understanding and use of print within books for reading. These checklists can be used in multiple ways. Teachers can check off skills when they observe mastery of a specific skill by a student while engaging in relevant classroom activities. Conversely, a teacher can sit down one-on-one with a student to evaluate all targeted skills in one sitting. In both cases, the teacher would check off skills that are correctly demonstrated by the student. Skills that are not evidenced would be reassessed using the checklist after time has passed and instruction has been provided. Otherwise, skills can also be checked off if they are successfully observed in other contexts. For instance, if a child has trouble tracking text left to right, the teacher may pay close attention when that child is at the literacy center pointing to text as he listens to a book on tape. The teacher would then update her concepts of print data sheet on that student when the targeted skill is observed. This form of observation is more structured than anecdotal observation because of the tool used to track the data collection.

Monitoring early reading skills can be a challenging task because of the number of skills that need to be tracked, including concepts of print, alphabet knowledge, sound/symbol relationships, phonological awareness, and early writing. Further, the challenge of tracking these skills is that not all students will need to be tracked on each skill. For instance, some students will enter kindergarten already having mastered concepts of print. With these students, there would not be a need to track students on this skill because they already have competency in this area. Other students may enter school knowing all of their upper and lower case letters, and ongoing tracking of these skills would not be necessary for those particular students. Because of the variability of student abilities, it is valuable for teachers to keep folders and binders for each student in the classroom that contain records of skill progression.

Early Progress Monitoring

With some skills, ongoing progress monitoring materials are available from curriculum publishers or research-based sources. One example of such material is the DIBELS assessment, which has research-based evaluation materials across multiple early reading areas. One of the areas monitored by DIBELS is letter naming fluency (LNF) where a student is asked to identify lower and upper case letters within a three-second time period for each letter. Teachers can easily use DIBELS materials by having a data sheet for each student who needs monitoring on this skill. The assessment is designed so students' skills in this area can be monitored more frequently than the screening time points. This type of assessment has standardized administration procedures and testing occurs at set times during the school year.

A Focus on Formal Assessment of Early Reading Development

While this chapter focuses on informal assessments of early reading development to inform instruction, there are circumstances where an educator might need information about how a student is doing related to other students of the same age or grade. In these instances, a formal assessment that is norm-referenced is needed. As you remember from Chapter 2, norm-referenced assessments are standardized and require specialized training to administer. These types of assessments cover a wide range of skills related to early literacy. Results provide an indication of how a student is performing compared to a norming sample of students in the same grade. A formal assessment of early literacy development would generally be used as a pre and post assessment of a student's performance as well as to determine whether a student's progress is sufficient to close an achievement gap with peers. An example of a formal assessment of early literacy is the BRIGANCE Inventory of Basic Skills.

BRIGANCE Inventory of Basic Skills	
Targeted Skills:	• Physical Development (gross motor and fine motor) • Language Development (receptive and expressive) • Academic Skills/Cognitive Development (literacy and mathematics) • Adaptive Behavior (daily living) • Social and Emotional Development (interpersonal and self-regulatory)
Ages:	0 to 7–11 years
Administration:	Individualized
Time Required:	15 minutes
Publisher:	https://www.curriculumassociates.com/Products/BRIGANCE

Instructional Supports for Struggling Readers

Oral language development and early reading skills serve as an important foundation for future reading proficiency. Numerous instructional approaches have been presented in this section of the book that foster these important skills. In Chapter 3, you learned that early language experiences that young children have before they enter school promote continued language development and provide exposure to literacy with print. These language experiences continue into the school years where teachers play an important role in setting the stage for learning. In addition, you learned in Chapter 4 that modeling, developmentally appropriate explicit instruction, and guided and independent practice through play are all important aspects of good early reading instruction. There are some aspects of instruction that are particularly crucial to remember for students who do not come to school with foundational learning experiences or who are at-risk for reading problems.

Selection of Instructional Materials

The vocabularies of struggling readers are much more limited than vocabularies of proficient readers. These students know fewer words and that knowledge is more shallow. Further, deficiencies in word knowledge begin in the earliest grades and grow larger over time. Therefore, it is important to expose students to a wide range of words beginning in the earliest grades. This means exposing students to rich conversations and a wide range of texts, including both informational texts as well as narrative texts and stories.

Considerations for Instruction

Students who are at-risk for reading problems, including English learners and students with language-based disabilities, are likely to need additional supports that may not be necessary for the typical learner. Additional input from the senses can help these students to hold information in working memory as they are processing new information. These supports can be auditory, visual, and tactile. **Auditory supports** are verbal prompts that help students attend to relevant information. **Visual supports** involve some sort of visual stimulus to support the learning task. **Tactile supports** involve some sort of physical manipulation of objects. Each of these cues can be used separately or in combination with each other.

All students can benefit from auditory supports; however, auditory prompts are more likely to be necessary for students who are at-risk for reading problems. You learned in Chapter 5 that, developmentally, students recognize beginning sounds of words first followed by ending sounds of words and finally the medial sounds of words. Some students have difficulty with recognizing ending sounds and especially the medial vowel sounds of words. In these instances, a teacher might provide an auditory prompt to cue students to the target sound. Ending consonant sounds are likely to be prompted by repeating the target sound sequentially numerous times. For example, for the word *cat*, the teacher might prompt /c/ /ă/ /t...t...t/, if the target sound the student was struggling to identify was the final sound in the word. Most struggling students have difficulty with both identifying and differentiating between medial vowel sounds in words. In this instance, a teacher would "stretch out" the vowel sound to help the students recognize the word. For example, in the word *pet* the teacher might provide an auditory prompt /p/ /ĕĕĕ/ /t/, giving the students more time to recognize and distinguish the medial vowel sound. This is important because many times students will confuse medial vowel sounds, for example, hearing *pit* for *pet* or *cop* for *cup*. Additional auditory prompts help these students to attend to the correct information. A full listing of prompts for sounds can be found in Chapter 5. You will notice in reviewing the practice chart that while all vowels are stretch sounds, consonants can be stretch or stop sounds (meaning they should be repeated).

Auditory prompts are also highly prevalent in early childhood classrooms that tend to use music, chants, repetitive stories, and poetry to foster awareness and manipulation of language. When walking into an early childhood classroom, for example, it would not be uncommon to hear a song playing from the children's singer Raffi (1996) about how he is going to "*eat eat eat apples and bananas*" and "*oot oot oot ooples and banoonoos*." This manipulation of sounds through music and other auditory mediums provide important cues to all students, but especially those who struggle to acquire language and early reading skills.

In a similar way, visual supports can be incorporated into instructional activities. When students are first learning phonological and phonemic awareness skills, the focus is on auditory recognition and discrimination, without recognition of the actual letters that represent those sounds. For this reason, picture cues are often used instead of letters in practice activities. For example, the teacher might show a picture of a cat and ask the students to "say the sound they hear at the beginning." If the student was a native Spanish speaker learning English, the student might respond /g/ as this is the beginning sound in *gato*—the Spanish word for *cat*. The student will be confused if the teacher then tells him that he is incorrect. Even for native English speakers, it is important to be cautious when using picture prompts. For example, a teacher may show a picture of a baseball cap and ask students to "say the sound they hear at the beginning." If a student identifies the word as a *hat* rather than a *cap* she may say /h/ while the other students respond /c/. Again, this can lead to confusion for the student and would be especially problematic for students who have language-based disabilities as it may become difficult to unlearn misinformation. Thus, when teachers use visual supports, it is important to clarify that the student and the teacher agree to the word that the picture represents.

You learned in Chapter 5 that modeling is an excellent way to help students learn concepts of print. In typical classrooms, teachers do this by reading "big books" that are large enough for all students to see and they point to each word as they are reading aloud as a model for students to attend to individual words. For students at-risk for reading problems, the teacher might also have a struggling student assist with pointing to each individual word using their finger or some other fun pointing device. This provides a visual–tactile

---

A Focus on Cueing to Support Phonological Awareness

Some students may need additional prompting to help them attend to and produce sounds correctly. For example, when modeling pronunciation of sounds in words, the teacher might put a finger near his mouth to cue students to look at the shape of his mouth when making the sounds. When pronouncing multiple sounds, the teacher may add a finger for each sound so that students have a visual cue of sound boundaries, for example /m/ (one finger), /ă/ (two fingers), /t/ three fingers.

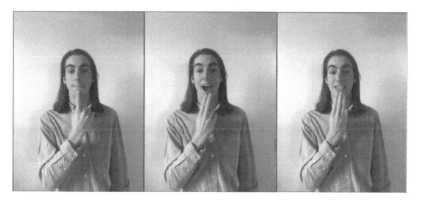

For students with disabilities who are really struggling to differentiate and produce sounds, speech–language clinicians will sometimes have a student use a mirror to see how his or her mouth looks and feels at the same time (visual–tactile support) when producing a sound.

Sometimes distinctions between sounds are subtle because the mouth and tongue are in a very similar position. In this case, it sometimes helps to have the student feel their larynx while saying a sound to feel whether there is a vibration (voiced sound) or not (unvoiced sound). This would be a tactile support to help a student differentiate between the sounds /f/ and /v/, for example.

Teachers might also use auditory–tactile supports to help students get their mouths in the correct position. For example, asking a student to smile wide when pronouncing the /ē/ sound or asking a student to make the sound of a ticking clock, paying attention to their tongue and the air coming out of their mouth (Bursuck & Damer, 2011).

support to the student to attend to those individual words from top to bottom and left to right (the sequence) that they may not learn as quickly from visual observation alone.

An example of visual–tactile supports was also presented in the description of Elkonin boxes presented in Chapter 5. In this activity, students manipulate chips that represent phonemes as a way to strengthen their phonemic awareness skills. While this type of activity is potentially beneficial for all students, it may be required for students who are at-risk for learning problems because it provides the visual–tactile and auditory supports that some students need to learn to manipulate phonemes. You will notice in the activity that chips were used to represent the sounds in words rather than letters. This ensures that the demands on the students are purely auditory, without requiring visual discrimination of print as well. The chips are a visual–tactical prompt that can help some students to better process and store the auditory information that they are learning.

Another example of a visual–tactile support includes using manipulatives to help students sequence information they hear in a story, fostering their listening comprehension. While some students may learn to retell events from a story without additional supports, others will need these cues to learn to efficiently process information. For example, a teacher could use a felt board with felt pieces representing aspects of the story that students hold and physically manipulate as they are putting the events of the story in order. Alternatively, students might complete an independent activity where they sequence pictures from the story in sequential order by gluing the pictures in sequence on paper. There is a photograph of this type of activity in Chapter 5.

Because play is so integral to early childhood classrooms, the use of visual–tactile supports tends to be more prevalent than in the upper grades. However, it is still important for teachers to be cognizant of why these prompts are important for at-risk learners in particular. For example, in Chapter 5, there is a photo of a student physically moving a card of the day of the week onto the correct sentence frame in the morning activity. This physical movement provides a tactile support for that student that reinforces retention of that sight word. Visual–tactile supports can also include the use of manipulatives, pictures, and multi-media in phonological awareness activities. For example, a teacher may present students with a box filled with toys and other classroom items that begin with the sound /d/. Students would select an item out of the box and identify both the name of the object and the sound that they hear at the beginning of that word. This provides a visual–tactile prompt for the students during the auditory task.

A Focus on Instructional Accommodations

Accommodations do not negate the need for explicit, direct instruction. However, in addition to quality instruction, some students with disabilities will need instructional accommodations in order to make progress in the curriculum or toward individualized education plan (IEP) goals. Accommodations are changes that are made for individual students and might include changes in time, input, output, and level of support (Hallahan et al., 2005). In the areas of oral language and early reading development, instructional accommodations might include:

- additional practice opportunities; longer time to respond (time),
- multi-modal presentation of new information; technology (input),
- use of a pencil grip; pointing to respond (output),
- individualized instruction; cross-age peer tutoring (level of support).

Additional Learning Opportunities

Multiple exposures to a word (or concept) helps all students learn more quickly; however, multiple exposures are critical for English language learners and students with language-based disabilities (McKeown, Beck, Omanson, & Pople, 1985; Stahl, 1999). In early childhood classrooms, that might mean (a) exposing students to a new term through an informational book read during circle time, (b) reviewing that word during small group instruction with an overt reference to it on the class word wall, (c) reading the same informational text in the library center, (d) practicing a computer game with the same term illustrated, and (e) completing a writing activity that lends to use of the new term. Multiple exposures to a word or concept across activities and contexts helps students to make connections and integrate the word or concept into their existing knowledge. This then becomes part of the students' existing knowledge that students can access in future learning activities.

In many modern classrooms, technology is a valuable resource to help support student learning because it can enable structured opportunities for additional practice and provide an additional modality for students to interact with new vocabulary and concepts. Numerous early reading programs can help reinforce language and literacy concepts that have been introduced through explicit instruction. For example, some programs like *A to Zap* (Sunburst) or *Earobics* (Houghton Mifflin) reinforce student understanding of the alphabetic principle and phonemic awareness. Websites like *BrainPOP, Jr.* (https://jr.brainpop.com/) support vocabulary development with animated curriculum-based content for a range of topics including science, health, writing, reading, social studies, and math. Regardless of the technology used, it is important for an adult to monitor student progress carefully. Just as students who are at-risk for learning problems may need additional

---

Specialized Instruction: Language and Early Reading

Lindamood-Bell programs use a sensory–cognitive approach. In these programs, intensive instruction is delivered to students individually or in small groups using multisensory techniques. Program content is structured through sequential lessons that foster concept imagery. Specialized training is needed to deliver instruction.

Seeing Stars

The *Seeing Stars* program focuses on symbol imagery to improve phonemic awareness, sight words, and spelling.

LiPS

The *LiPS* program focuses on the oral movements of phonemes to improve student ability to identify, number, and sequence sounds in words. These skills are then applied to reading, spelling, and speech.

Talkies

The *Talkies* program focuses on developing dual coding imagery and language as a means to foster language comprehension and expression. *Talkies* is the primer to the *Visualizing and Verbalizing* program (see Chapter 12 for a description).

support during modeling and explicit instruction to ensure that they are correctly applying learned skills, these students are likely to need similar prompting when independently practicing those newly learned skills on a computer.

References

American Speech-Language-Hearing Association (ASHA). (2019). Retrieved March 30, 2019 from *Speech & language disorders.* https://www.asha.org/public/speech/disorders/

Baker, S. K., Simmons, D. C., & Kame'enui, E. J. (1998). Vocabulary acquisition: Instruction and curricular basics and implications. In D. C. Simmons & E. J. Kame'enui (Eds.), *What reading research tells us about children with diverse learning needs: Bases and basics* (pp. 219–238). Mahwah, NJ: Erlbaum.

Bryant, D. P., Goodwin, M., Bryant, B. R., & Higgins, K. (2003). Vocabulary instruction for students with learning disabilities: A review of the research. *Learning Disability Quarterly, 26,* 117–128.

Bursuck, W. D., & Damer, M. (2011). *Teaching reading to students who are at-risk or have disabilities.* Boston, MA: Pearson.

Cunningham, A. E., & Stanovich, K. E. (1998). What reading does for the mind. *American Educator, 22,* 8–17.

Hallahan, D. P., Lloyd, J. W., Kauffman, J. M., Weiss, M. P., & Martinez, E. A. (2005). *Learning disabilities: Foundations, characteristics, and effective teaching* (3rd ed.). Boston, MA: Pearson.

Invernizzi, M. (2010). *Phonological awareness literacy screening (PALS).* Charlottesville, VA: University of Virginia.

Juel, C. (1988). Learning to read and write: A longitudinal study of 54 children from first through fourth grades. *Journal of Educational Psychology, 80,* 437.

Kilpatrick, D. (2016). *Equipped for reading success.* New York, NY: Casey & Kirsch Publishing.

Lovett, M. W., Barron, R. W., & Benson, N. J. (2003). Effective remediation of word identification and decoding difficulties in school-age children with reading disabilities. In H. L. Swanson, K. R. Harris, & S. Graham (Eds.), *Handbook of learning disabilities* (pp. 273–292). New York, NY: Guilford Press.

Mann, V. A. (2003). Language processes: Keys to reading disability. In H. L. Swanson, K. R. Harris, & S. Graham (Eds.), *Handbook of learning disabilities* (pp. 213–228). New York, NY: Guilford Press.

McKeown, M. G., Beck, I. L., Omanson, R. C., & Pople, M. T. (1985). Some effects of the nature and frequency of vocabulary instruction on the knowledge and use of words. *Reading Research Quarterly, 20,* 522–535.

Mercer, C. D., & Mercer, A. R. (2005). *Teaching students with learning problems* (7th ed.). Upper Saddle River, NJ: Prentice Hall.

Neuman, S. B., & Celano, D. (2012). *Giving our children a fighting chance: Poverty, literacy, and the development of information capital.* New York, NY: Teachers College Press.

Parish, H. (2009). *Amelia Bedelia's first day of school.* New York, NY: HarperCollins.

Raffi. (1996). *Apples and bananas.* Rounder.

Scarborough, H. S. (2009). Connecting early language and literacy to later reading (dis)abilities: Evidence, theory, and practice. In F. Fletcher-Campbell, J. Soler, & G. Reid (Eds.), *Approaching difficulties in literacy development: Assessment, pedagogy and programmes* (pp. 23–38). London, UK: Sage.

Scott, C. M., & Windsor, J. (2000). General language performance measures in spoken and written narrative and expository discourse of school-age children with language learning disabilities. *Journal of Speech, Language, & Hearing Research, 43,* 324–339.

Siegel, L. S. (2006). Basic cognitive processes and reading disabilities. In H. L. Swanson, H. R. Harris, & S. Graham (Eds.), *Handbook of learning disabilities* (pp. 158–181). New York, NY: Guilford Press.

Stahl, S. A. (1999). *Vocabulary development.* Newton Upper Falls, MA: Brookline Books.

University of Texas. (2019). *TPRI: Early reading assessment.* Retrieved March 30. 2019 from https://tpri.org/index.html

Wagner, R., Torgesen, J., & Rashotte, C. (1999). *Comprehensive Test of Phonological Processing (CTOPP).* Austin, TX: PRO-ED.

Wisconsin Center for Education Research. (2019). *The can do descriptors.* Retrieved March 26, 2019 from https://wida.wisc.edu/teach/can-do/descriptors

SECTION II: APPLICATION ACTIVITIES

Show What You Know!

In this section you learned about a wide range of early reading skills. Can you identify them? Take the quiz below to find out.

Directions:

Match each scenario to the corresponding early reading skill.

Scenario	Skill
1 Mr. Mason wondered aloud: "Who has a /b/ word to share with us?" as his students looked at the plastic pieces of fruit he handed them. Larry, who had a banana, said, "I have one, Mr. Mason." This student is developing _____.	A Phonemic awareness
2 At the beginning of the school year, a kindergarten teacher observes a child "pretend reading" a book in the independent reading area of the classroom. The child turns the pages in sequence, looking at the illustrations and quietly telling a story, but not referring to the printed text. This shows that the student has emerging _____.	B Phonological awareness
3 The teacher prompts a student: "Listen to these sounds: /s/.../a/.../t/. Say it fast." The student replies "/sat/": This shows the student is developing _____.	C Concepts of print
4 During writing time, the teacher observes Mika drawing a turtle. Underneath the picture she writes "t." This shows that she has emerging _____.	D Listening comprehension
5 After hearing a story read aloud to the class, the teacher asks "What happened first in the story?" Jose replies "The first pig made his house out of straw." This is an indicator of _____.	E Alphabetic knowledge

Answer Key: 1-B, 2-C, 3-A, 4-E, 5-D

Partner Activity/Discussion

Identification vs. production? In this chapter, you learned that production tasks are more challenging than identification tasks. This activity will help you decide for yourself!

Directions:

1. **Complete the activities**

    One person in the group will be the activity leader. This person (and only this person) should now turn to **Appendix B** for further directions.

The remainder of the group are participants and should follow the directions provided by the activity leader. Each participant needs a dry erase board, a dry erase marker, and an eraser (or paper towel). (*Tip*: If you do not have individual white-boards, a quick way to make a class set is to laminate 8 × 11 sheets of cardstock).

2. **After completing the activities, discuss the following questions in your group**

   • Which activity was the identification task and which was the production task?
   • Which did you find easier? Why?
   • When completing these activities, when might a student find a particular activity easier or more difficult than anticipated?

Learn More: Multimedia Activity

In this section you learned about oral language development and early reading. For this activity, you will go deeper in your learning by exploring the Reading Rockets website. This site houses a wealth of research-based strategies on helping students learn to read that serves as a valuable resource for teachers, parents, administrators, librarians, and childcare providers. Resources include videos, webcasts, articles, reports, and book recommendations. Have fun learning!

Directions:

1. **Before**
   In the first text box below, list key ideas you know (K) after reading this section of the textbook. In the next text box, write questions about what you want to learn (W) from completing this multi-media activity.

K (**K**now)	What do you already know about this topic? 1. 2. 3. 4.
W (**W**ant to learn)	What do YOU want to learn more about? 1. 2. 3. 4.

2. **During**

   Explore the Reading Rockets website at http://www.readingrockets.org/. Use the information you find here to answer your questions!

3. **After**

   After you have finished reading about the areas you wanted to learn more about, look back at what you indicated you knew before starting (K) and wanted to learn (W). Can you now answer the questions? How does this new information connect with what you knew before starting? Write the answers to your questions in the text box below. Be sure to add any additional unexpected information that you learned (L) as well!

L (Learned)	What did you learn? 1. 2. 3. 4.

Section III

Accessing Text

Section III: Overview

Being able to decode and recognize commonly used words is essential for reading proficiency, because it is necessary for reading comprehension of text. Teachers need knowledge
of the appropriate instructional progression for explicitly teaching sound constructions for
phonetically regular words, including multisyllable words, and strategies for helping students recognize and remember phonetically irregular words and sight words. Automaticity
with word recognition enables fluent reading of connected text, freeing up metacognitive
space needed for students to process and understand what they have read. In the first chapter
of this section, instructional approaches that help all students access text are presented. In
the second chapter of this section, intensive reading interventions are described. In the final
chapter of this section, characteristics of students who struggle with reading comprehension
will be described along with how to use assessment data to inform instructional choices for
these students.

- Chapter 7: Word Identification Skills and Fluency
- Chapter 8: Intensive Reading Intervention
- Chapter 9: Supporting All Students in Accessing Text

Guiding Questions

As you are reading, consider the following questions:

- How are words classified and why is it important to recognize the differences be-
tween them?
- What are the different types of text and when should they be used?
- What instructional approaches foster acquisition of basic reading skills and devel-
opment of reading fluency?
- What are the characteristics of students who need intensive intervention?
- How does the scope and sequence of intensive programs differ from general edu-
cation reading curriculums?
- In what ways is the instruction within intensive reading programs more explicit
than instruction in the general curriculum?
- What challenges do at-risk students have with acquiring basic reading skills?
- What assessments are used to informally assess a student's ability to access text?
- What additional instructional supports are needed for readers who struggle to ac-
quire basic reading skills?

Chapter 7

Word Identification Skills and Fluency

Fundamentals of Word Identification

Students are considered fluent readers if they read connected text quickly, accurately, and with expression—called reading fluency (Kuhn, Schwanenflugel, & Meisinger, 2010). If students are not able to recognize words in text quickly and accurately, they will not be able to understand the meaning of the print they have read. However, when a student reads text fluently, it "frees up" metacognitive space, which enables comprehension (Levy, Abello, & Lysynchuk, 1997; Temple, Ogle, Crawford, Freppon, & Temple, 2018). Accurate word recognition is at the heart of fluent reading, and as such, it is a necessary component of the reading process.

Word identification instruction is most effective when it is systematic. An important part of systematic instruction is the consideration of the types of words being taught. It is also important to carefully select texts that will be most beneficial for instruction and that students will practice reading independently to reinforce new skills that they have acquired during instruction. Finally, the learning environment itself can be structured to include supports to students as they are developing word recognition skills.

Types of Words

Words can be categorized into three types: phonetically regular words, phonetically irregular words, and sight words. A description of each follows.

Phonetically Regular Words

A variety of terms can be used to describe the relationship between graphemes (written letters) and phonemes (individual sounds), including: graphophonemic relationships, letter/sound associations, letter/sound correspondences, sound/symbol correspondences, and sound spellings (Armbruster, Lehr, & Osborn, 2001). Regardless of the terminology used, **phonetically regular words** are those in which letters represent their most common sound (Carnine, Silbert, Kame'enui, Slocum, & Travers, 2017). Phonetically regular words comprise letters and/or groups of letters that are predictable in their corresponding sounds. Some parts of words, such as rimes and affixes, are predictable as well. This means that both simple words and longer words can be phonetically regular.

Educators need to understand phonetic concepts in order to communicate effectively about the curriculum, assessment reports, and issues students are having. For example, you may have noticed that in some spaces in this book, letters were placed between slashes—/ă/, for example. These slashes indicate that the sound of the letter rather than the name of the letter is being referenced. In addition, you may have noticed symbols above some of the vowels, called **diacritical marks**, indicating a long or a short vowel pronunciation. For a listing of the most common sound notations, see Table 7.1. Although most teachers do not need to have every symbol committed to memory, they should understand the notation system and have a resource available to help them communicate with other relevant educators.

Table 7.1 Common Sound Notations

Diacritical Mark	Definition	Example
/ /	Indicates a letter sound	/b/ as in b<u>a</u>t
ˉ	Long vowel	/ā/ as in b<u>a</u>k<u>e</u>
ˇ	Short vowel	/ŏ/ as in t<u>o</u>p
ə	Schwa	/ə/ as in mount<u>ai</u>n
´	Primary stress	´stu dent
ˎ	Secondary stress	ˎsel ect

In Chapter 5, you learned the most common sounds for individual letters. Letters comprise **vowels** (A, E, I, O, U, and sometimes Y) and **consonants** (all other letters). Phonetically regular words can contain consonant blends, also called **consonant clusters**, such as "st" and "bl." Notice that the individual letters in consonant blends can be sounded out with the individual letter sounds: /s/-/t/, and /b/-/l/.

Some regular words contain vowel sounds that are influenced when followed by an "r" or "l"—these are called **r-controlled** and **l-controlled vowels**. For example, the sound that the letter "a" makes in the word *cat* is different from the sound it makes in the word *cart* where the vowel is influenced by the letter "r" that follows. Similarly, the sound that the letter "o" makes in the word *cot* is different from the sound it makes in the word *colt* where the vowel is influenced by the letter "l" that follows.

Phonetically regular words also include commonly used letter combinations with vowels or consonants, called digraphs and diphthongs respectively, that comprise commonly used sounds. Neither digraphs nor diphthongs can be sounded out using their individual letters because they make a new and distinct sound. "A **digraph** is a two-letter combination that represents a single speech sound" (Fox, 2010). For example, the digraph "ch" makes the distinct sound /ch/ that is not the same as the individual sounds of the letters: /c/ and /h/. "A **diphthong** is a single vowel phoneme, represented by two letters, resembling a glide from one sound to another" (Fox, 2010). For example, the diphthong "oy" makes a distinct sound where the first sound glides into the second sound; sounding out these letters separately would not produce the same sound. The most common letter combinations are shown in Table 7.2.

Once students have mastered the basic phonics skills involving **letter/sound correspondences** (the relationships between phonemes and graphemes), students begin to recognize familiar spelling patterns. Initially, children begin to separate single syllable words into their **onsets** (beginning consonant sound) and **rimes** (the vowel and consonant sound patterns that follow). For example, in the word *mine*, the onset is /m/ and the rime is /ine/. In the word *chair*, the onset is the phoneme /ch/ and the rime is /air/. Recognizing common spelling patterns, or **word families**, helps students to begin decoding unfamiliar words more efficiently. The 37 most common word families in English are: -ack, -ain, -ake, -ale,

Table 7.2 Common Sound/Letter Combinations

Vowel Digraphs			Consonant Digraphs			Diphthongs		
sound	letters	keyword	sound	letters	keyword	sound	letters	keyword
/a/	ai	bait	/n/	kn	know	/aw/	aw	raw
	ay	say	/f/	ph	graph		au	taught
/e/	ea	eat	/r/	wr	wren	/ew/	ew	few
	ee	meet	/w/	wh	when	/ow/	ow	sow
/i/	igh	sigh	/ch/	ch	chin		ou	out
/o/	oa	boat	/sh/	sh	shoe	/ar/	ar	far
/oo/	oo	moon	/th/	th	thin	/er/	er	her
			/th/	th	then		ir	sir
			/ng/	ng	sing		ur	fur
						/or/	or	for
						/ol/	ol	fold
						/oy/	oy	toy
						/coo/	qu	queen

Adapted from: Carnine, D. W., Silbert, J., Kame'enui, E. J., Slocum, T. A., & Travers, P. (2017). Direct instruction reading (6th Edition). Boston, MA: Pearson.

–all, –ame, –an, –ank, –ap, –ash, –at, –ate, –aw, –ay, –eat, –ell, –est, –ice, –ick, –ide, –ight, –ill, –in, –ine, –ing, –ink, –ip, –it, –ock, –oke, –op, –ore, –ot, –uck, –ug, –ump, and –unk (Wylie & Durrell, 1970). Some of the most common word families, progressing from basic to more complex, are shown in Table 7.3.

When students are at the point of decoding whole words, common **word notations** help educators communicate with one another about words that will be targeted for instruction. With common word notations, there are only two elements: consonants, noted with the shorthand C, and vowels, which are indicated with V. Educators communicate about the types of words using these two symbols. The most simple word constructions are indicated by CV and VC. CV words are ones that begin with a consonant and end with a vowel, such as *go, me, hi, so,* and *be.* VC words are ones that start with a vowel and end with a consonant, such as *on, it, an, up,* and *at.* In general, the notations are used to indicate word patterns that a student is currently working on and can be used to indicate simple patterns like the ones above or more complicated patterns, like consonant–consonant–vowel–consonant–consonant

Table 7.3 Sample Word Families

-at	-ake	-all	-ick	-unk	-ing	-ook	-ight
at	bake	all	brick	bunk	bring	book	bright
bat	brake	ball	chick	chunk	king	brook	fight
cat	cake	call	click	drunk	ping	cook	flight
fat	lake	fall	kick	dunk	ring	crook	fright
hat	make	hall	lick	flunk	sing	hook	knight
mat	quake	mall	pick	hunk	spring	look	light
pat	rake	tall	quick	junk	sting	nook	might
rat	shake	wall	sick	skunk	string	rook	night
sat	snake		stick	trunk	swing	shook	right
that	take		thick		thing	took	sight
	wake		trick		wing		tight

(CCVCC) words, which contain a short vowel sound with consonant digraphs or blends like *crush*, *drift*, *crisp*, *shift*, and *think*. The notations are useful because they clearly indicate progressively more complicated sound constructions in short and long single syllable words. When students begin to read more complex and multi-syllabic words, notations encompassing word parts are used. See Table 7.4 for common word notations.

Table 7.4 Common Word Notations

Notation	Meaning	Example
CV	Consonant–Vowel	go
VC	Vowel–Consonant	at
CVC	Consonant–Vowel–Consonant	top
CVCV	Consonant–Vowel–Consonant–Vowel	late
CVCC	Consonant–Vowel–Consonant–Consonant	bath
CCVCC	Consonant–Consonant–Vowel–Consonant–Consonant	block
CVVC	Consonant–Vowel–Vowel–Consonant	meet

When students have mastered individual phoneme decoding, recognition of word parts helps students to identify more complex words that have multiple syllables. Phoneme by phoneme decoding is effective when students are reading words that are one syllable with three to six phonemes. As words extend to seven or more phonemes, decoding one sound at a time becomes time-consuming and laborious, ultimately impeding what the student understands from what is read. Because multisyllable words can also be phonetically regular, students still use their basic phonics skills and sight word knowledge to help them decipher these **multi-syllabic words**, but they also use additional strategies for decoding beyond their ability to sound out each word phoneme by phoneme. These strategies include identification of sight words embedded within the word (called **base words**), word parts including syllables, and bound morphemes (discussed in Chapter 5), which are commonly called **affixes**. Focusing on decoding words with affixes is critical for students in 3rd grade and beyond. At the 3rd grade level is when most students begin reading multi-syllabic words, 80% of which have prefixes and suffixes as part of their word construction (Cunningham, 1998).

A **syllable** is a group of letters that typically encompasses one to a few consonant sounds but only one vowel sound (Searfoss, Readence, & Mallette, 2001). Syllables can be closed or open. **Closed syllables** consistently contain a vowel sound that may or may not be preceded by a consonant, but is always followed by a consonant sound. For example, *at*, *it*, and *up* are closed syllables with no beginning consonant sound, and *neck*, *clap*, and *shut* are closed syllables with consonant beginning and ending sounds. **Open syllables** generally begin with a consonant sound and end with a long vowel sound with no consonant sound at the end of the syllable, such as *go*, *me*, and *hi*. When reading multisyllabic words, a reader is likely to encounter open syllables that do not contain a beginning consonant sound either, like the "e" in *even*, the "o" in *open*, and the "a" in *acorn*.

An affix at the beginning of a word is called a **prefix**, and an affix at the end of a word is called a **suffix**. Affixes are **bound morphemes**—meaningful language pieces that cannot stand alone as their own word, but have essential meaning qualities that help shape the overall meaning of a given word. Table 7.5 displays the four most common prefixes and suffixes found in the English language. These affixes account for 97% of prefixed words in print (Honig, Diamond, & Gutlohn, 2000).

Table 7.5 Sample Affixes

Prefix	Example	Suffix	Example
anti-	antifreeze, antibiotic, anticlimactic, antithetical	**-ed**	hopped, pushed, invaded, skimmed, summarized
in- (im-, il-, ir-)	injustice, impossible, illegal, irrational	**-ing**	running, giving, analyzing, contradicting, writing
re-	return, retrace, regenerate, revise, resubmit	**-ly**	quickly, beautifully, significantly, interchangeably
un-	unfriendly, unfair, unrest, undo, uncivilized	**-es** (-s)	boxes, books, novels, experiments, subtracts

Phonetically Irregular Words

Irregular words do not follow phonetically regular patterns, such as *friend*. Pronounced phonetically, the "ie" in friend would make a long vowel sound as in *pie* or *tried*. You try. Which of the following words are irregular?

have

because

afternoon

through

great

question

toothpaste

oval

Monday

policeman

If you said that all words were irregular with the exception of *afternoon, question,* and *toothpaste,* you were correct!

Sight Words

Sight words are those words that the students should be able to identify automatically without sounding them out. Failure to develop a sight word vocabulary will prevent a student from becoming a fluent reader (Pikulski & Chard, 2005). This is because almost half of all the words in text are composed of 100 words, called **high-frequency words** (Fry, Fountoukidis, & Polk, 1985). Clearly, these words are important for developing reading proficiency because of the frequency with which they occur in text. For example, targeted sight words for a beginning reader would include: *a, and, is, it, my, no, said,* and *the,* while targeted sight words for middle elementary might include: *different, fall, number, other, picture,* and *sentence*. Notice that some of these words are phonetically regular. Because the desired outcome is for students to recognize them automatically, these words are generally learned through memorization even though they could be sounded out. Like when introducing new sounds, teachers should be careful that they limit the number of words that are introduced at one time and avoid visually similar words during initial instruction (e.g., *them* and *then; him* and *his; has* and *had*) (Bos & Vaughn, 2006). The most frequent sight words at each grade level can be found on sight word lists. Two common sight word lists are

Dolch (e.g., http://www.sightwords.com/sight-words/dolch/) and Fry (e.g., http://www.sightwords.com/sight-words/fry/).

As students become more proficient readers, they will recognize many other words and word parts by sight as well. This contributes to their ease with decoding more complex multisyllable words and their overall reading fluency. Thus, reading fluency requires students to actively apply the phonics skills they have been practicing with isolated target words to then decode both basic and more complex words within sentences and paragraphs—referred to as **connected text**.

Types of Text

Students can improve their word identification skills and reading fluency when they are provided opportunities for targeted practice. To this end, teachers will need to select texts that are at the appropriate level for both the needs of an individual student and the purpose of the reading activity (Bursuck & Damer, 2015). As such, it is also important for teachers to understand which texts are appropriate for instruction, which texts are appropriate for independent practice, and which texts are unreasonably difficult for a student.

Texts Appropriate for Instruction

In the classroom, with teacher instruction and supervision, learners benefit from practicing at the instructional level. An instructional level text is one where the student has between 90% and 94% accuracy for word recognition. Students recognize the majority of the words in text but may need teacher assistance with decoding difficult or newer sound patterns.

Texts Appropriate for Independent Practice

For fluency practice, students benefit from practicing independently in class or at home. In order for students to benefit from independent reading time, they need to practice reading texts that are at their independent reading level in the area of decoding. An independent level text is one where the student has 95% accuracy or higher for word recognition. At this level, students are easily able to decode and recognize words with little to no assistance.

Texts that Should be Avoided

A frustrational level text is one where the student can identify less than 90% of words (Armbruster et al., 2001). At the frustrational level students are overwhelmed by the decoding and word recognition needed to fluently read the text. If texts are at the student's frustrational level and cannot be avoided, additional supports are needed, or the text needs to be modified. A text modification is where a key facet of the text itself is changed to assist students in reading it. Modifications can take the form of reducing the number of words to be read, changing the amount and level of vocabulary words and minimizing of the complexity of the incorporated text sentences. Modifications should take place when the focus of a reading task is improving a student's decoding and fluency.

The Instructional Environment

The instructional environment can be a useful resource to help reinforce instruction. Like with classrooms in the early grades (see also Chapter 5), print-rich environments foster student learning throughout K–12. For example, a classroom in the primary grades is likely to display charts with word families. See Figure 7.1. Similarly, word walls are often used to display words that have been introduced in reading and writing instruction.

Figure 7.1 Example word families

Classroom libraries are another important source of environmental print. It is useful for students when the items in the classroom library are labeled in such a way that students can find a book at an appropriate reading level. In the upper grades, labels that indicate the genre can help students find books of interest. It is also important to ensure that the text options in the classroom library represent the range of reading levels of the students in the class. Because texts in the classroom library are generally intended for independent reading time, students' independent (rather than instructional) reading levels are the types of books that students should have access to. In the younger grades, this means ensuring that **controlled texts**—those that are easily decodable, are an option in the library. For older readers, age appropriateness of texts becomes a challenge when some students in the class have independent reading levels far below grade level. In these instances, high-interest/low-readability texts are a good addition to a class library. You will learn more about these types of texts in Chapter 9. Incorporating high-interest reading material is key to engaging many readers because students are more likely to read content that is meaningful to them personally. Another benefit of high-interest texts is that students will often persist in reading material of interest even if decoding of the text is a bit above their independent level.

Instructional Approaches

Readers use knowledge of sounds and word parts as well as their memory of intact words to effectively identify words within connected text. As students read, they use their knowledge of the rules of language and understanding of meaning from the surrounding words to correct any words that do not make sense as initially read. Eventually, these processes are used simultaneously and seamlessly, resulting in fluent reading.

Knowledge of sounds includes both phonemes and phoneme combinations, while knowledge of word parts includes rimes, syllables, and affixes. In order to use this knowledge to decode words, students must be able to quickly and accurately identify sounds and/or word parts—this is referred to as **automaticity**. For words that follow phonetically regular word patterns, phonics approaches are used for instruction. Teachers prompt students to practice what they have learned within connected text by drawing students' attention to the sound/symbol relationships within words. For words that are phonetically irregular or that appear in text with a high frequency, memory strategies are generally used to help students recognize these words automatically by sight. When students advance to more complex, multisyllable words, students are taught to use structural analysis to strategically decode the components of the words.

Finally, as students practice the word identification strategies that they have learned while reading connected text, there are prompting strategies that teachers can use to reinforce what has been taught and to encourage students to self-monitor their own reading— referred to as **context cues**. Context cues can refer to cues related to both semantics and syntax. As you will recall from Chapter 4, knowledge of the rules of language is referred to as syntax and understanding of the meaning of words is referred to as semantics. Figure 7.2 depicts the processes involved in word identification.

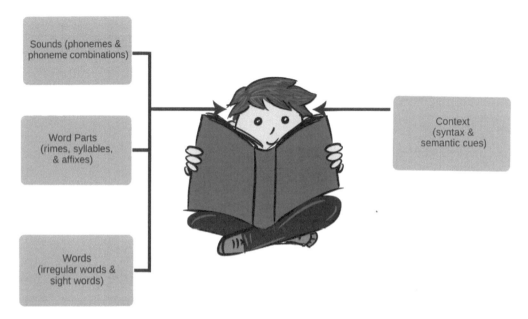

Sounds (phonemes & phoneme combinations)

Word Parts (rimes, syllables, & affixes)

Words (irregular words & sight words)

Context (syntax & semantic cues)

Figure 7.2 Word identification

Phonics

Phonics is an instructional approach that helps students recognize the relationship between letters and sounds, called the alphabetic principle (Armbruster et al., 2001). The most effective instruction in phonics is both systematic and explicit (National Reading Panel, 2000). **Systematic phonics instruction** includes the use of a curriculum with a specified range of letter/sound correspondences (referred to as **scope**), taught in a specified order (referred to as **sequence**) (Mesmer & Griffith, 2005). **Explicit phonics instruction** is direct, precise, and unambiguous, and includes practice using phonics to read words (Mesmer & Griffith, 2005). Further, explicit instruction is more effective when it focuses on teaching students to recognize linguistic patterns (phonological, orthographic, and morphological) rather than to memorize phonics rules (Moats, 2010).

One of the practices for improving students' phonics abilities for decoding words is developing their letter/sound manipulation skills. Letter/sound manipulation activities give students multiple opportunities to practice modifying existing words by changing out one letter (and its corresponding phoneme) one at a time and then identifying the newly formed word with the new letter/phoneme combination. Having students complete letter/phoneme manipulation activities can also be used to give students practice opportunities for segmentation and blending skills, which are foundational to effective decoding. Students with strong phonemic awareness skills will have an easier time with these activities because they have foundational early reading skills upon which to build.

While there are many ways to have students practice letter/phoneme manipulation, it is best to begin with identification activities. For instance, with younger students, teachers may have them "word hunt" around the classroom, school, or a particular book they are reading to find words that end in -at, -in, -up, or another word family (Bear, Invernizzi, Templeton, & Johnston, 2016, p. 62). For older students, an identification activity may involve having students see how many smaller words they can identify in larger multisyllabic words that are more difficult to decode (Cunningham & Hall, 1994).

After identification activities, teachers will move to more advanced practice, such as the use of **Elkonin boxes** (introduced in Chapter 5). The boxes provide a visual for the sound segmentation process. When addressing phonics, letters are placed in the Elkonin boxes to represent individual phonemes (rather than markers used when developing phonemic awareness skills). For example, letter/phoneme manipulation of the initial letter/sounds of words ending in -at might look like Figure 7.3.

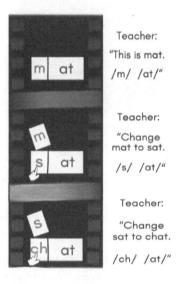

Figure 7.3 Elkonin boxes for letter/phoneme manipulation

To support student skill development with blending letter/sounds to form words, students can be encouraged to "slide" sounds of words together with the visual of a drawn playground slide. Using the slide visual, manipulative letters can be placed together at the top of the slide and moved down the slide together to provide overt and concrete practice blending the sounds. Teaching students to blend letters/phonemes together is a key decoding skill.

Other practice opportunities can be incorporated for blending and segmenting skills that incorporate the encoding process (further discussed in Chapter 13). One method of practicing letter/sound manipulation is using letter cards and a pocket chart. This works especially well for modeling letter/sound manipulation as well as fostering student interaction with words. Just like the Elkonin boxes can be used for breaking words into individual phonemes, in the pocket chart each letter/sound card can be moved and used to form words by putting the cards in order in the pockets to form real words. Then, one letter/sound card at a time can be changed out to modify the word (Beck, 2013). Instruction typically begins with words that have common phonetic spelling patterns to which students have already been introduced. Then, students form new words by changing out the initial letter/sound (onset) and keeping the end of the word with the particular spelling pattern (rime).

Besides pocket charts, another reading–writing practice connection with letter/sound manipulation is having students complete word sorts. In word sorts, the teacher gives students a list of words with familiar spelling patterns and students sort the words into groups. This gives learners practice with newly learned spelling patterns (Bear et al., 2016).

In addition to systematic and explicit phonics instruction in isolation, it is important for students to practice what they have learned with connected text. Practice should initially utilize controlled text that targets the skills that have been taught during instruction. While reading, students should be prompted to use graphophonic cues to assist them with applying the word reading strategies they have been taught. **Graphophonic cues** relate to the sounds and symbols of print (Searfoss et al., 2001). In reading the sentence *"The boy r___ down the street"* graphophonic cues would let the reader know that a short word is needed that begins with the sound /r/. Teachers need to remember though that the prompt "sound the word out" should only be used with phonetically regular words. Providing this sort of prompt with irregular words that cannot be sounded out will cause confusion and frustration for the student.

Memory Strategies

For irregular words and sight words, students will not be able to rely on their phonics abilities and instead will need to memorize them these words. While there are many types of **memory strategies** that work, there are some core practices with any of these strategies that are essential to their effectiveness.

When students are working on the initial stages of remembering words, it is critical that the teacher closely monitors student reading of these words. In this way, the teacher ensures from the outset that the student is accurately reading the word and committing the correctly read word to memory. At this stage in the learning process, it is important that the student has multiple opportunities to practice the word through repetition within engaging activities (Bear et al., 2016).

A key mechanism for irregular and sight word practice is using **flashcards** (Morrow, 2014). The following is a 1st grade teacher providing corrective feedback to a student during flashcard practice:

TEACHER: (shows student flashcard of the word "said")
STUDENT: (incorrectly reads word) "/s/-/ā/-/d/"
TEACHER: (providing corrective feedback) This word is "*said*." What word is it?
STUDENT: "*said*"
TEACHER: Perfect! Read "*said*" in a loud voice.
STUDENT: (much louder) "*said*"
TEACHER: Wow! That was great—very loud! Now read me the word "*said*" in a whisper.
STUDENT: (whispering) "*said*"
TEACHER: Nice work! Last time, read "*said*" for me in a silly voice.
STUDENT: (laughing) "*said*"
TEACHER: That's right—"*said*"! Now let's move on to our next word (moving the "*said*" flashcard to the back of the practice pile and going on to the next word).

In this example with the sight word "*said*," the student receives corrective feedback on how to accurately read the word. From there, the student is given multiple opportunities to practice the word while receiving teacher feedback on his reading, as well as having an accurate model presented by the teacher each time he is asked to repeat the target word. This practice process encompasses all the words selected for a particular flashcard practice set. In each set, students practice all the words, with any incorrect words moved to the back of the flashcard set for further repetition until mastered and then removed from the practice set.

Another key element of practice for instruction of sight and irregular words is **goal setting**. When students take an active role in helping to determine word recognition goals, it helps motivate them to practice. Students become more invested in their own learning when they are key players in determining word-learning goals with teacher guidance. As part of this process, learners can track their word learning by monitoring (and sometimes even graphing) their own progress. Student goal setting can also help make word learning more meaningful for each individual learner.

A final element of memorization strategies is to make word practice fun. Student **engagement** is essential to the success of any memory strategy for word learning. Students retain more when they are interested in their word learning. Teachers can develop and use memory strategies for new words that incorporate games for practice. Incorporating technology in these practice opportunities is another way to engage students.

Structural Analysis

Once students display mastery of letter/sound knowledge and are beginning to recognize small words and word parts by sight, they are ready to move on to the more difficult step of decoding multi-syllabic words. **Structural analysis** is an effective way to approach this process because it helps the reader break down multi-syllabic words into smaller more recognizable parts that include compound words, base words, syllables, and/or affixes (see Figure 7.4). Structural analysis also helps students with comprehension by helping them gain meaning from word morphology. (You will learn more about this in Chapter 11.)

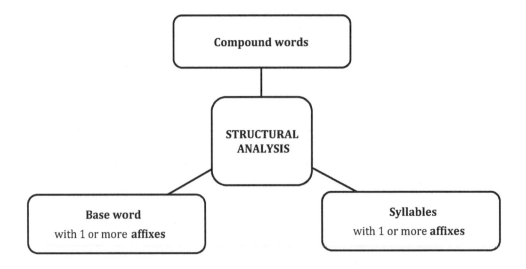

Figure 7.4 Structural analysis

When teaching students to read syllables, it is often best to start instruction with simple two syllable words where both syllables are actually smaller individual words, called free morphemes (see Chapter 4 for more information). When decoding multisyllabic words, free morphemes are typically called base words. In some cases, the student will recognize that the word comprises two adjacent base words—called **compound words**. For example, the word *baseball* comprises the base words *base* and *ball*. Similarly, the word *daydream* comprises the base words *day* and *dream*. In other cases, the word will comprise a base word or syllable with affix(es). As shown in Table 7.6, the construction of multisyllable words can become quite complex.

Table 7.6 Word Composition

Word Composition	Example
prefix + base	telephone, antibody, untrue, irregular, disorder, unearth
base + suffix	librarian, biology, fruitless, secondly, calculated
prefix + base + suffix	biannually, replanted, dishonorable, unimagined
base + suffix + suffix	helplessness, personally, powerlessly, forgetfulness
prefix + base + suffix + suffix	unquestioningly, noncommittedly, unsuccessfully, distrustfully

Structural analysis teaches students to approach these complex words systematically. With structural analysis strategies, students are first directed to look at the beginning and ends of multisyllable words to identify affixes. For example, in the word *baseballs*, the student would recognize the affix "s" in addition to recognizing the roots *base* and *ball*. This student may also make meaning from this observation by recognizing that the bound morpheme "-s" makes the word plural. In the compound word *daydreamed*, the student would recognize the affix "-ed" in addition to recognizing the roots *day* and *dream*. The student may also recognize that the bound morpheme "-ed" indicates the tense of the word.

Beginning instruction with base words that the student already recognizes will allow students to focus on recognizing affixes. At first, students should only be exposed to words with either a prefix or suffix. As students progress in their ability to see and decode different types of affixes, they then can be exposed to words with both a prefix and suffix, and eventually words with multiple prefixes and suffixes. Students should practice recognizing new affixes in multi-syllabic words in isolation at first. Like with sight word instruction, multiple exposures are important for facilitating automaticity—in this case, exposure would be to a variety of words with the targeted affixes. For example, if working on the suffix "-tion," practice words might include: *nation, position, pollution, revolution,* and *solution*.

Once students have mastered targeted affixes, words without recognizable bases should be added. For example, with the word *polynomial* a student would recognize the prefix "poly-" and the suffix "-ial" and recognize or sound out the remaining syllable "nom." Another example is the word *denominator*, where a student would recognize the prefix "de-" and the suffix "-or" leaving "nominat," which the student could sound out using the syllables /nom/-/in/-/āt/.

Approaches for Promoting Reading Fluency

As students increase in accurate recognition of individual words, they will practice reading these words in connected text. At this point, the focus shifts from accuracy alone to also include promoting fluent reading. Fluency involves both rate and prosody while reading connected text. **Rate** is the combination of both speed and accuracy and it is typically captured as correct words read per minute (CWPM). You will read more about this in Chapter 9. **Prosody** is the expression with which a student reads connected text. For example, a student with good prosody will read phrases of words together with appropriate inflection, pausing as indicated by punctuation in the text. Thus, prosody requires an underlying understanding of sentence structure and syntax (see Chapter 12 for more information). Following are activities to promote each of these areas.

Model Fluent Reading

It is important to ensure that students have the opportunity to hear fluent reading modeled by the teacher, or another adult. To further enhance the benefit to students, a visual support is used so that students are following along with the print at the same time that they hear it read aloud. Visual supports can include each student having an individual copy of the text or viewing a projection of the text on a screen or media device. Fluent reading can also be provided through media—such as material read aloud on a computer or a book on tape. Again, the most benefit is gained if the student reads along with the print while the text is read aloud. Finally, partner reading with a peer can be used where a stronger reader reads first.

Repeated Reading

Reading rate is often addressed through repeatedly reading a text multiple times after hearing a good model. Repeated reading can be enhanced by using reading material that is of high interest to a student. In addition, students often find it motivating to set goals. This is done by determining the student's rate on a first read, setting a goal for how many more words will be read after practice, reading the passage multiple times, and then checking to see if the goal was met. While rereading a passage can sometimes improve comprehension, benefits are limited and diminish after three readings (Chard, Vaughn, & Tyler, 2002). While repeated readings can help increase reading rate for the practiced passage, repeated readings do not generally influence prosody.

Reader's Theater

An approach for improving prosody is Reader's Theater. With **Reader's Theater**, a short story is selected that is then formatted as a script and each student is designated a part to read. It is critical that scripts have a variety of reading levels so that there are reading parts for students that are at different reading levels within the class. With Reader's Theater, students have multiple opportunities to practice reading the script because the end goal is a performance of the story being read just like a typical theater production. Beginning run-throughs may focus on accurate word identification, but then subsequent readings of the script move towards fluent and expressive reading of the text. In this way, students engage in meaningful practice to enhance prosody in addition to increasing reading rate.

Independent Practice

The amount of time spent reading has a positive relationship to reading performance. Students need to practice reading every day. Teachers can foster this by blocking off time in the school day for this to occur or assigning nightly independent reading as homework. Some schools approach this as a school-wide initiative where there is a designated time of the day where everyone in the school "drops everything and reads" (DEAR) or participates in "sustained silent reading" (SSR). However, time for independent reading, even school wide, is not sufficient. Students will not benefit if they only pretend to read during this designated time because the text is too difficult.

It is important to consider how to monitor students and hold them accountable when independently reading. In the classroom, teachers can simply observe student reading, looking for eyes on text, finger tracking left to right across the page, and the questions students ask about the text. Teachers can also utilize reading logs, which track what students have read both in school and at home. Reading logs can take many different forms but should allow students to note both the book and the number of pages read during a particular independent reading time. These logs can also take the form of student-made bookmarks like those shown in Photo 7.1 where students use their bookmark to note the number of pages read. Logs can be motivating to students as they participate in tracking their progression in a particular book. Additionally, teachers can use independent practice time to "touch base" informally with students about what they are reading.

Photo 7.1

A more formal option for monitoring independent reading can be asking students to share with the teacher or class they would or would not recommend a specific book they are reading. Book talks are another forum for monitoring, allowing students to talk about the book they are reading. In these talks, students present an overview of the story read as well as specific details and reader impressions of the text as a sales pitch to others to read the book.

Self-monitoring When Reading Connected Text

When students are reading connected text and read a word incorrectly, the other words in the sentence can help them recognize and correct their mistake; this process is referred to as **self-monitoring**. The surrounding words are helpful because they tap into the reader's existing knowledge of syntax and semantics (or word meaning). The grammar of a sentence (how words are ordered) is referred to as a **syntax cue** (Searfoss et al., 2001). For example, in the sentence "*The boy _____ down the street,*" one would expect the word to be a verb. Similarly, the sentence "*The boy run down street,*" would sound wrong because the verb is in an inaccurate tense (*runs* or *ran* would be grammatically correct) and an article (e.g., *the*) is missing. These types of cues can help a student recognize when a sentence "doesn't sound quite right" and help them predict words when they are not able to sound the word out successfully.

The meanings of words in a sentence are referred to as **semantic cues**, often called context cues. With this type of cue, students self-monitor what they read and recognize when something "doesn't make sense" (Bos & Vaughn, 2006). For example, if a student read "*The boy ran down the sweet,*" self-monitoring would prompt the student to recognize that the sentence does not make sense. The student would then go back and try to find and correct their mistake to understand the intended meaning.

While using context cues can be helpful for self-monitoring, it is important that students are not taught to over rely on them. Over relying on context cues can adversely impact student reading as texts become more difficult and have increasing numbers of words not in their speaking vocabularies. It can also undermine students' efforts to used phonics and structural analysis strategies they have been taught, particularly for students who struggle to learn to read.

References

Armbruster, B. B., Lehr, F., & Osborn, J. (2001). *Put reading first: The research building blocks for teaching children to read.* Washington, DC: U.S. Department of Education.

Bear, D. R., Invernizzi, M., Templeton, S., & Johnston, F. (2016). *Words their way: Word study for phonics, vocabulary, and spelling instruction* (6th ed.). Boston, MA: Pearson.

Beck, I. L. (2013). *Making sense of phonics: The hows and whys.* New York, NY: Guilford Publications.

Bos, C. S., & Vaughn, S. (2006). *Strategies for teaching students with learning and behavior problems.* Boston, MA: Pearson.

Bursuck, W. D., & Damer, M. (2015). *Teaching reading to students who are at risk or have disabilities* (3rd ed.). Boston, MA: Pearson.

Carnine, D. W., Silbert, J., Kame'enui, E. J., Slocum, T. A., & Travers, P. (2017). *Direct instruction reading* (6th ed.). Boston, MA: Pearson.

Chard, D. J., Vaughn, S., & Tyler, B. J. (2002). A synthesis of research on effective interventions for building reading fluency with elementary students with learning disabilities. *Journal of Learning Disabilities, 35,* 386–406.

Cunningham, P. (1998). The multisyllabic word dilemma: Helping students build meaning, spell, and read "big" words. *Reading & Writing Quarterly: Overcoming Learning Difficulties, 14,* 189–218.

Cunningham, P. M., & Hall, D. P. (1994). *Making words: Multilevel, hands-on, developmentally appropriate spelling and phonics activities.* Torrance, CA: Goodapple.

Fox, B. J. (2010). *Phonics and word study for the teacher of reading: Programmed for self-instruction* (11th ed.). Boston, MA: Pearson.

Fry, E., Fountoukidis, D. L., & Polk, J. K. (1985). *The new reading teacher's book of lists.* Englewood Cliffs, NJ: Prentice-Hall.

Honig, B., Diamond, L., & Gutlohn, L. (2000). *Teaching reading: Sourcebook for kindergarten through eighth grade.* Novato, CA: Arena Press.

Kuhn, M. R., Schwanenflugel, P. J., & Meisinger, E. B. (2010). Aligning theory and assessment of reading fluency: Automaticity, prosody, and definitions of fluency. *Reading Research Quarterly, 45,* 230–251.

Levy, B. A., Abello, B., & Lysynchuk, L. (1997). Transfer from word training to reading in context: Gains in reading fluency and comprehension. *Learning Disability Quarterly, 20,* 173–188.

Mesmer, H. A. E., & Griffith, P. L. (2005). Everybody's selling it—But just what is explicit, systematic phonics instruction? *The Reading Teacher, 59,* 366–376.

Moats, L. C. (2010). *Speech to print: Language essentials for teachers* (2nd ed.). Baltimore, MD: Brookes Publishing.

Morrow, L. M. (2014). *Literacy development in the early years: Helping children read and write.* Boston, MA: Pearson.

National Reading Panel. (2000). *Report of the national reading panel: Teaching children to read: An evidence-based assessment of the scientific research literature on reading and its implications for reading instruction: Reports of the subgroups.* National Institute of Child Health and Human Development, National Institutes of Health.

Pikulski, J. J., & Chard, D. J. (2005). Fluency: Bridge between decoding and reading comprehension. *The Reading Teacher, 58,* 510–519.

Searfoss, L. W., Readence, J. E., & Mallette, M. H. (2001). *Helping children learn to read: Creating a classroom literacy environment.* Boston, MA: Allyn & Bacon.

Temple, C., Ogle, D., Crawford, A., Freppon, P., & Temple, C. (2018). *All children read: Teaching for literacy in today's diverse classrooms* (5th ed.). Boston, MA: Pearson Education.

Wylie, R. E., & Durrell, D. D. (1970). Teaching vowels through phonograms. *Elementary English, 47,* 787–791.

Chapter 8

Intensive Reading Intervention

Fundamentals of Intensive Reading Interventions

The ability to access text is a prerequisite to reading comprehension and so it is vitally important to the academic success of all students. Most students will respond to reading instruction that is provided in the general education classroom; however, even high-quality instruction and interventions will not be effective for some students. Further, the reading problems of students in the elementary grades will be compounded over time as they face higher-level literacy demands in the upper grades (Biancarosa & Snow, 2006).

Students Who Need Intensive Intervention

Because the ability to access text is so pivotal to students' academic performance, schools strive to ensure that all students have basic word reading skills by the end of 3rd grade. Unfortunately, there are many students who, even with strong instruction and remediation efforts, do not master word reading skills in the primary grades and whose fluency and text comprehension are impacted as a result (Denton, Wexler, Vaughn, & Bryan, 2008). Further, many of these students continue to struggle with basic reading skills in the secondary grades persisting with the same decoding errors displayed by much younger children (Berkeley & Taboada Barber, 2015; Lovett, Barron, & Benson, 2008). Some researchers have suggested that perhaps as much as two hours a day of systematic instruction using age-appropriate materials is necessary for these students to make significant gains in reading (e.g., Archer, Gleason, & Vachon, 2003; Moats, 2001).

This type of systematic and intensive instruction generally occurs as part of "Tier 3 instruction" and/or special education. You will remember from Chapter 1 that "tiers" are in reference to school-wide models, such as response to intervention (RTI) and multi-tiered systems of support (MTSS), designed to systematically support the reading development of all students. Although models vary across states, generally, Tier 1 instruction refers to high-quality general education classroom instruction; Tier 2 instruction refers to initial small group remediation efforts for students who are not making as much progress as expected; and Tier 3 instruction is intended for students with the most significant challenges learning to read and for whom other remediation efforts have failed—sometimes referred to as "non-responders." Tier 3 instruction includes daily small group intensive explicit instruction, with frequent progress monitoring by a teacher with specialized training.

The reasons that these students do not respond to general education instruction and supplemental intervention attempts vary. Students who are second language learners who have not had educational experiences in their home country may fall into this group because they are just not able to make gains quickly enough to catch up to their native speaking peers. Students whose families are living in poverty may fall into this category because they do not have the same resources and experiences as other students. Students who are homeless are particularly likely to fall significantly behind because their basic needs are not being met, which draws attention away from learning at school. The vast majority of students receiving Tier 3 instruction are students with, or at-risk for, language-based learning disabilities that impede the acquisition of decoding skills and reading fluency (Katz, Stone, Carlisle, Corey, & Zeng, 2008).

As you learned in Chapter 1, a learning disability is a protected disability category under the federal legislation the Individuals with Disabilities Education Act (IDEA, 2004). These students have significant problems with language-based learning tasks despite having average to above average intelligence. These problems are thought to stem from underlying deficits in phonology and short-term memory—and working memory in particular (Swanson, Harris, & Graham, 2013). Students with the most severe form of language-based disability are referred to as having **dyslexia**.

Students with dyslexia experience multiple issues in reading, with one of the most prominent concerns being difficulties with phonological awareness and understanding and application of letter/sound relationships (International Dyslexia Association, 2002). Other significant difficulties involve letter ordering and reversals, decoding longer multi-syllabic words, misattending to smaller words, and an overall slower reading rate that impacts both oral and silent reading (The Dyslexia Resource, 2019). With older students, letter reversals when reading and writing are one of the "red flags" for indicating dyslexia. One of the assessments used as part of evaluation in determining dyslexia is rapid automatic naming (RAN). Within a RAN assessment, students are presented with letters, colors, numbers, and objects and are asked to name them as quickly as they can (Ziegler et al., 2010). Research has shown connections between students' in abilities to identify these common language items with automaticity at an early age and later reading development difficulties. Students who struggle with these naming tasks are often the ones with the most significant reading difficulties, which are associated with dyslexia (Norton & Wolf, 2012).

Another group of students who may experience significant reading delays are dually-identified learners. Dually-identified learners are English language learners who are also identified with a learning disability, in essence demonstrating the same difficulties with phonology in their L1 that they also demonstrate in English (Park, Martinez, & Chou, 2017). In general, before deciding whether a dually-identified student needs intensive reading instruction, it is important to determine if that student is within the silent period of language development mentioned in Chapter 1. Students who are within the silent period are unable to express learning that is occurring and may need more time to acquire language rather than intensive reading instruction. Fully understanding student needs and abilities is therefore important for determining whether intensive reading instruction is warranted.

Comprehensive Intensive Reading Programs

Intensive reading programs utilize a tightly controlled sequence of instruction with specialized teaching methods. Intensive programs that are comprehensive are also sufficiently broad in scope to address the major areas of reading instruction where students with the most significant challenges struggle. While teachers could develop their own tightly controlled materials, this is rarely feasible because of the intensive time and specialized skill set needed to do so. As such, use of a published program that has been developed by experts and extensively field tested is a more realistic option. While there are many packaged reading programs available, this chapter will focus on two of the most intensive and commonly used approaches: Direct Instruction and the Orton-Gillingham method. Table 8.1 lists some of the most commonly used published programs that are grounded in these approaches. Teachers need specialized training to learn how to implement both of these programs effectively.

Table 8.1 Published Program Descriptions

Published Program	Website for Program Description
Direct Instruction	
Corrective Reading (decoding and comprehension strands) McGraw-Hill	https://www.mheducation.com/prek-12/program/corrective-reading-20082008/MKTSP-URA04M0.html?page=1&sortby=title&order=asc&bu=seg
Reading Horizons Discovery Reading Horizons	https://www.readinghorizons.com/
Reading Horizons Elevate Reading Horizons	https://www.readinghorizons.com/
Language for Learning McGraw-HIll	https://www.mheducation.com/prek-12/program/language-learning-20082008/MKTSP-USA07M02.html?page=1&sortby=title&order=asc&bu=seg
Reading Mastery McGraw-Hill	https://www.mheducation.com/prek-12/program/reading-mastery-signature-edition-2008-2008/MKTSP-UQM08M02.html?page=1&sortby=title&order=asc&bu=seg
REWARDS Voyager Sopris Learning	https://www.voyagersopris.com/literacy/rewards/overview
Orton-Gillingham	
Explode the Code EPS	http://eps.schoolspecialty.com/products/literacy/phonics-word-study/explode-the-code/about-the-program
FUNdations Wilson Language Training	https://www.wilsonlanguage.com/programs/fundations/
Just Words Wilson Language Training	https://www.wilsonlanguage.com/programs/just-words/
Mega Words EPS	http://eps.schoolspecialty.com/products/literacy/phonics-word-study/megawords-2nd-edition/about-the-program
Recipe for Reading EPS	http://eps.schoolspecialty.com/products/literacy/reading-intervention/recipe-for-reading/about-the-program
SPIRE EPS	http://eps.schoolspecialty.com/products/literacy/reading-intervention/s-p-i-r-e-3rd-edition/about-the-program
Wilson Reading System Wilson Language Training	https://www.wilsonlanguage.com/programs/wilson-reading-system/

Direct Instruction Approaches

Direct Instruction is an intensive, scripted reading program that uses highly controlled teaching materials and instructional techniques to ensure that all students master skills taught in each lesson. According to the National Institute for Direct Instruction (2019), there are five philosophical principles for Direct Instruction:

1. All children can be taught.
2. All children can improve academically and in terms of self-image.

3. All teachers can succeed if provided with adequate training and materials.
4. Low performers and disadvantaged learners must be taught at a faster rate than typically occurs if they are to catch up to their higher-performing peers.
5. All details of instruction must be controlled to minimize the chance of students misinterpreting the information being taught and to maximize the reinforcing effect of instruction.

There are many published programs grounded in Direct Instruction methods that have gone through field testing and revision before publication. Published programs all have several features in common. First, Direct Instruction programs require that a student be placed into the level of a program that matches the student's skill level. In other words, even though Direct Instruction is provided through group instruction, the groups are homogeneous rather than heterogeneous. Second, all Direct Instruction programs are mastery programs. This means that all students need to show mastery of the target skills before moving forward in the program. For this reason, Direct Instruction programs have specific correction procedures and routines that enable instruction to be modified to accommodate each student's rate of learning and to ensure that all students are able to master skills.

Orton-Gillingham Approaches

Orton-Gillingham is an intensive approach to reading, writing, and spelling instruction versus a specific reading method or program. According to the Academy of Orton-Gillingham Practitioners and Educators (2019), literacy instruction using this approach is "direct, explicit, multi-sensory, structured, sequential, diagnostic, and prescriptive" and is intended for learners that struggle with acquiring reading skills especially caused by dyslexia. The approach uses multiple exposures to skills across reading, writing, and spelling employing multisensory techniques that include visual, auditory, tactile, and kinesthetic learning and response opportunities. When utilizing this approach, instruction should be guided by ten critical components (Orton-Gillingham Online Academy, 2019):

1. Multi-sensory elements include visual, auditory, tactile, and kinesthetic learning opportunities.
2. Instruction is specifically on the letter/sound relationships between graphemes and phonemes.
3. Both synthetic and analytic phonics are taught emphasizing understanding individual phoneme/grapheme relationships, as well as decoding words by individual sounds.
4. Connections are built between lessons and predictable lesson structure.
5. Sequencing of instruction builds from less to more complex reading decoding concepts.
6. Activities and instruction have repetition and practice built in for automaticity of skills.
7. Instruction is mastery driven and cumulative, with current instruction building on previous learning.
8. Teaching of decoding skills is rules based and logical for students to follow and apply when reading independently.
9. Ongoing monitoring of student reading progress is incorporated to assess student response to instruction.
10. Individual student response to instruction is used to guide and determine pacing of future reading instruction.

There are many published programs that use a multisensory approach. While not all of the programs interpret the Orton-Gillingham approach in exactly the same way, many key similarities can be seen across programs that implement the approach. First, programs individualize instruction for students in a one-on-one or small group setting. Second, students typically have multiple methods of responding during each part of the lesson, allowing for many practice opportunities using different sensory modalities. Finally, progress in these programs typically has a mastery level expectation with each skill before students progress to the next skill area for instruction.

Scope and Sequence of Intensive Reading Program Curriculums

In Chapter 7, you learned that programs are evaluated on both the scope and sequence of the curriculum as well as the pedagogical approach used (Mesmer & Griffith, 2005). In this section, examples from different intensive programs will be used to illustrate these important concepts.

Intensive reading programs are similar in scope. All comprehensive intensive programs focus narrowly on skills that build and reinforce a student's capacity to recognize words with automaticity. Intensive programs are heavily phonics based, but also include foundational phonemic awareness practice to ensure all students have the solid knowledge of phonemes and the alphabetic principle to support success in subsequent skills. To further reinforce learned skills, programs have spelling components to reinforce and support sounds and word patterns that are the focus of instruction. Similarly, intensive programs include connected text where students have practice applying new word identification skills that foster reading fluency. Although word identification is the primary focus of comprehensive programs, there is always a comprehension component as well. The purposes of these components are two-fold. First, it is important to explicitly teach and monitor how well students are attending to the content of the text they are reading. Second, surrounding words give context that can give students clues to the pronunciation and meaning of unknown words (vocabulary). Although context is not the first or primary strategy that students are prompted to use, inclusion of these components ensures that students are balanced in their strategies and approaches to accessing text.

Intensive reading programs are also similar in that they require an intentional sequence for instruction. This includes both the sequence of skills that are taught as well as sequence in the lessons themselves. For example, in Direct Instruction programs, content within each lesson is pared back to the essential skills needed for that lesson; these skills are then taught and practiced to mastery resulting in steady skill building across lessons and program levels. From the very first lesson, the sequence for each lesson includes phonemic awareness manipulation, explicit word-attack instruction and practice with overt corrective feedback, supported reading of controlled passages to mastery, comprehension practice, independent application activities, and progress monitoring of fluency development. In Orton-Gillingham programs, concepts are also taught in a specified sequence with purposeful practice and monitoring of student skill development. However, in this approach skills are mastered in isolation before advancing to application with reading words in sentences and passages. In addition, substeps are practiced to proficiency before moving on to the next substep within each multisensory lesson component (sound cards drill, concepts for reading, word cards, wordlist reading, sentence reading, sound card review, concepts for spelling, written dictation, controlled text passage reading, listening comprehension). As students progress, sentence reading and passage reading are added substeps.

A Focus on Reading Recovery

Reading Recovery is a one-to-one tutoring program implemented in the primary grades, and primarily first grade, as an intervention for students who are struggling. According to the *Reading Recovery* website (https://readingrecovery.org/), each lesson involves:

- reading familiar books,
- reading yesterday's new book and taking a running record,
- working with letters and/or words using magnetic letters,
- writing a story,
- assembling a cut-up story,
- reading a new book.

Unlike the tightly controlled intensive reading programs discussed in this chapter, the focus is on supporting students as they develop their own strategic behaviors to use for reading and writing.

Although this program is highly popular and widely used, evaluations of its effectiveness are mixed. Proponents of *Reading Recovery* refer to the program's inclusion as an effective practice in the What Works Clearinghouse and its widespread use. Opponents of this approach cite (a) empirical research that indicates that while this program is effective for students above the 25th percentile, it has no meaningful effect on students below the 25th percentile, (b) the program's practice of "dropping" students who do not perform well enough (potentially inflating appearance of beneficial outcomes), (c) lack of retention of skills for students who do complete the program, and (d) questionable cost effectiveness of the program (Elbaum, Vaughn, Tejero, Hughes, & Watson Moody, 2000; Moats, 2007).

Types of Words

Words can be categorized as being phonetically regular, phonetically irregular, or sight words (see also Chapter 7). Phonetically regular words are words where letters represent their most common sounds. Phonetically irregular words do not follow these same phonetic patterns and needs to be remembered. Sight words can be a combination of phonetically regular or irregular words; however, they are important for students to memorize because they occur frequently in text. As students progress in their decoding abilities, they will need to decode and break down words into parts or syllables through structural analysis rather than solely focusing on decoding at the sound level. Intensive reading programs treat types of words differently during instruction by providing additional supports to help students recognize and remember consistent sound patterns and words.

Phonetically Regular Words

Phonetically regular words are constructed using individual letters, groups of letters, rimes, and affixes that follow predictable sound patterns (Carnine, Silbert, Kame'enui, Slocum, & Travers, 2017). Many students will pick up on these phonetic patterns through exposure in core instruction, but some students will need more explicit intensive instruction to recognize and decode phonetically regular word constructions. Intensive reading programs take the approach of instructing students to decode phonetically regular words with more systematic and specific cueing to draw student attention to specific phonological patterns.

In *Corrective Reading* (a Direct Instruction program), words are introduced by having students attend to specific targeted sounds and then read the words. For example, if the sound combination "oa" was a target of instruction, students would read a list of words containing that word combination by first saying the sound for "oa" underlined in the word, and then read the entire word. When reading the word *boat* the students would first say the sound "oa" and then read the word *boat*. Students would repeat this pattern through an entire list of "oa" words. In later lessons, "oa" words will be mixed in with other mastered sounds and decoded using the same "say the sound" then "read the word" pattern.

In *Explode the Code* (an Orton-Gillingham based program), words are introduced by specific sound patterns and then are practiced with picture cues and other practice opportunities for the word in isolation before progressing to the word in connected text. For example, if students are practicing the "ur" sound combination, they would practice connecting "ur" to pictures that illustrate "ur" words, like *hurt*, *burn*, and *churn*. Then, the students might be asked to complete a practice activity with similar "ur" words where they would circle the "ur" sound pattern in each word in isolation. Finally, the student would wrap up "ur" sound work with filling in the correct "ur" word in a sentence blank from a word bank of two or three words.

In addition, specialized programs have intentional features designed to help students recognize and remember phonetically regular phonetic patterns. For example, many programs provide visual cues for students to help them attend to meaningful information. These sorts of visual cues are important for learners who are having severe issues learning to decode, because it helps them to focus their attention accurately and consistently on the phonetic patterns in words.

For example, in the *Reading Mastery* program (a Direct Instruction Program) letters have different sizes of fonts to highlight specific sound aspects within words. Notice in the image below of a teacher's whiteboard (Photo 8.1) that there are several alterations to standard text that can help students recognize important aspects of the letters both in isolation and within actual words. For example, in the first row, notice that the letters "th," "er," and "oo" are physically touching. This is intentional to assist students in recognizing that these letters go together to make a single sound. In the second row, you will see that the construction of the letter "d" is adjusted to make it more easily distinguishable from its commonly confused counterpoint, the letter "b." In addition, notations are sometimes used to help students, such as the swoop over the "ng" to indicate that these letters make a common sound and the macron above the letter "e" in *he* to overtly indicate that the "e" in this word makes a long vowel sound. These special notations are also used within words. In the word *made*, a macron is placed over the "a" to indicate a long vowel sound and the "e" is made small to remind students that it should be silent. The word *rain* uses similar notations with the macron over the "a" and a small "i" to remind the student that it should remain silent. Notations are made under words as well to draw student attention to sound combinations that are newly learned, such as the "ar" in *far*. As students progress through the program, these text alterations are systematically faded as students no longer need them.

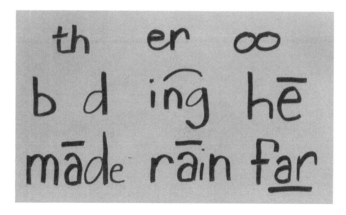

Photo 8.1
Inspired by: Reading Mastery (Decoding A). McGraw Hill.

Visual supports are also utilized in teacher modeling of segmenting and blending. In Figure 8.1, notice that the teacher is providing a visual cue for sounding out the word cat. The dots below the sounds cue the students to what they will be segmenting aloud and the solid line reminds them to "say it fast"—the program prompt to blend the letters. As students become proficient with attending to sounds in words, these prompts are faded in the program.

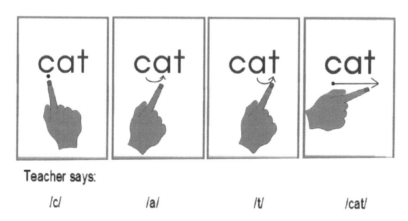

Teacher says:

/c/   /a/   /t/   /cat/

Figure 8.1 Visual cues for blending words

In the *Wilson Reading* program (an Orton-Gillingham based program), regular decodable words are constructed using color-coded sound cards. Consonant letters are a light beige color and vowels are a coral color. When decodable words are constructed, students are cued into word construction and sound patterns by the colored sound cards. The teacher in Photo 8.2 is using sound cards to help students recognize and manipulate decodable words. Notice how she has cards separated into groups by consonants and vowels, and she is using the cards to focus in on individual letter/sound relationships.

Photo 8.2

These components all serve the function of helping students attend to the specific phonetic patterns that are a focus of instruction to ensure that they apply what they have learned
to real word reading. For typically developing readers, this level of prompting is not necessary, but for students with significant problems learning to decode, this level of explicitness
is critical. Without this level of explicitness, these students are unlikely to generalize what
they practice in isolation to reading of words within connected text.

Phonetically Irregular Words and Sight Words

Intensive programs are also purposeful in how they teach students to recognize both phonetically irregular words that cannot be sounded out and sight words. In both Direct Instruction and Orton-Gillingham approaches, repeated practice helps serve as a memory
technique to help students memorize these words as part of their sight word vocabulary.
Note that the phrase "sight word vocabulary" refers simply to automatic recognition of
words, and not necessarily to the meanings of words.

In Direct Instruction programs, this is accomplished by teaching students to spell rather
than sound out irregular words. For example, during initial practice reading the word *friend*
in isolation, students would say each of the letters in friend—"f-r-i-e-n-d"—and then read
the entire word *friend*. They would continue practicing targeted words in this way until the
end of the practice list.

In *FUNdations* (an Orton-Gillingham based program), the primary focus on instruction
is decoding of phonetically regular words; however, students are also taught irregular words
and sight words on an as-needed basis to support student reading when they encounter these
words within lesson sentences. Students in the FUNdations program maintain a word study
book, and during each lesson students add two to five sight words that will be immediately
used during that lesson while reading connected text. Irregular and sight words are practiced with flash cards, in sentences and paragraphs, and through written practice at the end
of lessons when students write dictated sentences.

Multi-syllable Words

Intensive programs also have specialized methods for helping students learn how to decode longer, multi-syllable words. These methods extend what students have been taught when learning to read phonetically regular single-syllable words by providing visual cues that help students attend to phonetic patterns in longer words. These patterns include prefixes and suffixes that are highly prevalent in multi-syllable words. Like with single-syllable words, typically developing readers may not need this level of prompting; however, students with severe reading problems are likely to face significant challenges learning to decipher longer words without this level of support.

For example, *REWARDS* (Reading Excellence: Word Attack and Rate Development Strategies) utilizes Direct Instruction principles to make structural analysis of longer words overt for students with intensive reading needs through tactile notations on the words themselves. Specifically, *REWARDS* teaches students a flexible strategy for recognizing common word patterns using a combination of overt and covert strategies. Overt strategies include identifying affixes and physically circling them and then underlining the vowel sounds in the rest of the word to delineate the syllables in the word. Students then blend these word "chunks" to sound out the word. See Figure 8.2 below for an example of what this might look like. Because all syllables contain at least one vowel, this takes any guess-work out of breaking a longer word into syllables. Students then say each of the parts of the word and blend them together. If the word does not make sense—for example, the student reads "hŏtel" instead of "hōtel" the student will "fix up" the word to make it a real word. As students master this overt step, they transition to a covert approach where they look for word parts at the beginning and end of the words and mentally note the vowels. Then they say each of the parts of the word and blend them together, followed by "fixing up" the word to make it a real word if needed.

Figure 8.2 Structural analysis strategy
Inspired by: REWARDS. Voyager Sopris Learning

The *SPIRE* program (Specialized Program Individualizing Reading Excellence) also makes decoding of multi-syllabic words more overt through the use of an Orton-Gillingham based multi-sensory approach. Within this program, students receive instruction using structured multi-step lessons that begins by manipulating individual syllable cards. The use of these cards is similar to the use and manipulation of consonant and vowel sound cards described earlier in this chapter with other Orton-Gillingham based programs. Within *SPIRE*, students use syllable cards and manipulative letters to build words with multiple syllables while orally reading each word part during word construction.

In both programs, students have multiple opportunities for practice with words in isolation before reading words in sentences and paragraphs within controlled text that targets syllables taught and reviewed in the specific lesson. In addition, within each lesson, students practice both decoding the multi-syllabic words and encoding these same words. There are multiple opportunities within both programs to practice encoding the words in isolation, sentences, and longer connected text as well to help students build meaningful application skills for writing multi-syllabic words in different contexts.

Types of Text

As discussed in Chapter 3, as students are learning to read, students have varying levels of proficiency depending on the difficulty level of text. For this reason, teachers need to be purposeful when selecting text for instruction or independent student reading. Texts at a student's instructional level should be used for instruction. Texts at a student's independent level should be used for independent reading and homework. Texts at a student's frustrational level should be avoided because these texts are too difficult for students even with support from an adult. In other words, independent text is easy, frustrational text is too hard, and instructional level text is "just right." General education teachers should follow this "Goldilocks principle" for all students. However, for students with intensive reading needs, text selection needs to be even more intentional.

The texts used in intensive reading programs are highly controlled to restrict words to those with sound patterns that have been taught or reviewed during the target lesson. In some programs sight words are also highly controlled. This is critical for the success of students with the most intensive reading problems because it minimizes the opportunity for potential errors or confusion as students are beginning to master sound patterns. In addition, it increases the likelihood that the student will be successful with the reading experience. For students with significant reading disabilities, and older students in particular, these successful experiences are vital for their motivation to attempt to improve their reading and their feelings of worth as learners (Elbaum & Vaughn, 2006).

In order for students to attain automaticity with word recognition, they need ample amounts of independent practice that reinforces instruction and helps them map letter/sound associations into memory (Bursuck & Damer, 2011). For students with intensive reading needs, not only should this independent practice be with texts at the grade level that is the student's independent level, the texts should also be restricted to the specific decoding skills that have been targeted in instruction. These types of texts are sometimes called **"decodable texts"** because the text is restricted to words that have sound/letter relations the student has previously learned and to a limited number of high-frequency sight words that the student has mastered (Chard & Osborn, 1999).

Increased Explicitness of Instruction in Intensive Reading Programs

You learned in the last chapter that **explicit phonics instruction** must be direct, precise, unambiguous, and reinforced through practice (Mesmer & Griffith, 2005). Phonics instruction can assist all students in understanding the alphabetic principle, but it is essential for students with significant reading concerns to receive explicit instruction on the relationship between letters and sounds that they may not intuitively recognize (Armbruster, Lehr, & Osborn, 2001). Intensive reading programs use linguistic patterns (phonological, orthographic, and morphological) that are sequential and systematic versus having students memorize phonics principles without meaning or context (Moats, 2010).

In order for intensive reading programs to be effective, it is important that teachers implement them with **fidelity**, which means incorporating all pieces or steps of a specific program in the correct order. Intensive programs' lessons are set up with specific steps in a certain order to ensure struggling readers have many opportunities using multiple modalities to learn and practice phonics skills. Sequencing of specific skills within these programs is also purposeful, building from foundational skills to higher-level ones that rely on previous student learning and connections within the program as students progress. Because of these design elements, teachers who implement intensive reading programs should ensure that program fidelity is maintained during instruction because the effectiveness of the programs rely on their faithful implementation. Modifications in lesson steps themselves, reordering of these steps, or step deletion can result in phonics instruction that lacks needed intensity within a program. Changes in skill sequences being taught within a program may break from the logical progression of skill development within the program, confusing the student or leaving gaps in their phonics understandings. Teachers should also steer away from combining elements of different reading programs together, because programs may differ in their philosophy, approach, and skill progression.

Teachers can keep in mind that published comprehensive reading programs are constructed intentionally and each component serves a purpose. Skill development has also been carefully thought through, ensuring that students are prepared to begin instruction in a particular skill based on earlier concepts and skills covered within the program. Fidelity of program implementation can be enhanced by targeted teacher training in the specific program. Training in one program assists a teacher with using that program with fidelity, but not necessarily with other programs. Many times, teachers who work consistently with students who struggle with reading have been trained in multiple programs so they can effectively implement the most appropriate program for each individual student's needs. The key area where implementation may vary slightly is from elementary level to secondary level in terms of how and where the program is implemented. At the elementary level, time is allotted daily for small group reading instruction, so time for instruction is already built into the day but a separate setting and trained staff may not be. At the secondary level where each individual student's daily schedule is content-area course driven, intensive reading instruction often needs to be scheduled within a separate reading course that already has time, space, and a teacher allotted to it.

Instructional Environment and Arrangement

In Chapter 7 the importance of having a print rich environment that can include word family charts, word walls, and classroom libraries was discussed. With students who need intensive reading instruction, additional environmental supports are helpful. Additionally, teachers need to further evaluate the classroom environment, ensuring students are receiving reading instruction in the place that is most conducive for this learning. Additional considerations for print support in the environment would include visual displays posted on classroom walls that are specific to the intensive reading program being used. However, since many students who receive intensive instruction need to be narrowly focused on the instruction at hand, it is advisable that there are not too many visual distractions on the walls other than those specifically geared at enhancing the students' immediate literacy skills. Teachers should steer away from other classroom displays and visuals that may distract students from their reading focus. Students who require intensive reading instruction can also be those who struggle to focus in general, and thus need a reduced number of visual distractions.

The location of where reading instruction takes place is also a key consideration. Many intensive programs require a setting for small group or individualized instruction. Most elementary classrooms are not conducive to this type of instruction and require a separate space or classroom for students with intensive reading needs. At the middle and high school level, students may also need an additional course scheduled specifically for intensive reading instruction to ensure the scheduled time and space for that small group or one-on-one instruction. At the same time, especially at the secondary level, privacy for intensive reading instruction is important, because students will feel more comfortable participating in reading instruction at their instructional reading level when their typically reading peers are not present. Additionally, besides the privacy factor, the separate environment for instruction typically provides a physical environment with less overall distractions. Teachers' thoughtful consideration of visuals and location for intensive reading instruction can help this teaching to be as effective as possible.

When providing intensive reading instruction, the instructional arrangement for teaching is a critical element. Grouping is a key factor with intensive reading programs. With most Orton-Gillingham based programs, the major concern is to provide needed individualized instruction to best meet specific student needs. With most Orton-Gillingham programs the suggested small group size for instruction is two to three students, often with one-on-one instruction being preferred. The idea behind the small group size or one-on-one teaching is the ability to individualize instruction, provide immediate reinforcement of ideas and skills, and also deliver the most targeted and specific corrective feedback possible. On the

---

A Focus on Read 180

Read 180 is a reading program that combines digital, small group, and whole group instruction for older students in Grades 4 and higher that struggle with reading. Each lesson is structured for 90 minutes, and is recommended for use 5 days a week with a maximum of 24 students. The program's target populations are students at-risk for reading difficulties, English language learners, and students with learning disabilities. According to the *Read 180* website (https://www.hmhco.com/products/read-180/instructional-approach.php), skills of focus include:

- phonological awareness,
- word study,
- fluency,
- comprehension,
- vocabulary,
- spelling,
- handwriting.

Lessons are structured to begin with a skill-focused whole group lesson. Then, the program uses the instructional arrangement of small groups, dividing students into three groups with up to eight people in each. The three groups then rotate through student application, small group instruction, and independent practice. In student application, students work on the *Read 180* app, which has content and instruction personalized to each individual student's reading abilities. Within small group instruction, students receive skills-based instruction to meet their individual reading needs. During independent practice, students can choose from a variety of content area texts on their instructional reading level to practice vocabulary and comprehension skills. In the end of the lesson, students are pulled together again to tie up learning for the day and revisit targeted skills.

other hand, Direct Instruction programs operate differently using a larger group approach. Direct Instruction programs can have small groups or larger groups of up to approximately 15 students, while still providing reading instruction that addresses significant reading difficulties. Direct Instruction approaches use behavior plans embedded within the programs to help structure on-task behaviors and attention that enables meaningful reading instruction.

Both types of intensive reading programs have advantages as well as disadvantages. Orton-Gillingham programs provide individualized instruction tailored to one or just a few students' strengths and difficulties. However, at times progress and pacing can be slow, because instruction does not move forward until each individual student is ready for that move. Additionally, finding time for individualized instruction or additional small group reading meeting times can be challenging for teachers on a regular basis outside of the typical literacy block. Most of the Orton-Gillingham programs require instruction three to five times a week for meaningful gains to be seen. Direct Instruction programs can be used with more students at once, which is a benefit because a much higher ratio of students can receive needed intensive instruction from just one teacher. In this way, providing additional reading instruction time at both the elementary and secondary levels is an easier task. One drawback of Direct Instruction programs can be making homogeneous instructional groupings of students with similar reading profiles, particularly for relatively larger instructional groups. Like with Orton-Gillingham programs, if appropriate homogeneous grouping does not occur, some students may be ready to move forward before others.

Instructional Techniques

Within intensive reading programs, the instructional techniques that are used work together to provide instruction that includes multiple student supports for reading growth. Across intensive programs, mastery expectations are key to student progress. Within a typical whole class reading curriculum, there is often a wide range of student skill development as a result of instruction. However, the goal of intensive program instruction for students is much different. Most intensive programs are structured so that the next skill or step in the program is not started until the current skill is mastered by all students with at least 80% proficiency or above. This approach ensures that the program moves as the student actually progresses in skill development and not before. In the same vein, pacing and sequencing of skills is a key underpinning of intensive programs. While teachers may choose specific

Specialized Instruction: Skill Specific Supplemental Reading Programs

The programs discussed earlier in this chapter are comprehensive intensive reading programs geared at developing the overall reading skills of struggling readers. While some readers will struggle significantly across areas, other readers will have difficulties in one or just a few specific skill areas of reading. With these students, more focused reading instruction in the particular area of weakness may be what is needed. To this end, the chart below includes a listing of skill specific reading programs. The programs are not comprehensive in nature, but instead target a few related skill areas together. For each reading program, the chart indicates which specific skills are targeted to assist teachers in their decision-making process for program selection for student use.

Program	Phonemic Awareness	Phonics	Structural Analysis	Sight Words	Fluency	Comprehension	Vocabulary	Spelling
Lexia	*	+						
Lexia SOS	*	+	*				*	
Lindamood-Bell								
LIPS	+	*						*
Seeing Stars		+						*
Talkies							+	
Visualizing and Verbalizing						+	*	
Read Naturally								
Read Naturally Masters					+			
Read Naturally Live		*			+	*	*	
Read Naturally Encore		*			+	*		
Read Naturally GATE	*	+		*	*	*		
Word Warm-ups	*	*			*			
Take AIM! At Vocabulary					*	*	+	
Signs for Sounds	*	*						+
Funēmics	+							
Direct Instruction								
Compre-hension Strand						+	*	

pieces of the general reading curriculum to use with students while omitting others, in-struction using intensive programs requires following the specific pacing and sequencing of lessons. The pacing of each lesson is tightly structured with learning opportunities built in to engage students and work on skill building. In addition, lessons are sequenced to build skills sequentially.

Ongoing corrective feedback is another hallmark feature of intensive reading programs. In general reading curriculums, feedback may be given to students as they participate in guided practice with the teacher, but this feedback tends to be incidental within teachable moments. However, in intensive programs, students are immediately given prescribed and intentional corrective feedback to ensure that the student will correctly apply the skill learned in all subsequent practice opportunities. In this way, students have the opportunity to more quickly fine tune skills through a cyclical feedback and practice model. While the goal of intensive programs is for students to constantly build new reading skills, the programs use the tool of predictability within each lesson, having the same core elements in the same order. Students feel comfortable and supported by the lesson structure which can facilitate student learning of increasingly complex reading skills.

Another strength of intensive programs is the number and type of student response opportunities. These programs have greater opportunities for students to respond and practice skills than in typical reading curriculums. Practice opportunities are also usually structured to provide more positive skill experiences for students, such as the use of **choral responding**—where all students respond in unison when practicing a new skill so the students have peer support. Additionally, practice opportunities can be structured to span modalities such as visual, tactile, and auditory to help students have practice opportunities that vary in type, as well as being greater in number.

References

Academy of Orton-Gillingham Practitioners and Educators (2019). What is the Orton-Gillingham approach? Retrieved from https://www.ortonacademy.org/resources/what-is-the-orton-gillingham-approach/

Archer, A. L., Gleason, M. M., & Vachon, V. L. (2003). Decoding and fluency: Foundation skills for struggling older readers. *Learning Disability Quarterly, 26*, 89–101.

Armbruster, B., Lehr, F., & Osborn, J. (2001). *Put reading first: The research building blocks for teaching children to read.* Washington, DC: National Institute for Literacy.

Berkeley, S., & Taboada Barber, A. (2015). *Maximizing effectiveness of reading comprehension instruction in diverse classrooms.* Baltimore, MD: Brookes Publishing.

Biancarosa, G., & Snow, C. E. (2006). *Reading next—A vision for action and research in middle and high school literacy: A report to Carnegie Corporation of New York* (2nd ed.). Washington, DC: Alliance for Excellent Education.

Bursuck, W. D., & Damer, M. (2011). *Teaching reading to students who are at risk or have disabilities* (2nd ed.). Boston, MA: Pearson.

Carnine, D. W., Silbert, J., Kame'enui, E. J., Slocum, T. A., & Travers, P. (2017). *Direct instruction reading* (6th ed.). Boston, MA: Pearson.

Chard, D. J., & Osborn, J. (1999). Phonics and word recognition instruction in early reading programs: Guidelines for accessibility. *Learning Disabilities Research & Practice, 14*, 107–117.

Denton, C., Wexler, J., Vaughn, S., & Bryan, D. (2008). Intervention provided to linguistically diverse middle school students with severe reading difficulties. *Learning Disabilities Research & Practice, 23*, 79–89.

Dyslexia Resource. (2019). *What is dyslexia?* Retrieved March 31, 2019 from https://dyslexiaresource.org/information-about-dyslexia/what-is-dyslexia/

Elbaum, B., & Vaughn, S. (2006). Self-concept and students with learning disabilities. In H. L. Swanson, H. R. Harris, & S. Graham (Eds.), *Handbook of learning disabilities* (pp. 229–241). New York, NY: Guilford.

Elbaum, B., Vaughn, S., Hughes, M. T., & Moody, S. W. (2000). How effective are one-to-one tutoring programs in reading for elementary students at risk for reading failure? A meta-analysis of the intervention research. *Journal of Educational Psychology, 92*, 605–619.

Individuals with Disabilities Education Act, 20 U.S.C. § 1400. (2004).

International Dyslexia Association. (2002). Definition of dyslexia. Retrieved March 31, 2019 from https://dyslexiaida.org/definition-of-dyslexia/

Katz, L., Stone, A., Carlisle, J., Corey, D., & Zeng, J. (2008). Initial progress of children identified with disabilities in Michigan's reading first schools. *Exceptional Children, 74*, 235–256.

Lovett, M. W., Barron, R. W., & Benson, N. J. (2008). Effective remediation of word identification and decoding difficulties in school-age children with reading disabilities. In H. L. Swanson, K. R. Harris, & S. Graham (Eds.), *Handbook of learning disabilities* (2nd ed., pp. 273–292). New York, NY: Guilford Press.

Mesmer, H. A. E., & Griffith, P. L. (2005). Everybody's selling it—But just what is explicit, systematic phonics instruction? *The Reading Teacher, 59*, 366–376.

Moats, L. C. (2001). When older students can't read. *Educational Leadership, 58*, 36–40.

Moats, L. (2007). *Whole-language high jinks: How to tell when "scientifically based reading instruction" isn't*. A report to the Thomas B. Fordham Institute. Retrieved March 30, 2019 from https://fordhaminstitute.org/national/research/whole-language-high-jinks

Moats, L. C. (2010). *Speech to print: Language essentials for teachers* (2nd ed.). Baltimore, MD: Brookes Publishing.

National Institute for Direct Instruction. (2019). *Basic philosophy of direct instruction (DI)*. Retrieved February 2019 from https://www.nifdi.org/what-is-di/basic-philosophy.html

Norton, E., & Wolf, M. (2012). Rapid automatized naming (RAN) and reading fluency: Implications for understanding and treatment of reading disabilities. *Annual Review of Psychology, 63*, 427–452.

Orton-Gillingham Online Academy. (2019). *10 essentials of the Orton-Gillingham approach*. Retrieved March 31, 2019 from https://ortongillinghamonlinetutor.com/10-essential-elements-of-the-orton-gillingham-approach/

Park, S., Martinez, M., & Chou, F. (2017). *CCSSO English learners with disabilities guide*. Washington, DC: Council of Chief State School Officers.

Swanson, H. L., Harris, K. R., & Graham, S. (Eds.). (2013). *Handbook of learning disabilities*. New York, NY: Guilford Press.

Ziegler, J. C., Bertrand, D., Tóth, D., Csépe, V., Reis, A., Faísca, L., … Blomert, L. (2010). Orthographic depth and its impact on universal predictors of reading a cross-language investigation. *Psychological Science, 21*, 551–559.

Chapter 9

Supporting All Students in Accessing Text

Students Who Struggle with Word Identification

Basic reading skills are needed in order for students to become fluent readers who can quickly and accurately access text. Reading comprehension is dependent on this access. Yet, even with strong instruction in this important area, some students will struggle to acquire the skills needed to be fluent readers. In particular, students who struggle with basic decoding skills will continue to fall behind their typically achieving peers over time (Judge & Bell, 2011). Therefore, in addition to possessing an array of instructional strategies for teaching students to read text quickly and accurately, teachers must also be able to recognize when students are struggling and how to intervene effectively. This is particularly important because student failures in reading affect their motivation and self-concept over time making it more likely that they will disengage from any attempts to improve their reading skills. This in turn results in an ever-widening gap with their same age peers. Minority students, students living in poverty, students who are learning English, and students with disabilities are all at-risk for failing to acquire basic reading skills (Biancarosa & Snow, 2006).

Challenges Stemming from English Language Development

Students who are learning English as a second language develop early reading skills at a slower pace than their native English-speaking counterparts, largely because of differences between the orthography of English and students' first language (L1; see Chapter 6 for more information). This is also true for the development of word identification skills. Some phonetically based languages, such as Spanish, have a one-to-one correspondence between sounds and letters, while English is less consistent. Differences in the orthographies of languages encompass morphology (variations in word meanings) and syntax (variations in sentence structures) as well. These differences put English learners at a disadvantage when learning to identify printed words in English.

Additionally, oral language use is often delayed due to the developmental nature of acquiring a second language (see Chapter 1 for more information). This slow or delayed development is observed for acquisition of word identification skills and reading fluency as well (August & Shanahan, 2006). Knowledge of morphology and syntax of English assists native speakers when they are learning to communicate and read connected text; however, English learners do not have this same background knowledge, limiting the tools at their disposal when learning to read. In essence, English language learners do not have the same common knowledge of how the English language "works" that native speakers do, which slows their development of skills.

Challenges Stemming from Disability

Students may have difficulty acquiring basic reading skills due to a disability. There are a variety of areas that might impede these students' ability to efficiently decode phonetically regular words that are primarily language based. Common problems in the area of phonology can include issues with articulation of phonemes as well as auditory discrimination of phonemes (Mercer, Mercer, & Pullen, 2010). Issues with phonology are particularly likely in students with severe language-based disabilities, such as dyslexia.

As you learned in Chapter 6, **auditory processing** problems interfere with a student's ability to identify sounds in words, particularly medial vowel sounds and sounds that are auditorily similar. Auditory processing problems will continue to create challenges for students when they are trying to decode longer words because they may have difficulty "hearing" the components of a longer succession of sounds in multi-syllabic words. In addition, students may have difficulty with phonological tasks because of problems with working memory—holding information in short-term memory while processing new information (see also Chapter 1). For example, a student may not be able to retain common rimes when a teacher is working on manipulation of initial sounds to develop phonics or be able to recall common affixes to assist with structural analysis of longer words. Problems with working memory can also affect a student's fluency because he or she may spend so much mental energy on sounding out words or recalling sight words that reading slows and becomes choppy or disfluent. Mental energy used to read text fluently leaves few resources for the student to attend to the meaning of the text or to decipher the meaning of unknown words within the text (Swanson & O'Connor, 2009).

A Focus on Dyslexia

The International Dyslexia Association has adopted the following definition of **dyslexia**:

> Dyslexia is a specific learning disability that is neurobiological in origin. It is characterized by difficulties with accurate and/or fluent word recognition and by poor spelling and decoding abilities. These difficulties typically result from a deficit in the phonological component of language that is often unexpected in relation to other cognitive abilities and the provision of effective classroom instruction. Secondary consequences may include problems in reading comprehension and reduced reading experience that can impede growth of vocabulary and background knowledge.

As can be discerned from this definition, dyslexia is a severe language-based learning disability that significantly impacts decoding and spelling. Further, these difficulties are rooted in deficits that impede a student's ability to process the phonology and orthography of language. These students need intensive intervention to learn to read that is direct, systematic, and explicit. In addition, the International Dyslexia Association recommends that instruction should involve multiple senses (hearing, seeing, touching) at the same time. Without intervention, deficiencies in decoding at the phoneme level persist into adulthood (Shaywitz, 1996).

Refer to the International Dyslexia Association for more information: https://dyslexiaida.org/

Students with language-based disabilities are likely to fail to attend to the nuance of other areas of language form—morphology and syntax. The ability to self-monitor understanding of language and process linguistic information is referred to as **metalinguistic awareness** (Bialystok, 1993). Problems with metalinguistic awareness are thought to interfere with a student's ability to utilize knowledge of meanings of words and sentence structures to help themselves identify new words and their meanings when reading—called using context cues (see Chapter 7 for more information). Students with language-based disabilities either tend to underuse or overuse context cues. Both scenarios diminish the usefulness of this strategy. When students do not attempt to use context at all, they have not learned to actively engage with the text in a meaningful way and are missing opportunities both to improve their word recognition skills as well as to build their vocabularies. Over-reliance on context cues is especially common in students with language-based disabilities because these students often have under-developed phonics strategies.

Challenges for Older Struggling Readers

As students transition from elementary school to middle school, they face content area classes such as language arts, social studies, math, and science, where they are expected to read and understand increasingly difficult text (Bryant et al., 2000). However, in the upper grades, instruction no longer focuses on teaching students how to read, but instead focuses on the content of material read (Saenz & Fuchs, 2002). For at-risk students who have not yet mastered basic reading skills, content-area reading can be overwhelmingly difficult. This is particularly true for students with language-based disabilities, because a large number of these students read several years below grade level upon reaching middle school (Archer, Gleason, & Vachon, 2003; Mastropieri, Scruggs, & Graetz, 2003). If the ability to hear and manipulate individual phonemes and/or larger units of sound is not mastered before middle school, students will require "intensive, focused, sustained instruction to help them catch up with their peers" (Hock & Deshler, 2003, p. 52). This includes direct instruction across all areas of reading including decoding, fluency, vocabulary, comprehension, and spelling (National Institute of Child Health and Human Development & National Institute for Literacy, 2007).

Further, reading problems in older students are detrimental to both their motivation and their feelings of themselves as learners. "When students experience repeated failures, it generally results in low perceptions of ability, negative academic self-concept, tendencies toward learned helplessness, and lower expectations for future school success" (Berkeley & Taboada Barber, 2015, p. 111). This can lead to student disengagement from all reading related activities, which impacts their academic performance overall (Guthrie & Wigfield, 2000). It is no wonder that it is so difficult to remediate reading problems in older students!

Assessment of Student Ability to Access Text

The ability to quickly and accurately access text is necessary for comprehension to occur, and as such, it is an important skill to closely monitor. With all word identification and fluency assessments, teachers listen to students read aloud to determine any word identification errors students may have. Some assessments are given as screeners to quickly identify students who may not be progressing sufficiently compared to grade level peers. When students do not perform as expected, the teacher is likely to collect additional information through targeted assessments and/or analysis of student errors. This information is then used to design instruction for entire classes, groups of students, or individuals. For students identified as at-risk, the teacher will also put in place a plan to monitor student progress;

data from these assessments will be used to determine whether the student is responding to instruction and to adjust instruction as appropriate. Because error analysis can be completed with any oral reading assessment, it is helpful to have an understanding of what this entails before learning about specific assessments.

When looking for patterns in student oral reading errors, called **error analysis**, teachers look for a number of common errors. Errors in shorter phonetically regular words include incorrectly reading beginning, ending, or medial sounds in words, including vowel digraphs and diphthongs. Errors in reading longer words tend to include miscues with adding or deleting endings like -*s*, -*ed*, or -*ing*. Another common error in multi-syllabic word decoding is the deletion and addition of syllables. For example, some learners may read *reinspect* as "respect" by omitting a medial syllable or read *usually* as "unusually" by adding a syllable to the beginning of the word. Students may also make errors where they inaccurately approximate a word using the visual features of the word, which may be of similar length and include similar beginning and ending letters. For example, a word like *gram* may be approximated with the visually similar word "game;" similarly, the word *coat* might be misread as "cost."

Students can also make consistent errors when reading phonetically irregular words or sight words. These errors are important to identify because they can indicate a lack of student memorization of high-frequency words. Students may also omit words when there is a phonetic pattern with which the student is struggling. Finally, failure to attempt words can also give some important insights into a student's level of confidence as a learner.

A teacher can create an error log to systematically evaluate errors that a student makes. An **error log** is a recording tool where all miscues are listed and then categorized by the type of error. An error log helps a teacher to systematically analyze student errors to determine if there are any consistent error patterns. Conducting this error analysis can help teachers identify specific phonics difficulties that should be targeted for instruction. For instance, if a teacher reviews an error log and sees multiple errors where a student misidentifies the medial sound in words (such as reading *pet* for *pot* or *cot* for *cut*) and deletes word endings -*ed* and -*ing*, she can determine that medial vowel sounds and ending sounds should be a focus for future decoding lessons.

As teachers become more experienced at assessing and monitoring student decoding and fluency, they will begin to note if students are using any context cues to help themselves identify words. For example, it might become apparent when a student is over or under reliant on context cues. A younger student might always look at pictures as the only cue to assist in word recognition rather than attempting to decode the print. An older student may not use surrounding words to help themselves determine an unknown target word. Similarly, teachers may notice that students are incorrectly using, or failing to use, sentence structures when attempting to figure out an unknown word. Error analysis can be completed with all of the skill specific assessments described in the next section.

Observation/Authentic Assessment

Informal observation of students reading aloud in class is a primary form of authentic assessment of students' ability to access text. For example, a teacher might note a concern about a student's decoding abilities if the student struggles to sound out individual words or reads connected text word by word rather than fluently reading sentences. Subtler indicators of decoding problems may include an observed reluctance of a student to read aloud in class. This reluctance might also present as a misbehavior during class that enables the student to avoid a reading activity altogether. Similarly, a student may make direct statements about not liking reading.

Observations might also include evidence of a student reading less than peers or gravitating toward texts that are at a lower difficulty level than peers. As you learned in Chapter 7, reading logs are often used to track the types of things that students read as well as how long and how often they read. Information from reading logs can help teachers see at a glance how much time is being spent on independent reading, including reading outside of school, and how much reading is completed in that time.

Leveled Word Lists

Word lists are often used to determine students' general abilities to recognize words in isolation or to identify the appropriate entry point to a specific reading program or more comprehensive assessment. Word lists are generally leveled by difficulty or grade and can include phonetically regular real words, phonetically regular **nonsense words**—made up words that follow the phonetic rules in English, and/or high-frequency sight words. Nonsense words are used to discern whether the student is using knowledge of phonics to identify words or whether they are memorizing words as a strategy. For example, if a student is using phonics, they should be able to read words on both a real word list and a nonsense word list. However, if the student is memorizing words without using phonics, they would be able to read real words, but would struggle with the made up words. There are many sources for sight words and high-frequency words including *Dolch* and *Fry* word lists, but individual school districts may have their own lists that they prefer that

A Focus on Formal Assessment of Decoding

While this chapter focuses on informal assessments of word identification to inform instruction, there are circumstances where an educator might need information about how a student is doing related to other students of the same age or grade. In these instances, a formal assessment that is norm-referenced is needed. As you remember from Chapter 2, norm-referenced assessments are standardized and require specialized training to administer. These types of assessments cover a wide range of skills related to basic reading and results provide an indication of how a student performed compared to a norming sample of students in the same grade. A formal assessment of basic reading would generally be used as a pre and post assessment of a student's performance as well as to determine whether a student's progress is sufficient to close an achievement gap with peers. An example of a formal assessment of decoding is the *Test of Word Reading Efficiency 2nd Edition* (TOWRE-2).

Test of Word Reading Efficiency (TOWRE)	
Test Description:	• Sight word recognition (real words) • Phonemic decoding (nonsense words)
Ages:	6–0 through 24–11 years
Administration:	Individualized
Time Required:	5–10 minutes
Publisher:	https://www.proedinc.com/Products/13910/towre2-test-of-word-reading-efficiencysecond-edition-complete-kit.aspx

teachers use. Regardless of the type of word list, accurate identification of words with automaticity (within three seconds) is used for scoring. If miscue notations are used, an error analysis can be completed to discern error patterns.

Informal Reading Inventories

Informal reading inventories (IRIs) are comprehensive informal assessments that provide important information about students' word identification skills and fluency in addition to students' reading comprehension abilities. IRIs include both leveled word lists and connected text in passages that provide a breadth of information across reading skill areas that can help teachers know where to begin instruction. Chapter 3 contains an in-depth description of the administration and interpretation of IRIs.

Computer-based Assessments

While reading individually with a student provides the most accurate picture of his or her ability to identify words and read fluently, it is time-consuming to achieve with an entire class of students. Yet, teachers need information about students' reading abilities to ensure that they are selecting the appropriate level of reading materials for all students in the class. With advances in technology, more and more schools are using computerized assessments that allow an entire class of students to be evaluated at one time. These assessments generally provide a reasonably accurate approximation of students' basic reading skills. For example, the HMH Reading Inventory (2019; formerly called the Scholastic Reading Inventory or SRI) can be used to assess students' reading levels based on underlying foundational reading skills in decoding and fluency. This is done not by evaluating a student's oral reading, but by estimating a student's foundational skill levels based on his responses to comprehension questions about text at varying difficulty levels. This produces a lexile that can be used to select the appropriate level of text to use in instruction and for homework.

Running Records

A **running record** is an informal reading assessment primarily used in the early elementary grades. This assessment of student reading is easy to complete because instructional reading materials are used. To administer, the teacher selects a reading passage of the same type and level at which a student has been receiving instruction. For instance, a teacher may select a reading passage that has not yet been read from the same reading unit. The length of time is not firm in a running record and the entire passage does not need to be read; however, they generally last for at least one to two minutes.

To administer a running record, the student will read the passage aloud while the teacher notes words read correctly or incorrectly on a photocopy of the text. As shown in Figure 9.1, the most critical notations are of words the student reads correctly—indicated by check marks above each word, and incorrectly—indicated by writing how the word was actually read (Tompkins, Campbell, Green, & Smith, 2014). It is also important to note the words that students self-correct when reading. The self-corrected words are counted with check marks, and help teachers identify areas where the student is not yet solid. After the assessment is given, the teacher can perform an error analysis to determine patterns in student errors that indicate a need for further instruction.

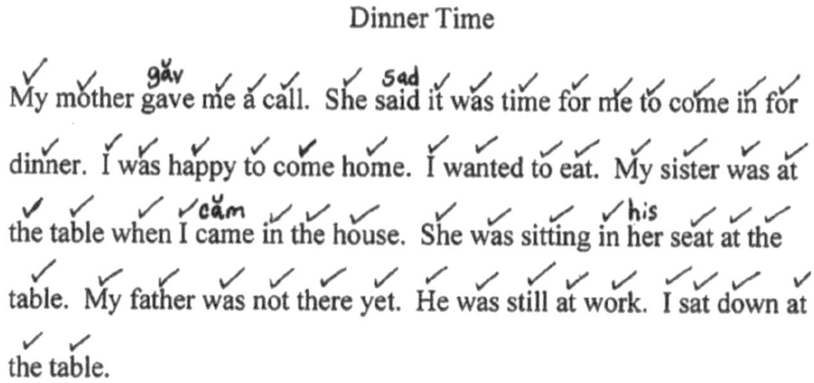

Dinner Time

My mŏther găv me ă cáll. Shĕ sáid it wăs tiĭme fŏr nĕ tŏ cŏme iń fŏr

dińner. Ĭ wăs háppy tŏ cŏme hóme. Ĭ wanted tŏ eat. My sister wăs ăt

thĕ table when I cắm cȧm in thĕ house. Shĕ wăs sitting in her seat at thĕ

table. My father wăs not there yĕt. He wăs still at work. I sat down at

thĕ table.

Figure 9.1 Running record

Oral Reading Fluency Assessments

You learned in Chapter 3 that reading fluency is generally assessed by determining the number of words that a student reads aloud correctly in one minute, called correct words per minute (CWPM). This is obtained by listening to a student read for one minute, noting any miscues and then subtracting the number of errors from the total number of words read in the minute, resulting in the student's reading rate. For example, if a student read 100 words in one minute and made five errors, their reading rate would be 95 CWPM. The student's reading rate is then compared to other peers in the same grade or the student's own past performance to determine whether progress has been made. This process is referred to as an **oral reading fluency (ORF) assessment**. Although prosody is a component of fluency, it is not addressed in ORF assessments; prosody assessments will be further discussed in Chapter 12.

Assessing students' abilities to read with speed and accuracy is a quick and easy way to determine if particular students are struggling in the areas of word recognition. In addition, ORF is a strong predictor of reading competence because there is a well-established relationship between fluency and student performance on standardized tests of reading comprehension (Fuchs, Fuchs, Hosp, & Jenkins, 2001; Kuhn & Stahl, 2003). For these reasons, ORF assessments are the most commonly used form of curriculum-based measures (Wayman, Wallace, Wiley, Tichá, & Espin, 2007). In the elementary grades, in addition to using ORF assessments as a curriculum-based measure, reading fluency is assessed as part of screening and/or benchmark processes. In these early grades, the general education classroom teacher and/or a specialist, such as a reading specialist or special education teacher, may be responsible for administering the fluency assessment. At the middle and high school levels, fluency is not ordinarily assessed on a regular basis for the typical learner, but is likely to continue for students identified with reading problems. In the upper grades, a reading specialist or a special education teacher usually gives fluency assessments.

Because an ORF assessment is the most commonly used curriculum-based measure, there are many free resources available as well as a wide range of published resources. One free resource includes the DIBELS materials developed by the University of Oregon (2019),

Table 9.1 Fluency Tracking Resources

Resource	Website for More Information
AIMSweb	www.aimsweb.com
DIBELS	https://dibels.uoregon.edu
Edcheckup	www.edcheckup.com
McGraw-Hill	www.yearlyprogresspro.com
CBM Warehouse	www.interventioncentral.org

Adapted from: Berkeley, S., & Riccomini, P. J. (2017). Academic progress monitoring. In J. M. Kauffman, D. P. Hallahan, & P. C. Pullen (Eds.), *Handbook of special education* (2nd ed., pp. 334–347). New York, NY: Routledge.

which span from kindergarten to 8th grade. DIBELS resources are available for download online and include benchmark assessments and ongoing progress monitoring materials for evaluating student fluency in naming upper- and lowercase letters, phonemic segmentation, nonsense word reading, and real word reading, as well as reading fluency of connected text (University of Oregon, 2019). An example of a commercially available ORF assessment is the Reading Fluency Benchmark Assessor (RFBA) (Read Naturally, 2008). This assessment consists of leveled passages from 3rd to 8th grade used to monitor students' fluency rate through tracking students' speed and accuracy using CWPM. This assessment includes norms that can be used to compare a student's performance to peers. These norms are benchmarked at several time points of the school year and so can be a useful tool to help a teacher determine whether students are making enough progress. Because the use of ORF assessments is so prevalent in schools, there are also resources available to help teachers graph and interpret student fluency performance and growth. See Table 9.1 for some of the most widely used resources.

Even if a teacher does not have access to formal fluency probes, fluency can be assessed with any text that is leveled by grade. Student performance can then be compared to published grade level norming tables (e.g., Hasbrouck & Tindal, 2006). While teacher-made assessments will not be as tightly controlled for difficulty, they can still be useful for giving the teacher an idea of a student who is much further behind peers as well as gauging the difficulty level of a text selected for use in instruction.

In some cases, a student's instructional reading level will be significantly below his or her actual grade level and additional steps will be taken to evaluate and monitor the student's progress. First, just as with all students, the teacher will administer an on grade level ORF and compare the student's performance to peers at that grade level. This information will give an indication of how far behind the student is performing. However, tracking student performance with grade level text has little utility if it is at the student's frustrational level, because this is not where instruction should be occurring and immediate growth is unlikely. Therefore, teachers will also track the student's progress with text at the level where instruction is occurring, as this is where gains should be immediately seen. Norming tables can be used to help teachers determine how many words the student should be able to read at that grade level before moving up to more difficult material. However, teachers should *not* interpret out of level fluency rates as being indicative of how fluently same grade peers are able to read as this is not how the norms were developed.

Instructional Supports for Struggling Students

Numerous instructional approaches have been presented in this section of the book that foster word identification and reading fluency. These basic skills serve as a gateway for reading comprehension. In Chapter 7, you learned how the instruction of basic reading skills is direct and explicit. You also learned that the instructional environment sets the stage for learning, and in particular, a print-rich environment sets the stage for reading and writing. In Chapter 8, you learned that while some students acquire basic reading skills regardless of the instructional approach, some students need direct explicit instruction in order to learn to access print, including introducing letters and sounds in an intentional sequence that fosters skill development. Additionally, some aspects of good instruction are particularly crucial for these students.

Selection of Instructional Materials

Effective instruction takes into consideration the nature of different types of words which can include phonetically regular words whose letters represent their most common sounds, phonetically irregular words that do not follow phonetically regular patterns and need to be memorized, and sight words that can be phonetically regular or irregular and are uniquely important because of the high frequency of their appearance in within text. Good instruction also takes into consideration the types of text that are appropriate for instruction—called instructional level text. Texts that a student can read at an independent level are also important because these texts are assigned for independent practice such as homework to provide reinforcement of basic reading skills that have been taught. Frustrational texts should be avoided, even in instruction, unless modified. For more on how to determine whether a student is reading at an instructional, independent or frustrational level, refer to Chapter 3.

In addition to considering whether texts are at a student's independent, instructional, or frustrational level, it is also important to consider what topics are of interest or are personally meaningful for students when giving them options of text to read. Students are more likely to persist with difficult text when they are interested in what they are reading about (Jennings, Caldwell, & Lerner, 2010). With younger students, this means ensuring that students have access to nonfiction trade books in addition to stories and other fiction genres, such as fairy tales or mysteries. With older students, it is sometimes a challenge to find appropriate reading because topics of interest to students are not always written at a reading level that is independent for them. In these cases, the teacher may be able to alter the difficulty level of the text to make it more accessible to the student. Alternatively, there are increasing options of collections of text that are of high interest but low readability, such as High Noon Books (https://www.highnoonbooks.com/HNB/abouthnb.tpl) or HIP (High Interest Publishing) Books (https://hip-books.com/books/).

Considerations for Instruction

Just as with early reading, students who are at-risk for reading problems are likely to need additional prompting that may not be necessary for the typical learner. You learned in Chapter 8 that some students with significant learning disabilities will need explicit and intensive instruction in order to make progress in word identification skills. There are also students who fall somewhere in between—they need more support than typically developing students, but not as intensive as for students with significant learning disabilities or dyslexia. These supports can include visual supports, tactile supports, and auditory supports. Visual stimuli to support a learning task are called a **visual supports**. Physical manipulation of objects is referred to as a **tactile support**. Finally, verbal prompts that help students attend to relevant information are referred to as **auditory supports**. These supports can be used separately or in combination.

Reading is inherently a visual process. However, some students do not attend to similarities between words unless overtly directed to do so. Visual displays in the child's environment can help them to attend to word patterns within words. For example, displays of word family charts can help students attend to words that sound and are spelled the same at the end of words. In addition, awareness of letter patterns in words can be fostered through word manipulation activities where some letters stay constant while others are manipulated. This type of visual manipulation can also include visual–tactile supports, such as the use of Elkonin boxes (see Chapter 7). In this type of activity, students physically move letters they are manipulating within a word.

Students with language-based disabilities are more likely to need auditory prompting to attend to specific information, although it can be beneficial to any student who is having trouble distinguishing sounds. Some sounds can be cued by "stretching" them out (stretch sounds), while other sounds need to be repeated (stop sounds). For example, if a student was having trouble attending to the "s" at the end of the word *dog*, the teacher might prompt /dogs-sssss/. Medial vowel sounds are the most difficult sounds for students to distinguish and they are all stretch sounds. If a student was having trouble distinguishing between the sounds /b/ and /d/ the teacher would repeat the stop sound to prompt /b/-/b/-/b/-/bill/ being careful not to add a schwa to /b/. A full listing of prompts for sounds can be found in Chapter 5.

You learned in Chapter 7 about how the context of a sentence can help a student to identify words in the sentence through knowledge of the meanings of the surrounding words and correct sentence syntax. However, it is important that this is not the only word identification strategy emphasized in a classroom, particularly for students with learning disabilities. Further, according to Spear-Swearling (2006):

> Because youngsters with reading disabilities typically have problems involving poor phonological skills, they generally benefit from instructional approaches that provide highly explicit, systematic teaching of phonemic awareness and phonics. However, if children are taught systematic phonics in one part of the reading program but are encouraged to use context to guess at words when reading passages, they may not apply their phonics skills consistently. Thus, the phonics component of the reading program may be seriously undermined.

Therefore, not only is it important that these students are taught phonics and structural analysis strategies to help themselves figure out unknown words, but these students also need overt prompts to practice the phonics that they have learned when they encounter phonetically regular words in text. In the instances where auditory prompting of students to use context cues is appropriate, it is important to ensure that students are attending to the morphology and syntax of the sentences rather than simply telling students to use the surrounding words to "figure it out."

When providing targeted instruction on different sound patterns for decoding, some students will need small group instruction. At the elementary level, all learners are pulled for

A Focus on Instructional Accommodations

Accommodations do not negate the need for explicit, direct instruction. However, in addition to quality instruction, some students with disabilities will need instructional accommodations in order to make progress in the curriculum or toward IEP goals. Accommodations are changes that are made for individual students and might include changes in time, input, output, and level of support (Hallahan, Lloyd, Kauffman, Weiss, & Martinez, 2005). In the areas of word identification skills and reading fluency, instructional accommodations might include:

- extra time to read assignments or tests (time),
- reading a test aloud to a student reading below grade level (input),
- use of a mask to help a student keep place while reading aloud (output),
- small group or individualized instruction (level of support).

It is important to note that accommodations often vary by context. For example, reading a test aloud to a student who is reading below grade level is listed above as a potential accommodation. While this accommodation would be perfectly appropriate to give to a 5th grade student reading multiple years below grade level when taking a grade level science test, it would *not* be an appropriate accommodation for the student in his reading class where the purpose of the lesson was to improve decoding and fluency of text written at the student's instructional level. Indeed, a student who is reading far below grade level actually needs more practice to master basic reading skills, *not* less.

small group reading instruction because this small group arrangement is a core component of elementary literacy instruction. At the middle and high school levels, small group instruction is not typically part of instruction in English/Language Arts nor are basic reading skills a part of the secondary curriculum. As a result, teachers will need to build in small group instruction during another time of the school day slated for independent practice or review of class content. For students far below grade level, this extra support is likely to occur through a formal remedial reading class.

Additional Learning Opportunities

The reading of struggling students is generally slow and laborious (Moats, 2001). This causes these students to become frustrated and to avoid reading tasks resulting in less time spent practicing acquired skills than their typically developing peers (Archer et al., 2003). Therefore, in order for students who are behind in reading to "catch up" with their peers, they need to spend ample amounts of time reading text that allows them to reinforce word identification skills they have learned and to increase their fluency. In other words, these students need to read *a* lot! Therefore, it is important that teachers find ways to foster the independent reading of students both in and out of school. See Chapter 7 for some initial ideas.

As in early childhood classrooms, technology can be a valuable resource for providing additional practice activities for students who are in the process of acquiring basic reading skills. For this reason, technology is sometimes used to give students extra time to practice learned skills. Using technology to supplement instruction is sometimes called **computer-assisted instruction**, or CAI. This approach is particularly useful in the upper grades where basic word identification instruction is no longer a part of the curriculum. Further, computer-assisted instruction is inherently individualized to the needs of the learner who can work at his or her own pace (Stetter & Hughes, 2010). As with any computer program, teachers need to monitor students carefully to ensure that they are practicing skills correctly and intervene if additional explicit instruction is needed (Regan, Berkeley, Hughes, & Kirby, 2014).

Specialized Instruction: Basic Reading Skills

Lexia

Lexia Core5 Reading contains a series of learning paths through scaffolded activities in areas where students have gaps in learning:

- Phonemic awareness activities include identifying, segmenting, blending and manipulating syllables and sounds in words.
- Phonics activities include applying knowledge of letter/sound correspondence to reading and spelling words.
- Structural analysis activities include work on recognizing meaningful parts of multi-syllabic words derived from Latin and Greek.
- Fluency is addressed through activities that involve analysis of sentence structure and ultimately the timed silent reading of passages.
- Vocabulary activities are structured to teach word-learning strategies, to provide exposure to rich and varied vocabulary words and to allow students to develop an awareness of word relationships and associations.
- Comprehension activities develop the ability to understand information at a concrete level as well as an abstract level through the application of higher order thinking skills.

The program is designed for students in grades PreK–8.

For more information: https://www.lexialearning.com/products/core5

Read Naturally

Read Naturally Live is a web-based program that utilizes a teacher model, repeated reading practice, and self-monitoring of progress to help students improve their fluency. The program also includes a preview of key vocabulary, a quiz, and retell components that support student improvements in vocabulary and comprehension. Students choose readings from a range of high-interest text options and set their own goals for improvement, which fosters motivation and engagement. The program is designed for students in Grades 1–8.

For more information: https://www.readnaturally.com/intervention-programs

References

Archer, A. L., Gleason, M. M., & Vachon, V. L. (2003). Decoding and fluency: Foundation skills for struggling older readers. *Learning Disability Quarterly, 26,* 89–101.

August, D., & Shanahan, T. (2006). *Developing literacy in second language learners: Report of the National Literacy Panel on language-minority children and youth.* Mahwah, NJ: Lawrence Erlbaum.

Berkeley, S., & Riccomini, P. J. (2017). Academic progress monitoring. In J. M. Kauffman, D. P. Hallahan, & P. C. Pullen (Eds.), *Handbook of special education* (2nd ed., pp. 334–347). New York, NY: Routledge.

Berkeley, S., & Taboada Barber, A. (2015). *Maximizing effectiveness of reading comprehension instruction in diverse classrooms.* Baltimore, MD: Brookes Publishing.

Bialystok, E. (1993). Metalinguistic awareness: The development of children's representations of language. In C. Pratt & A. Garton (Eds.), *Systems of representation in children: Development and use* (pp. 211–233). London: Wiley & Sons.

Biancarosa, G., & Snow, C. E. (2006). *Reading next—A vision for action and research in middle and high school literacy: A report to Carnegie Corporation of New York* (2nd ed.). Washington, DC: Alliance for Education.

Bryant, D. P., Vaughn, S., Linan-Thompson, S., Ugel, N., Hamff, A., & Hougen, M. (2000). Reading outcomes for students with and without reading disabilities in general education middle-school content area classes. *Learning Disability Quarterly, 23,* 238–252.

Fuchs, L. S., Fuchs, D., Hosp, M. K., & Jenkins, J. R. (2001). Oral reading fluency as an indicator of reading competence: A theoretical, empirical, and historical analysis. *Scientific Studies of Reading, 5,* 239–256.

Guthrie, J., & Wigfield, A. (2000). Engagement and motivation in reading. In M. Kamil, P. Mosenthal, D. Pearson, & R. Barr (Eds.), *Handbook of reading research* (pp. 518–533). Mahwah, NJ: Earlbaum.

Hallahan, D. P., Lloyd, J. W., Kauffman, J. M., Weiss, M. P., & Martinez, E. A. (2005). *Learning disabilities: Foundations, characteristics, and effective teaching* (3rd ed.). Boston, MA: Pearson.

Hasbrouck, J., & Tindal, G. (2006). Oral reading fluency norms: A valuable assessment tool for reading teachers. *Reading Teacher, 59,* 636–644.

Houghton Mifflin Harcourt (HMH). (2019). *HMH Reading Inventory.* Retrieved March 26, 2019 from https://www.hmhco.com/products/assessment-solutions/literacy/sri-index.htm

Hock, M. F., & Deshler, D. D. (2003). Don't forget the adolescents. *Principal Leadership, 4*(3), 51–56.

International Dyslexia Association. (2012). *Definition of dyslexia* (adopted by the IDA Board of Directors, Nov. 12, 2002). Retrieved January 3, 19 from https://dyslexiaida.org/definition-of-dyslexia/

Jennings, J. H., Caldwell, J. S., & Lerner, J. W. (2010). *Reading problems: Assessment and teaching strategies.* Boston, MA: Pearson.

Judge, S., & Bell, S. M. (2011). Reading achievement trajectories for students with learning disabilities during the elementary years. *Reading & Writing Quarterly, 27,* 153–178.

Kuhn, M. R., & Stahl, S. A. (2003). Fluency: A review of developmental and remedial practices. *Journal of Educational Psychology, 95,* 3.

Mastropieri, M. A., Scruggs, T. E., & Graetz, J. E. (2003). Reading comprehension instruction for secondary students: Challenges for struggling students and teachers. *Learning Disability Quarterly, 26,* 103–116.

Mercer, C. D., Mercer, A. R., & Pullen, P. C. (2010). *Teaching students with learning problems* (8th ed.). Boston, MA: Pearson.

Moats, L. C. (2001). When older students can't read. *Educational Leadership, 58,* 36–40.

National Institute of Child Health and Human Development & National Institute for Literacy. (2007). *What content-area teachers should know about adolescent literacy.* Washington, DC: National Institute for Literacy.

Read Naturally. (2008). *Reading Fluency Benchmark Assessor.* Saint Paul, MN: Read Naturally.

Regan, K., Berkeley, S., Hughes, M., & Kirby, S. (2014). Computer-assisted instruction for struggling elementary readers with learning disabilities. *Journal of Special Education, 48,* 106–119.

Saenz, L. M., & Fuchs, L. S. (2002). Examining the reading difficulty of secondary students with learning disabilities: Expository versus narrative text. *Remedial & Special Education, 23*, 31–41.

Shaywitz, S. E. (1996). Dyslexia. *Scientific American, 275*, 98–104.

Spear-Swerling, L. (2006). *The use of context cues in reading.* Retrieved March 24, 2019 from http://www.readingrockets.org/article/use-context-cues-reading

Stetter, M. E., & Hughes, M. T. (2010). Computer-assisted instruction to enhance the reading comprehension of struggling readers: A review of the literature. *Journal of Special Education Technology, 25*, 1–16.

Swanson, H. L., & O'Connor, R. (2009). The role of working memory and fluency practice on the reading comprehension of students who are dysfluent readers. *Journal of Learning Disabilities, 42*, 548–575.

Tompkins, G., Campbell, R., Green, D., & Smith, C. (2014). *Literacy for the 21st century.* Australia: Pearson.

University of Oregon. (2019). *DIBELS 8th Edition.* Retrieved March 30, 2019 from https://dibels.uoregon.edu/

Wayman, M. M., Wallace, T., Wiley, H. I., Tichá, R., & Espin, C. A. (2007). Literature synthesis on curriculum-based measurement in reading. *Journal of Special Education, 41*, 85–120.

SECTION III: APPLICATION ACTIVITIES

Show What You Know!

In this section you learned how important it is for a teacher of reading to have a strong foundation in phonics. How are your phonetic skills? Take the quiz below to find out.

Directions:

1. **Step 1:** Take the phonics test in **Appendix C**.
2. **Step 2:** Score your test.

Answer Key: 1- a; 2- a; 3- c; 4- c; 5- d; 6- d; 7- a; 8- d; 9- b; 10- c; 11- c; 12- d; 13- c; 14- b; 15- d; 16- a; 17- b; 18- b; 19- d; 20- a

3. **Step 3: Learn more.**
    If your test results indicate that your phonics skills are rusty or that you do not have a strong foundation in phonics, we encourage you to practice more. Effective reading teachers are able to automatically recognize phonetic errors that students make and very quickly see patterns to those errors. Teachers who do not have a solid foundation in phonics themselves are not able to do this. One of our favorite resources is Barbara Fox's self-study:
    Fox, B. J. (2014). *Phonics and word study for the teacher of reading: Programed for self-instruction (11th ed.).* Boston, MA: Pearson.

Partner Activity/Discussion

In this chapter, you learned how important it is for teachers to correctly model sounds of corresponding letters. In this activity, you will work with a partner to determine how proficient you are. Be sure to practice any letters you miss!

Directions:

For this activity, one of you will be the activity leader and the other will be the participant.

Round 1: The activity leader (and *only* the activity leader) should turn to Table 5.1: Sound/Symbol Relationships for Single Letters in Chapter 5. Ask your partner the following questions for each letter in the chart and check his/her response.

1. **What is the sound for the letter "____"?** (Note: For vowels, indicate whether the vowel is "short" or "long".)

    *   **CHECK**—Use the keyword in the next column to determine whether your partner's answer matches the sound in the keyword. If your partner's response is NOT correct, ask him/her to repeat the keyword after you and then say the sound again.

2. **Is the sound voiced or unvoiced?**

   - **CHECK**—If your partner's response is NOT correct, ask him/her to touch his/her vocal chords while he/she says the sound to help him/her understand the correct answer.

3. **Is the sound a stretch or stop sound?**

   - **CHECK**—If your partner's response is NOT correct, use the "Teaching Cues for Students" column to model the correct cueing.

4. **How would you cue the student during instruction?**

   - **CHECK**—If your partner's response is NOT correct, use the information in the "Teaching Cues for Students" column to model the correct cueing. Then ask him/her to repeat the cue.

Round 2: Switch roles so that the participant is the activity leader and repeat the steps from Round 1.

Learn More: Multimedia Activity

In this section you learned about word reading skills and fluency. For this activity, you will go deeper in your learning about how reading interventions occur within an RTI framework by exploring the Center on Response to Intervention website. The site houses a wealth of information about the essential components of RTI, numerous resources, and an expert blog. In completing the activity, you will also be exposed to some excellent online resources for related topics as well. Have fun learning!

Directions:

1. **Before**
   In the first text box below, list key ideas you know (K) after reading this section of the textbook. In the next text box, write questions about what you want to learn (W) from completing this multi-media activity.

K (Know)	What do you already know about this topic?
	1.
	2.
	3.
	4.

W (Want to learn)	What do YOU want to learn more about? 1. 2. 3. 4.

2. **During**

Explore the Center on Response to Intervention website at https://www. rti4success.org/. Use the information you find here to answer your questions!

3. **After**

After you have finished reading about the areas you wanted to learn more about, look back at what you indicated you knew before starting (K) and wanted to learn (W). Can you now answer the questions? How does this new information connect with what you knew before starting? Write the answers to your questions in the text box below. Be sure to add any additional unexpected information that you learned (L) as well!

L (Learned)	What did you learn? 1. 2. 3. 4.

Section IV

Understanding Text

Section IV: Overview

Reading comprehension is the purpose of reading. As students progress through their schooling, they will be increasingly expected to read independently to learn new information. Their success in doing this will be dependent on whether they have acquired the basic reading skills needed to access the text as well as their background knowledge of the topic being read about. This background knowledge includes the depth and breadth of students' vocabularies. The first chapter in this section focuses on instructional strategies that help students approach text in the strategic ways that good readers do. The second chapter in this section focuses on how to help build background knowledge and vocabulary to help students make connections between newly read information and their existing knowledge. The last chapter in this section presents the characteristics of students who struggle with reading comprehension and describes how to use assessment data to inform instructional choices for these students.

- Chapter 10: Reading Comprehension
- Chapter 11: Background Knowledge (Including Vocabulary)
- Chapter 12: Supporting All Students in Understanding Text

Guiding Questions

As you are reading, consider the following questions:

- What are the major processes of reading comprehension?
- How are reading strategies most effectively taught?
- What instructional approaches foster reading comprehension?
- What types of vocabulary words are important to teach?
- What instructional approaches support building and activating background knowledge?
- What instructional approaches foster vocabulary acquisition?
- What challenges do at-risk students have with understanding text?
- What assessments are used to informally assess a student's ability to understand text?
- What additional instructional supports are needed for readers who struggle to understand text?

Chapter 10

Reading Comprehension

Fundamentals of Reading Comprehension

The purpose of reading is **comprehension**—the construction of meaning from print (Kintsch & Kintsch, 2005). Reading comprehension requires simultaneous proficiency in both the automatic identification of words as well as the language processes required to derive meaning from those words (Chard, Vaughn, & Tyler, 2002; Joseph & Schisler, 2009; Perfetti, Landi, & Oakhill, 2005). Additionally, reading comprehension is an active rather than a passive process that requires engagement from the reader before, during, and after reading (Berkeley & Taboada Barber, 2015). As such, readers need to be both purposeful and active if comprehension is to occur (National Reading Panel, 2001). Fortunately, students can be taught to be purposeful and active readers by teaching them how to approach text strategically.

Types of Text

Demands on the reader can vary based on the type of text being read. There are numerous ways to categorize and discuss types of text; however, the most common terms used are narrative text and expository text (Kent, 1984). In the early elementary grades when students are beginning to learn to read, students are predominantly exposed to narrative texts. By the end of high school, however, students are required to read predominantly expository texts, such as textbooks (Barton, 1997; Vidal-Abarca, Martínez, & Gilabert, 2000).

Narrative Texts

Narrative texts are fictional stories written with the purpose to entertain. The components of narrative text, called text structure, are referred to as **story grammar**. In its simplest form, the story grammar of narrative text refers to characters, setting, and plot (Fountas, 2001; Keene, 2008). Story grammar of narrative text can also include theme, perspective, antagonist, protagonist, movement through time, change, goals, conflict, rising action, climax, falling action, and resolution.

Many genres of text tend to be written in a narrative text structure, including fables, historical fiction, science fiction, and mysteries, to name a few. Because narratives are also conveyed through oral language and conversation, students are likely to enter school with exposure to storytelling, which helps with understanding of narrative stories in print (Morrow, 2014). As students move through the grades, narrative texts become increasingly complex with non-sequential story lines, multiple points of view, and complex storytelling devices (such as foreshadowing, irony, and hyperbole). As the complexity of text increases, students will need additional guidance and instruction.

Expository Texts

Nonfiction texts that are written to help a reader learn something new are called **expository texts**, also called informational texts. Unlike narrative texts, expository texts generally contain a variety of text structures that can vary among chapters, paragraphs, and even sentences (Berkeley, King-Sears, Hott, & Bradley-Black, 2014). These **text structures** include descriptive, explanatory, sequential, compare/contrast, problem/solution, and cause/effect (Meyer & Poon, 2001). See Table 10.1 below for a description of each. This complexity of text structure is part of the reason that expository texts are more challenging for students to read and understand than narrative texts (Sáenz & Fuchs, 2002).

Among others, genres of expository texts include textbooks, newspapers, manuals, and biographies. Textbooks are a particularly challenging form of expository text because they are typically written above grade level—containing large numbers of unfamiliar multi-syllabic words, highly variable text structures, and large numbers of novel concepts and vocabulary terms (Berkeley, King-Sears, Vilbas, & Conklin, 2016). Textbooks are relied on heavily in content area classrooms (Issitt, 2004; Nokes, 2010), so it is important for teachers to understand the challenges inherent to this type of text and strategies that can help students understand more of what they read. Although expository texts are predominantly used in the upper grades, secondary teachers are not the only teachers who need to understand how to help students with this type of text. It is also important for teachers in the elementary school grades to expose students to these types of texts early so that they are familiar with some of these text structures later when they are expected to independently read to learn new information. See Chapter 5 for an example of how to incorporate expository text into classrooms as young as kindergarten.

Table 10.1 Text Structures

Text Structure	Definition	Example
Description (also called explanatory)	lists of related facts (order is not important)	• description of the parts of a microscope • description of a desert topography
Sequential	temporal listing where time order is important	• historical events in chronological order • steps to complete an algebraic equation • the sequence of the water cycle
Compare/Contrast	similarities and differences between people, events or concepts	• comparison of democracies and dictatorships • comparison of characteristics of fruits and vegetables
Problem/Solution (also called cause/effect)	description of a response to an event (problem)	• causes and outcome of the Revolutionary War • causes and effect of soil erosion

Adapted from: Kinder, D., Bursuck, B., & Epstein, M. (1992). An evaluation of history textbooks. *The Journal of Special Education, 25*, 472–491.

Reading Comprehension Strategies

Students understand more of what they read when they approach text strategically (Deshler, Ellis, & Lenz, 1996; Gersten, Fuchs, Williams, & Baker, 2001; Pressley & Ghatala, 1990). While some students are naturally strategic in how they approach reading, many students are not and will need to be taught how to do so. Because reading comprehension is not a visible behavior, students will not "pick up" strategic behaviors by observing their peers. Rather, they will need direct instruction that makes these invisible cognitive behaviors visible. The benefit of improved reading comprehension extends far beyond the reading lesson. When students learn to approach text strategically, it enables them to learn independently from text in content areas, such as social studies and science, as well (Scruggs, Mastropieri, Berkeley, & Graetz, 2010; Therrien, Taylor, Hosp, Kaldenberg, & Gorsh, 2011).

A wide array of **reading comprehension strategies** have been developed to help students approach the reading process systematically. As shown in Figure 10.1, these processes can be conceptualized as the "4 Ps": *plan, pay attention and problem solve*, and *process information*. Planning generally occurs before readers begin reading and helps them be more efficient in their efforts. During reading, strategic readers pay attention to what they are understanding and problem solve steps they should take when they recognize that comprehension has broken down. After students have finished reading, they actively process and synthesize the information read and integrate it into their existing knowledge base.

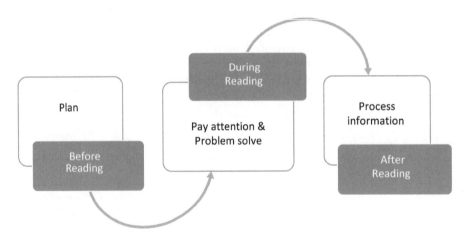

Figure 10.1 The 4 Ps of reading comprehension

Plan

A part of planning is strategy awareness. **Strategy awareness** involves understanding the demands of a task and whether a strategy would assist with comprehension as well as knowing the steps of the selected strategies (Pressley & Ghatala, 1990). This seems rather straightforward, but for many students this awareness does not occur naturally and needs to be overtly taught (Wixson & Lipson, 1991).

Strategy use is more likely to be sustained when students understand why, how, and when to use a strategy. Both of these processes are important for sustained strategy use. Table 10.2 presents these key instructional features of strategy instruction.

Activities that occur before students begin reading can be instrumental in reading comprehension. Therefore, it is important that instruction is front-loaded to have maximum impact on student learning (Berkeley & Taboada Barber, 2015). In other words, teachers should take care to adequately prepare students before they begin reading, as students will then be better able to access and understand what they read independently.

Table 10.2 Strategy Planning Guide

Instruction Component	Purpose
Why to use a strategy.	Students are more motivated to use strategies when reading if they understand why the strategy will help.
How to use a strategy.	Students need to know how to follow the steps of the strategy. Sometimes a mnemonic or visual cue is used to help students remember all of the steps.
When to use a strategy.	Students need to understand when a strategy will be appropriate. This is an important step because students who rigidly apply strategies to texts that do not fit the strategy may abandon the strategy altogether.

Pay Attention and Problem Solve

During reading, it is important to teach students that they should pay attention and problem solve when comprehension breaks down. In other words, readers need to self-monitor their own comprehension to become aware of their understanding or lack thereof. This metacognitive process is referred to as **comprehension monitoring** (National Reading Panel, 2001). Unfortunately, many students do not actively monitor their own understanding while reading and need instruction and practice to make this a habit.

In addition to targeting specific cognitive processes, strategy instruction needs to include aspects that promote self-monitoring of self-regulation and metacognition (see Figure 10.2). **Self-regulation** is the cyclical process individuals use to sustain their own learning through active engagement in the learning process that helps them reach learning goals (Zimmerman, 2000). **Metacognition** is a student's awareness of his or her own thinking (LaJoie, 2008; Lenz, Ellis, & Scanlon, 1996; Pressley & Ghatala, 1990). Metacognition also helps students to monitor their selection and use of strategies.

When understanding breaks down, good readers problem solve by considering which strategies might help them to "fix-up" their comprehension (Berkeley & Riccomini, 2013; Roberts, Torgesen, Boardman, & Scammacca, 2008). In order to do this successfully, students need to be aware of reading strategies. Then, students need to remember and follow the steps to the strategy that they have selected. Students who are able to do this tend to understand more of what they read (Deshler et al., 1996).

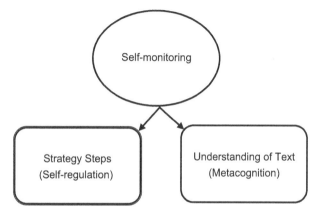

Figure 10.2 Self-monitoring components

Process Information

Reading is a complex process. Numerous interactions between the reader and the text itself are required for reading comprehension to occur (Klingner, Vaughn, & Boardman, 2007). There are two overarching ways that reading results in improved understanding— synthesizing information as a means to interpret and evaluate what has been read and making connections between new information read and what the reader already knows (Pressley & Afflerbach, 1995; Sampson, Rasinski, & Sampson, 2003).

Synthesizing information involves both getting the **gist**, or the essence of the meaning, of what is being read and making distinctions between main ideas and details. A **main idea** is the most important idea in a section of text, while **details** are the supporting information that supports the main idea (Klingner, Morrison, & Eppolito, 2011). Sometimes main ideas are stated directly in text, but more often, they need to be inferred.

There are several types of connections that can be helpful to a reader (Keene & Zimmerman, 2007); these are depicted in Figure 10.3. Some connections help the reader relate what is read to personal knowledge and experiences. Other connections help the reader relate information between different texts, which includes knowledge of genres and text structures. Connections can also help the reader relate what is read with the reader's knowledge of the world. Connections can be critical in helping students make sense of what they are reading. Students can tie information from the reading to their own previous experiences—their background knowledge—and then meaningfully apply what is read to novel learning situations in the future. You will learn more about this in Chapter 11.

CONNECTIONS WHILE READING

Figure 10.3 Connections while reading

Instructional Approaches

It is important for teachers to help students learn strategies to help themselves plan, pay attention, problem solve, and process information. However, knowing what strategies to teach is only half of the equation; a large body of research tells us that *how* we go about teaching strategies is just as important as the strategies themselves.

Fostering Acquisition and Self-regulation of Reading Strategies

When teaching students comprehension strategies, a teacher cannot simply introduce the strategy, but rather must facilitate the entire process, including identifying an appropriate strategy, correctly applying all the steps, monitoring the effectiveness of the strategy and making adjustments as needed. A large body of research tells us that this can be most effectively accomplished through instruction that utilizes modeling, guided and independent practice, and corrective and strategy focused feedback (Mastropieri, Scruggs, & Graetz, 2003; Swanson, 1999; Vaughn, Gersten, & Chard, 2000). See Figure 10.4 below for a visual depiction of these elements of instruction.

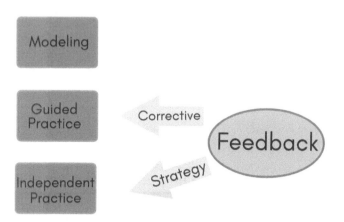

Figure 10.4 The instructional process

Modeling Strategy Use

Initially, students are exposed to a new strategy through modeling (Methe & Hintze, 2003; Rupley, Blair, & Nichols, 2009). **Modeling** is the process that teachers use to help students conceptualize new skills and strategies. This phase is fertile ground for discussing the strategy instruction components highlighted earlier in this chapter. Modeling is important because reading comprehension is an internal cognitive process. In other words, students cannot see or hear what is going on in another person's head. For this reason, a teacher may use "**think-alouds**" to model the teacher's thought process while thinking aloud, to enable students to see how the strategy is applied and hear the reasoning behind the application of the strategy components (Block & Israel, 2004). The most effective think-alouds are specific and explicit, and overtly demonstrate flexibility in strategy use (Regan & Berkeley, 2012). Think-alouds in the upper grades are similar to shared reading experiences in the earliest grades (see Chapter 5).

Guided Practice of Strategy Use

Guided practice is the process where students use a newly introduced strategy with support from a teacher. During this part of the process, the teacher walks students through the strategy's application, providing clarification on how to correctly use different strategy elements (Mercer, Mercer, & Pullen, 2010). One of the key aspects of instruction in this phase is fostering students' self-regulation skills through selection, application, and self-monitoring of a strategy (Mastropieri & Scruggs, 2018). This might include use of a strategy steps checklist that students will use only until they have internalized the strategy steps and use them automatically while reading.

An important aspect of guided practice is providing corrective feedback to students. **Corrective feedback** comprises explicit responses to student efforts to use a strategy that redirects students to correctly use the strategy steps in order. Like all feedback to students, corrective feedback should be direct and explicit, constructive to learning, and encouraging. Notice in the example in Table 10.3 that the teacher begins by acknowledging and praising the student's efforts, provides clear feedback about the things that the student did correctly in addition to the item that needs to be corrected, and finally, she encourages the student to try again. In the first non-example in the next column, you notice that the teacher's feedback is direct, but vague—the student is told that she did not do the strategy correctly, but not why, and there is no acknowledgment of the effort that she has put in to trying to learn. In the second non-example, the teacher's feedback acknowledges the student's efforts and is positive and encouraging, but there is no direct feedback about what the student has done incorrectly and should continue to work on. In fact, the student may walk away from this exchange mistakenly thinking that she has applied the strategy correctly and may continue to repeat the same mistake in the future, impeding the efficiency or effectiveness of the strategy.

Table 10.3 Corrective Feedback

Example	*Non-Example*
Teacher: I like how hard you are trying to follow all of the steps of the strategy. It looks like you missed one of the steps. You remembered to _____ and _____, but you forgot to _____. Next time, remember to _____. Try again!	**Teacher:** You did not do the strategy correctly. Do it again, please. **Teacher:** Great job! If you keep working, you will get this down in no time!

Independent Practice of Strategy Use

Once students have had the experience of applying the comprehension strategy with support, they are ready to begin implementing the learned strategy by themselves—called independent practice. Independent practice is important because students need opportunities to independently apply strategy steps to ensure that it becomes an automatic part of their reading.

As students move into independent practice, they can begin to be given strategy feedback. **Strategy feedback** is intended to help students make connections between effort and success, and conversely, between insufficient effort and failure (Berkeley, Mastropieri, & Scruggs, 2011). This type of feedback might include phrases like:

- *"Awesome job working hard and using all the steps in the strategy to write a great summary!"*

This statement reinforces effort and strategy use by the student that resulted in a positive learning outcome. At other times, students might need feedback that redirects them to expend greater effort and implement other learned strategies, such as

- *"It sounds like you forgot to use one of the strategies that you learned in class and are having trouble figuring out the answer to this question. Which strategy could you use to help yourself figure it out?* [wait for student response] *What are the steps in that strategy?* [wait for student response] *Great! Give it a try!"*

These feedback statements serve to help students make the connection between failing to use strategies and failure to comprehend, rather than reading comprehension failure being some internal factor inherent to the student or otherwise out of the student's control. Notice that this feedback serves to coach the student through the thought process used by strategic readers in order to problem solve. Strategy feedback intentionally leaves ownership for comprehension and action in the student's hands. In other words, the teachers are not the sole holders of the correct answers and actions that should be taken. This is a critical step in fostering student persistence with strategy use when the teacher is not present to support the process.

Strategies that Help Students Plan

There are many ways to help students get into the habit of making a plan prior to reading. Common strategies include setting a purpose for reading, previewing the text, and activating background knowledge. An explanation for each of these approaches and exemplar strategies follows.

Setting a Purpose for Reading

One way for a student to plan is to **set a purpose for reading**. When students are attempting a reading task, they are usually more successful when they have set a specific purpose for reading, because it helps them to stay focused on the reading task. This is also referred to as **goal setting**, which is the first step in self-regulating one's learning. When setting a meaningful goal, it is important that the goal is challenging but attainable. In addition, it should be related to the student's understanding of what was read rather than solely completion of the reading. For example:

- *"I need to find out what countries were on the Allies' side in World War II."*
- *"I need to read carefully so I am able to answer the questions for the homework assignment. This information will be on the test next week!"*

Goals are also most effective when they are specific, because the reader is then better able to evaluate later whether they have successfully achieved their purpose for reading.

A Focus on Types of Goals

Goal setting is an important part of the self-regulation process. There are many different ways to conceptualize goal setting, but one common way is to think of them in two categories: as achievement goals and as process goals. People are often inclined to set achievement goals, but research shows that achievement goals alone are not sufficient for helping a student self-regulate their learning. Process goals, on the other hand, are generally regarded as being helpful for learning. However, the most effective approach is a combination of both process and achievement goals. Each are described next with an example of what these types of goals might look like in the area of reading.

Achievement Goals

As the term implies, achievement goals are long-term goals that are focused on the end result—achievement. These types of goals are most effective when the goal matches the motivation of the individual. Some people are motivated by competition and so for this individual, a goal to outperform another might be most effective. Some people are motivated by the quality of the end outcome and so for this individual, a goal to have a great product might be most effective. Some people are motivated by the process itself and so for this individual, a goal that involves personal development of a skill might be most effective.

Process Goals

Process goals tend to be short-term goals that are focused on successful completion and performance of the steps needed to reach their long-term goal. These goals are most effective when they are specific, challenging, and attainable.

In the example below (Photo 10.1), a 3rd grade student wrote about her New Year's resolution to improve her reading.

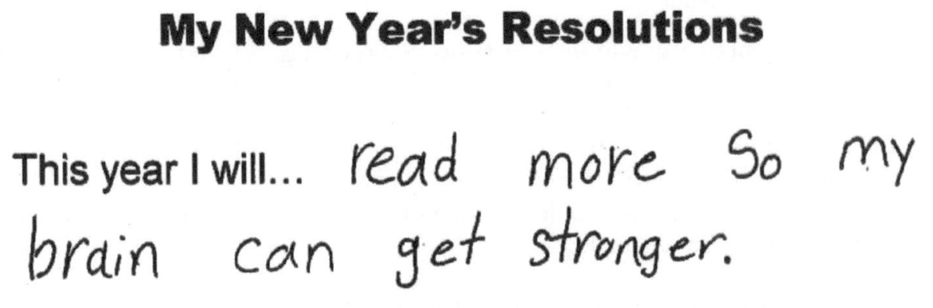

My New Year's Resolutions

This year I will... read more So my brain can get stronger.

Photo 10.1

To *read more so my brain can get stronger* is the student's long-term outcome goal. To reach that goal, the student plans to work on the following short-term process goal: "to read 'Virginia Reader's Choice' books for 20 minutes before bed every night." The combination of these two types of goals are very powerful tools for helping her self-regulate her learning. The fact that the student developed these goals independently shows that she has some nicely developing self-regulation skills.

Previewing

Strategic readers take time before reading to look for key features within the text—this process is called **previewing**. Previewing is particularly helpful before reading expository texts because expository texts tend to have a wide range of features that support understanding of the content. Text features can include both features in text (such as headings, bolded vocabulary with definitions), supplemental figures (such as maps, graphs, photographs), and reader supports (such as graphic organizers, bullet key points). Previewing the text gives readers a sense of what they will be reading about and helps them make a plan for how they might best utilize supports that are included with the text. For example, if there are maps included in the text, he or she might make a mental note to study those maps to better understand what the text is communicating. Alternatively, if the reader sees that vocabulary words are in bold and defined in the margins, the student might make a mental note to remember to look at those definitions if there is a bolded word they do not understand while reading.

Activating Background Knowledge

Another way that good readers plan before reading is by purposefully activating their background knowledge prior to beginning to read so that their memory is primed to make connections with new information in the text. This includes thinking about vocabulary that they already know related to the topic. Background knowledge is so important for effective comprehension that the entire next chapter, Chapter 11, is devoted to it.

Strategies that Help Students Pay Attention and Problem Solve

Students understand more of what they read when they are actively engaged during the reading process. Strategies can help students to pay attention while they are reading and problem solve when they run into obstacles to their understanding. A powerful way to help students pay attention while reading is to teach them to ask and answer questions while reading (National Reading Panel, 2001). This is why many strategies include some sort of questioning. A student's ability to problem solve when comprehension problems occur is also important. In order to problem solve, however, students first need to be aware that their understanding has broken down. Comprehension monitoring strategies can help students to recognize when they have not understood what they have read. Often, these strategies employ questioning as well. Examples of questioning and comprehension monitoring are presented next.

Self-questioning

Paying attention to text for sustained periods of time can be difficult for readers. One of the strategies for fostering this attention is helping students to develop self-questioning skills. **Self-questioning** is a process where readers ask themselves questions and then answer those questions while reading. This process helps readers to self-regulate their engagement with text and understand more of what they read. For many students, this self-questioning does not come naturally and has to be explicitly taught and incrementally developed. Most students do not conceptualize reading in this way. However, when students approach reading with this mindset, reading becomes an active rather than passive process. Initially, the teacher may provide students with pre-set questions that they can ask and answer before reading. As students become proficient, scaffolded instruction is provided to help them develop their own questions.

In the earliest grades, questions might be used to help students attend to and sequence the most basic aspects of plot by asking:

- What happened at the *beginning* of the story?
- What happened in the *middle* of the story?
- What happened at the *end* of the story?

The more consistent teachers are with asking these questions after reading, the more students will begin to anticipate them and attend to this information while listening to stories and in their earliest attempts to read beginner books.

Next, students might be introduced to utilizing "W" words to help them remember information that they read. "W" questions might include:

- *Who* is the story about?
- *What* happened in the story?
- *Where* does the story take place?
- *When* does the story take place?
- *Why* do you think those events happened?

"Who" and "what" questions are the most basic, with "where," "when," and "why" questions becoming increasingly difficult. Students may be introduced to questioning initially as a listening comprehension strategy—where students listen to a teacher read the story aloud and practice asking and answering questions about what they hear in the story. As students begin reading connected text on their own, students would be encouraged to continue asking and answering these questions when reading on their own. Notice that these questions draw students' attention to the underpinnings of story grammar. Student ability to ask and answer these sorts of questions in the early grades will serve as a foundation to support understanding of increasingly complex narrative text structures as they progress through the grades.

As students become more proficient with their self-questioning abilities, the teacher can move to helping students think about the nature of questions and the types of answers that they unveil. Answers to some questions are directly stated in a single sentence of text—called **explicit questions**. Other questions require that information from two or more sentences be used to infer an answer—called **implicit questions**. Still other questions require that the student rely on their existing knowledge in addition to what is in text in order to construct an answer—called **scriptal questions**. A strategy that helps students to understand and take advantage of knowledge about questions is called the Question Answer Relationships Strategy, or QAR (Kinniburgh & Prew, 2010). QAR teaches students to identify four types of question/answer relationships:

1. "right there" questions (explicit questions),
2. "think and search" questions (implicit questions),
3. "author and you" questions (scriptal questions),
4. "on your own" questions (reader background knowledge).

When students are able to identify types of questions, it will give them direction for the best approach for trying to answer questions (Adler, 2001). Further, questions help students to focus their attention on the most relevant information needed to answer the question. For a *"right there"* question, skimming and scanning for the answer would be a strategic way to locate the answer. For a *"think and search"* question, using a strategy for summarizing or making connections between important points would be effective. For an *"author and you"* question, students will want to activate and include their background knowledge while making connections. Finally, for an *"on your own"* question, students will want to activate and reflect on their background knowledge. Although this strategy seems straightforward, students will need sufficient practice in order to master and make this strategy a habit. The teacher's end goal is to develop student self-questioning skills to the point of independence. In this way, students will begin any reading task ready to ask questions of all types with the goal of understanding what is read.

Comprehension Monitoring

Similar to self-questioning, comprehension monitoring strategies are strategies that prompt students to actively engage with text they are reading. Comprehension monitoring strategies foster metacognition during reading. Metacognition is the ability to monitor one's own understanding during the reading task (National Reading Panel, 2001). Just like with self-questioning, many students do not intuitively develop metacognitive skills without explicit instruction. Initially, metacognition is taught at the sentence level and then progresses to longer sections of text.

One example of a strategy that incorporates metacognitive components is Survey, Question, Read, Recite, Review (SQ3R) (Adams, Carnine, & Gersten, 1982). The acronym SQ3R helps students to remember the steps to the strategy:

1. *Survey*—preview the text for text features (headings, maps, graphs, illustrations).
2. *Question*—develop your own questions by rephrasing headings and subheadings as questions.
3. *Read*—read the material taking notes as necessary.
4. *Recite*—recite information that you remember.
5. *Review*—reread and check notes to refresh your memory of the content.

In this strategy, the final two "r" steps—recite and review, involve metacognition. If a student is able to recite what he remembers, then it is an indicator to himself that he has understood what he has read. If a student is not able to recite what he remembers, then it is an indicator to himself that he has not understood what he has read and the final review step gives the student a next step for helping repair comprehension.

Another example of a comprehension monitoring strategy is QRAC-the-Code (Berkeley & Riccomini, 2013). This strategy is similar to SQ3R in that it uses natural prompts in text (headings and subheadings) to cue students to reflect on whether or not they have understood what they have read. The steps to the QRAC-the-Code strategy are:

1. *Question*—turn headings into questions.
2. *Read*—read the section and STOP.
3. *Answer*—ask yourself: "*Can I answer my question?*"
4. *Check*—check to be sure your answer was correct.

In addition to an acronym of the strategy steps, a memorable image and auditory prompt is used (see Figure 10.5). A "duck-tective" reminds students to "QRAC-QRAC-QRAC" the code. When said aloud, "QRAC-QRAC-QRAC" sounds like "quack, quack, quack." Students know that a duck says "quack," which jogs their memory of the similar-sounding acronym for the strategy.

Figure 10.5 Mnemonic for QRAC-the-code strategy

The metacognitive component of QRAC-the-Code is in the final step "check." If a student is able to answer her own question, then she will circle "yes" on her strategy sheet, to indicate that she has understood. If a student is unable to answer her own question, then she will circle "no" on her strategy sheet, which indicates that she has not understood and she needs to try some other strategies to "fix-up" her comprehension. Question prompts are provided as a part of the strategy to help students determine which "fix-up" strategy would be most helpful. In keeping with the "duck-tective" theme, prompts are in a section titled "*Need more clues?*":

- Did you understand <u>vocabulary</u>? *Look for the definition of bold words.*
- Were there clues in the <u>text features</u>? *Study maps and graphs.*
- Do you know anything else about the topic? *Use your prior knowledge.*
- Was your question not answered? *Try to summarize the section instead!*
  1. Who was the section about?
  2. What happened in the section?
  3. Tell what the section was about in less than two sentences.
- Really, really stuck? *Reread the section and try again!*

Student responses on their strategy sheets serve as a powerful tool to teachers as they monitor student progress, because it gives teachers a visual cue to whether students think they are understanding or not. Teachers can then query students about the answers they gave on their strategy sheets to inform strategy feedback to students that helps them develop accuracy in their self-evaluation of their comprehension.

Strategies that Help Students Process Information

Comprehension strategies can also help students to process information that they have read as a means to make sense of information. Strategies that help students recall and summarize read information helps them to synthesize that information. Students who connect what they are reading to what they already know have a deeper level of understanding of the material read. Visual representations can help students to make these important connections as well.

Using Retelling and Summarizing Strategies to Synthesize Information

As you learned in Chapter 5, students' earliest efforts to comprehend information include recognizing and remembering the beginning, middle, and end of a story in sequence. Next, they will advance to remembering more of the important information from a story in order—called a **retelling**. Then they will advance to summarizing larger chunks of information and distinguishing between main ideas and details. Numerous simple strategies can help students practice and become proficient with synthesizing information.

One such strategy is Peer Assisted Learning Strategies (PALS), which utilizes peer tutoring to support student comprehension (McMaster, Fuchs, & Fuchs, 2006; Sáenz, Fuchs, & Fuchs, 2005). When using this strategy with students, a stronger reader is purposefully paired with a weaker reader. Pairs of students work through the following steps:

1. *Partner reading*—the stronger reader reads a passage aloud while the weaker reader follows along. Then the weaker reader reads the same passage while the stronger reader follows along.
2. *Paragraph shrinking*—partners work together to summarize what they have read and to state the main ideas from the passage.
3. *Prediction relay*—one partner tries to predict what will happen in the next part of the text and then tries to see if the prediction was correct when reading.

Step number two, paragraph shrinking, requires students to work together to practice summarizing information. In turn, summarizing information will help students to identify the main idea. Further, utilizing peer tutoring maximizes the structured practice opportunities for students in the classroom. Notice also that the final step, prediction relay, has a metacognitive component; students need to check their understanding by confirming whether their prediction was correct.

There are also several strategies that students can learn to use independently to help themselves synthesize information. For example, the RAP strategy (Katims & Harris, 1997; Schumaker, Denton, & Deshler, 1984) has three steps:

1. **R**ead the paragraph.
2. **A**sk yourself—*"What are the main ideas and details of this paragraph?"*
3. **P**ut the main ideas and details in your own words.

Steps number two and three prompt students to distinguish the main ideas and details and to put the information in their own words. Although this information seems simple, it can be quite challenging for students to learn to apply and scaffolded support may be needed.

A similar three-step strategy gives students a systematic process for summarizing text (Berkeley et al., 2011; Jitendra, Hoppes, & Xin, 2000). The steps are:

1. Who (or what) is the paragraph about?
2. What is happening to the who (or what)?
3. Create a summary sentence in your own words using less than ten words.

Notice that this strategy uses *who* and *what* questions that students have likely practiced since the earliest grades. In addition, the final step prompts students to create a word bank with words that will enable them to write a summary. Again, this strategy seems simple on its face, but it will be difficult for many students and so teachers will need to have a plan to scaffold supports.

Using Text Structure and Graphic Organizers to Make Connections

Reading comprehension is always contextualized within an individual's own experiences; it never occurs in a vacuum. As such, good readers actively make connections between what they are reading and what they already know. Visual representations can assist students with making these important connections, generally through the use of a graphic organizer. Some graphic organizers support student recognition of the structure of the text itself, while other organizers help students to attend to specific content and ideas.

For example, a story map is a type of graphic organizer that can help a student to attend to and reflect on important components of a narrative text. In narrative text, it is important to pay close attention to the characters in the story, as these characters are important to the meaning of the story. Because characters are inherently human, or at least have human experiences, purposefully considering the characteristics of those characters and their relative importance in the story can help students to relate to them and make connections to people in their own lives who have similar characteristics. In the same way, the setting is important within a narrative text structure. When students are prompted to carefully consider the setting for the story and why it is important to the events of that story, it can help them draw parallels to their own experiences in similar settings. In cases where they do not have personal experiences with the type of setting in the story, it can help them to ask questions about what that setting might be like. This will help them to think more deeply about why the setting is important for communicating the events of the story. Finally, the events of the story itself are important in a narrative story structure. As you learned earlier in this chapter, students will have been exposed to other strategies that help them identify and sequence the beginning, middle, and end of the story. As students get older, this basic concept advances and students need to also consider which events are central to the story (the rising action) as well as determine when events are so important that they change the direction of the story altogether (the climax). A story map captures all of this information in a diagram enabling students to make all of this internal thinking visible so that they are better able to process their thinking.

As you learned earlier in this chapter, expository texts do not follow the same structure of narrative texts, and in fact, can contain a variety of structures within and across texts. One common structure found within expository texts is a compare–contrast structure. In this structure, the reader needs to identify differences in information being read. One graphic organizer that can support this type of reading is a compare–contrast chart. An example of this type of organizer is depicted in Photo 10.2 below. After finishing a class reading of a trade book on living and non-living things, the early-grades teacher is recording students' oral statements about what was read using the classification chart. When they are finished, she will go back over the chart, overtly helping students synthesize information in the living things column, followed by synthesizing information in the non-living things column.

As text and content becomes more complex, students will need to not only classify items, but also recognize how concepts are the same as well as how they are different. The content of this type of text structure is often displayed using a graphic organizer called a Venn diagram. In a Venn diagram, students fill in two partially overlapping circles with information. Where the circles overlap, students note how the content is the same (or similar) and where the circles are not overlapping the student notes how the content is different. This process helps the reader to actively think about and classify information. In Photo 10.3, after reading a section of her civics textbook, a student has used a Venn diagram to help herself compare and contrast a democracy and a dictatorship.

Photo 10.2

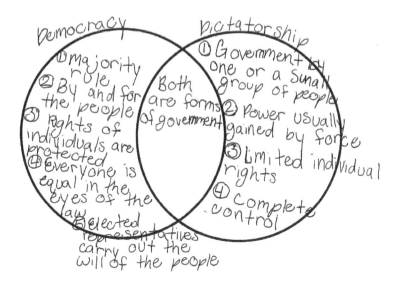

Photo 10.3

There are several other types of expository text structures that students might encounter while reading. When teachers are first introducing graphic organizers as a means to support student processing of information, they carefully consider the nature of the text structure and select a graphic organizer that represents the concept being conveyed through that structure. For example, when reading a history book, if the key takeaway is for students to sequence the historical events in order, a graphic organizer of a timeline would be a logical choice. However, neither a Venn diagram nor timeline would be a logical choice if the main point of the reading was to identify the causes and effects of the Civil War. In this latter scenario, a graphic organizer that visually represented the cause–effect relationships would better help students to attend to the appropriate information needed to make meaningful connections and understand the key point of the reading. Over time, teachers will help students to identify text structures and corresponding graphic supports on their own so that they can use these visual representations independently to help themselves understand what they read.

References

Adams, A., Carnine, D., & Gersten, R. (1982). Instructional strategies for studying content area texts in the intermediate grades. *Reading Research Quarterly, 18*, 27–55.

Barton, K. C. (1997). "I just kinda know": Elementary students' ideas about historical evidence. *Theory & Research in Social Education, 25*, 407–430.

Berkeley, S., King-Sears, M., Vilbas, J., & Conklin, S. (2016). Textbook characteristics that support or thwart comprehension: The current state of social studies texts. *Reading & Writing Quarterly, 32*, 247–272.

Berkeley, S., King-Sears, M. E., Hott, B. L., & Bradley-Black, K. (2014). Are history textbooks more "considerate" after 20 years? *Journal of Special Education, 47*, 217–230.

Berkeley, S., Mastropieri, M. A., & Scruggs, T. E. (2011). Reading comprehension strategy instruction and attribution retraining for secondary students with learning and other mild disabilities. *Journal of Learning Disabilities, 44*, 18–32.

Berkeley, S., & Riccomini, P. J. (2013). QRAC-the-code: A comprehension monitoring strategy for middle school social studies textbooks. *Journal of Learning Disabilities, 46*, 154–165.

Berkeley, S., & Taboada Barber, A. (2015). *Maximizing effectiveness of reading comprehension instruction in diverse classrooms.* Baltimore, MD: Brookes Publishing.

Block, C. C., & Israel, S. E. (2004). The ABCs of performing highly effective think-alouds. *The Reading Teacher, 58,* 154–167.

Chard, D. J., Vaughn, S., & Tyler, B. J. (2002). A synthesis of research on effective interventions for building reading fluency with elementary students with learning disabilities. *Journal of Learning Disabilities, 35,* 386–406.

Deshler, D. E., Ellis, E. S., & Lenz, B. K. (1996). *Teaching adolescents with learning disabilities* (2nd ed.). Denver, CO: Love Publishing Company.

Fountas, I. C. (2001). *Guiding readers and writers, grades 3–6: Teaching comprehension, genre, and content literacy.* Portsmouth, N.: Heinemann.

Gersten, R., Fuchs, L. S., Williams, J. P., & Baker, S. (2001). Teaching reading comprehension strategies to students with learning disabilities: A review of research. *Review of Educational Research, 71,* 279–320.

Issitt, J. (2004). Reflections on the study of textbooks. *History of Education, 33,* 683–696.

Jitendra, A. K., Hoppes, M. K., & Xin, Y. P. (2000). Enhancing main idea comprehension for students with learning problems: The role of a summarization strategy and self-monitoring instruction. *Journal of Special Education, 34,* 127–139.

Joseph, L. M., & Schisler, R. (2009). Should adolescents go back to the basics? A review of teaching word reading skills to middle and high school students. *Remedial & Special Education, 30,* 131–147.

Katims, D. S., & Harris, S. (1997). Improving the reading comprehension of middle school students in inclusive classrooms. *Journal of Adolescent & Adult Literacy, 41,* 116–123.

Keene, E. O. (2008). *To understand: New horizons in reading comprehension.* Portsmouth, NH: Heinemann.

Keene, E. O., & Zimmerman, S. (2007). *Mosaic of thought: The power of comprehension strategy instruction* (2nd ed.). Portsmouth, NH: Heinemann.

Kent, C. E. (1984). A linguist compares narrative and expository prose. *Journal of Reading, 28*(3), 232–236.

Kinder, D., Bursuck, B., & Epstein, M. (1992). An evaluation of history textbooks. *The Journal of Special Education, 25,* 472–491.

Kinniburgh, L. H., & Prew, S. S. (2010). Question answer relationships (QAR) in the primary grades: Laying the foundation for reading comprehension. *International Journal of Early Childhood Special Education, 2*(1), 31–44.

Kintsch, W., & Kintsch, E. (2005). Comprehension. In S. G. Paris, & S. A. Stahl (Eds.), *Children's reading: Comprehension and assessment* (pp. 71–92). Mahwah, NJ: Lawrence Erlbaum Associates.

Klingner, J. K., Morrison, A., & Eppolito, A. (2011). Metacognition to improve reading comprehension. In R. E. O'Connor & P. F. Vadasy (Eds.), *Handbook of reading interventions* (pp. 220–253). New York, NY: Guilford Press.

Klingner, J. K., Vaughn, S., & Boardman, A. (2007). *Teaching reading comprehension to students with learning difficulties.* New York, NY: Guilford Press.

Lajoie, S. P. (2008). Metacognition, self-regulation, and self-regulated learning: A rose by any other name? *Educational Psychology Review, 20,* 469–475.

Lenz, B. K., Ellis, E., & Scanlon, D. (1996). *Teaching learning strategies to adolescents and adults with learning disabilities.* Austin, TX: Pro-Ed.

Mastropieri, M. A., & Scruggs, T. E. (2018). *The inclusive classroom: Strategies for effective differentiated instruction* (6th ed.). Boston, MA: Pearson.

Mastropieri, M. A., Scruggs, T. E., & Graetz, J. E. (2003). Reading comprehension instruction for secondary students: Challenges for struggling students and teachers. *Learning Disability Quarterly, 26,* 103–116.

McMaster, K. L., Fuchs, D., & Fuchs, L. S. (2006). Research on peer-assisted learning strategies: The promise and limitations of peer-mediated instruction. *Reading & Writing Quarterly, 22,* 5–25.

Mercer, C. D., Mercer, A. R., & Pullen, P. C. (2010). *Teaching students with learning problems* (8th ed.). Boston, MA: Pearson.

Methe, S. A., & Hintze, J. M. (2003). Evaluating teacher modeling as a strategy to increase student reading behavior. *School Psychology Review, 32*(4), 617–623.

Meyer, B. J. F., & Poon, L. W. (2001). Effects of structure strategy training and signaling on recall of text. *Journal of Educational Psychology, 93,* 141–159.

Morrow, L. M. (2014). *Literacy development in the early years: Helping children read and write.* Boston, MA: Pearson.

National Reading Panel. (2001). *Put reading first: The research building blocks for teaching children to read.* Jessup, MD: Author.

Nokes, J. D. (2010). Observing literacy practices in history classrooms. *Theory & Research in Social Education, 38,* 515–544.

Perfetti, C. A., Landi, N., & Oakhill, J. (2005). The acquisition of reading comprehension skill. In M. J. Snowling & C. Hulmee (Eds.), *The science of reading: A handbook* (pp. 227–247). Oxford, UK: Blackwell.

Pressley, M., & Afflerbach, P. (1995). *Verbal protocols of reading: The nature of constructively responsive reading.* Mahwah, NJ: Erlbaum.

Pressley, M., & Ghatala, E. S. (1990). Self-regulated learning: Monitoring learning from text. *Educational Psychologist, 25,* 19–33.

Regan, K., & Berkeley, S. (2012). Effective reading and writing instruction: A focus on modeling. *Intervention in School & Clinic, 47,* 276–282.

Roberts, G., Torgesen, J. K., Boardman, A., & Scammacca, N. (2008). Evidence-based strategies for reading instruction of older students with learning disabilities. *Learning Disabilities Research & Practice, 23,* 63–69.

Rupley, W. H., Blair, T. R., & Nichols, W. D. (2009). Effective reading instruction for struggling readers: The role of direct/explicit teaching. *Reading & Writing Quarterly, 25,* 125–138.

Sáenz, L. M., & Fuchs, L. S. (2002). Examining the reading difficulty of secondary students with learning disabilities: Expository versus narrative text. *Remedial & Special Education, 23,* 31–41.

Sáenz, L. M., Fuchs, L. S., & Fuchs, D. (2005). Peer-assisted learning strategies for English language learners with learning disabilities. *Exceptional Children, 71,* 231–247.

Sampson, M. B., Rasinski, T. V., & Sampson, M. (2003). *Total literacy: Reading, writing, and learning* (3rd ed.). Belmont, CA: Wadsworth/Thomson Learning.

Schumaker, J. B., Denton, P. H., & Deshler, D. D. (1984). *The paraphrasing strategy: Instructor's manual.* Lawrence, KS: University of Kansas Institute for Research on Learning.

Scruggs, T. E., Mastropieri, M. A., Berkeley, S., & Graetz, J. E. (2010). Do special education interventions improve learning of secondary content? A meta-analysis. *Remedial & Special Education, 31,* 437–449.

Swanson, H. L. (1999). Reading research for students with LD: A meta-analysis of intervention outcomes. *Journal of Learning Disabilities, 32,* 504–532.

Therrien, W. J., Taylor, J. C., Hosp, J. L., Kaldenberg, E. R., & Gorsh, J. (2011). Science instruction for students with learning disabilities: A meta-analysis. *Learning Disabilities Research & Practice, 26,* 188–203.

Vaughn, S., Gersten, R., & Chard, D. J. (2000). The underlying message in LD intervention research: Findings from research syntheses. *Exceptional Children, 67,* 99–114.

Vidal-Abarca, E., Martínez, G., & Gilabert, R. (2000). Two procedures to improve instructional text: Effects on memory and learning. *Journal of Educational Psychology, 92,* 107.

Wixson, K. K., & Lipson, M. Y. (1991). Perspectives on reading disability research. In R. Barr, M. Kamil, P. Mosenthal, & P. D. Pearson (Eds.), *Handbook of Reading Research* (pp. 539–570). New York, NY: Routledge.

Zimmerman, B. J. (2000). Self-efficacy: An essential motive to learn. *Contemporary Educational Psychology, 25,* 82–91.

Chapter 11

Background Knowledge (Including Vocabulary)

Fundamentals of Background Knowledge

The experiences and knowledge that students have prior to reading are referred to as **background knowledge**, also known as prior knowledge (Dochy, Segers, & Buehl, 1999). Background knowledge is important to the reading process because it influences comprehension (Goldman & Rakestraw, 2000). The reason for this is that background knowledge enables students to make connections between what they already know and new information that they are reading about (Sampson, Rasinski, & Sampson, 2003). As such, a lack of background knowledge prevents the opportunity for connections to be made.

Making Connections

You learned in the last chapter (Chapter 10) that connections can be critical for helping students make sense of what they are reading. In order for students to make these meaningful connections and apply what they have learned after reading, they need to have background knowledge to "hang" new learning on. Connections made while reading can be related to background knowledge the student has from personal experiences (text-to-self connections), factual knowledge gained through reading (text-to-text connections) or other learning (text-to-world connections) (Keene & Zimmerman, 2007). See Figure 11.1.

Students who do not have background knowledge of a topic, or who do not make connections between this existing information and new information, do not understand as much of what they read as students who do make these connections (Goldman & Rakestraw, 2000). When students actively make connections between their background knowledge

CONNECTIONS WHILE READING

Figure 11.1 Connections while reading

and new learning, they develop their schema. **Schema** is the mental map of information, relationships, and understandings related to a particular idea. One of the most important connections when developing schema is to existing vocabulary knowledge.

One critical aspect of a student's background knowledge is his or her knowledge of the meaning of words, or vocabulary. Like with background knowledge in general, vocabulary knowledge has a strong relationship to reading comprehension. Those with larger vocabularies tend to understand more of what they read, while students with smaller vocabularies tend to understand less (Nagy & Stahl, 2000; Pullen & Cash, 2017).

The Role of Vocabulary

Vocabulary is "the set of words in a language that a person knows and uses" (Berkeley & Taboada Barber, 2015, p. 31). Sometimes people refer to vocabulary as the words that a student is able to decode, for example, referring to a student's "sight word vocabulary." This is misleading, however, because vocabulary is about the *meaning* of those words. Vocabulary typically develops naturally and includes words learned through reading. As you learned in Chapter 4, oral language is the start of a student's vocabulary development. Initially, a child's vocabulary helps them to communicate survival needs and as their language development progresses, they begin to develop their vocabulary for objects, people, and actions in the child's immediate environment. As students are exposed to books at home and at school, their vocabularies continue to grow as they are exposed to new words. In addition, as students progress through school, they are continuously exposed to new words related to the curriculum, the classroom, and other social contexts. As students become more sophisticated in word learning, they become able to decipher meanings of words used both in and out of context (Beck, McKeown, & Omanson, 1987).

In Chapter 1, you learned that not all students enter school with the same language experiences and that the level of language exposure in a child's early years can set a child up for success or set them back in their academic trajectory. Stanovich (1986) coined this phenomenon as the Matthew Effect to describe an ongoing cycle where the "rich get richer, and the poor get poorer." Vocabulary is an area where educators see this phenomenon play out, profoundly affecting a student's experiences and success in school. For this reason, it is critically important for schools to provide meaningful experiences where students can expand their vocabularies, through both direct and indirect learning experiences. Direct learning experiences include explicit classroom instruction. Indirect learning experiences include discussion and reading.

You may be surprised to see reading highlighted as being as important as explicit instruction for fostering a student's vocabulary development. This is because reading plays a significant role—for better or worse. Students who read more are exposed to a larger number of novel words and concepts, and as a result, tend to have larger vocabularies (Berkeley & Taboada Barber, 2015). Conversely, students who read less do not benefit from exposure to new words and concepts, and as a result, tend to have limited vocabularies (Baker, Simmons, & Kame'enui, 1998). Students with limited vocabularies struggle more with reading and writing tasks as well as understanding the content in the curriculum, which negatively affects their overall academic performance (Lesaux & Marietta, 2012).

Types of Vocabulary Words

Many new teachers will have questions about what types of vocabulary words should be targeted for instruction and how they should decide which of these words to teach. The National Reading Panel (2001) suggests teaching three categories of words: important words, useful words, and difficult words.

Important words are specific academic vocabulary and key terms related to core content in the curriculum (Juel & Deffes, 2004). Core concepts are the essential underpinnings of the curriculum that students should understand after instruction or reading a subject area text. At the elementary school level these words might include *sum, difference, product* and *quotient* in mathematics or *fiction* and *nonfiction* in reading/language arts. At the secondary level, important words might include *integer* in mathematics, *mole* in chemistry, and *federalism* in government studies.

Useful words are words that a student will often see in any printed text—called high-frequency words. As you learned in Chapter 5, high-frequency words include sight words—the 200–300 basic words such as *the, in, at, does,* and *said* (e.g., Dolch, 1941; Fry, Fountoukidis, & Polk, 1985). High-frequency words also include general academic words that cut across content areas, such as *problem, paragraph, comprehend,* and *identify.* Not only do these words frequently appear in published texts, but they also appear on assessments. Not knowing the meaning of a general academic term might prevent a student from correctly demonstrating learning because it is likely to interfere with the student's understanding of the question.

Difficult words are a group of words that can be just that—difficult or troublesome for students. Difficult words include words that have multiple meanings and those used within idiomatic expressions. Multiple meaning words can throw students off as they are attempting to determine a word's meaning in a particular situation. Students are also likely to run across these difficult words in academic readings (Carnine, Silbert, Kame'enui, Slocum, & Travers, 2017). An example of such a word is *bark,* which may seem like a simple word on the surface. *Bark* can mean the noise a dog makes. But, *bark* can also mean the hard outer covering of a tree. Additionally, *bark* can refer more abstractly to someone that will "*bark an order*" by talking loudly and in a gruff voice. Words can also be deemed difficult if they are a part of idiomatic expressions where the combination of words has a meaning that is not literal. In these phrases, fairly typical words may have an entirely different meaning, for instance if someone says "*piece of cake*," "*hold your horses!*" or "*when pigs fly.*" None of these phrases contain words that are difficult in themselves, but the phrasing makes the expression figurative rather than literal. The key to teaching students to understand these "difficult" words is to recognize why they are hard for students to understand. Take a look at the pictures below (Figure 11.2) to appreciate what a student might visualize if they are unfamiliar with the example idioms. You can see why a student might become confused!

Figure 11.2 Idiomatic expressions

Depth of Word Understanding

It is easy to think that a student either knows a word or does not. However, this is an oversimplification. Vocabulary knowledge is better conceptualized as a continuum

(Phythian-Sence & Wagner, 2007). As Figure 11.3 shows, at one end of the continuum, a student may never have heard a word at all. At the other end of the continuum a student has a deep understanding of the word including being able to identify the word out of context, detect nuances in word meaning in relationship to other similar words, and understand metaphorical uses of the word (Berkeley & Scruggs, 2010). Between these ends of the continuum lies a deepening progression of understanding based on the student's experiences with and exposures to a new word.

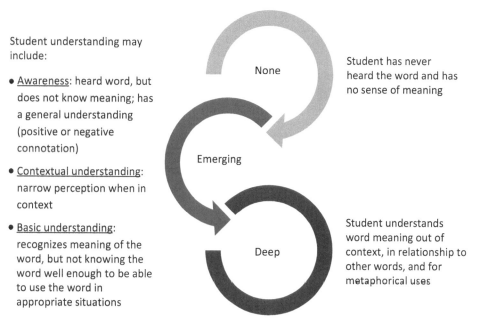

Student understanding may include:

- <u>Awareness</u>: heard word, but does not know meaning; has a general understanding (positive or negative connotation)

- <u>Contextual understanding</u>: narrow perception when in context

- <u>Basic understanding</u>: recognizes meaning of the word, but not knowing the word well enough to be able to use the word in appropriate situations

None

Student has never heard the word and has no sense of meaning

Emerging

Deep

Student understands word meaning out of context, in relationship to other words, and for metaphorical uses

Figure 11.3 Continuum of vocabulary knowledge

While teachers should always be working on expanding students' base of vocabulary knowledge, students do not need the same level of understanding of all newly learned vocabulary words. It is important for students to have a deep understanding of some words that they will encounter throughout their academic career. These might include direction words such as *solve, analyze,* or *describe.* However, not all words require this deep level of understanding initially. For example, when the term *scientific method* is first introduced in elementary school, the goal may be to generally introduce the scientific method as a process and steps needed for undertaking scientific investigation, rather than for students to have a deep and nuanced understanding of this complex procedure. Understanding the depth of knowledge of particular words students will need is important to consider when planning instruction.

Instructional Approaches

Because background knowledge and vocabulary influence a student's reading comprehension, it is important that instruction directly addresses these areas. There are multiple approaches to helping students build their background knowledge and vocabulary as well as for activating knowledge that students already have.

Building Background Knowledge

Throughout their schooling, students will read increasingly challenging texts on a variety of topics. To support this reading, teachers can help students develop foundational background knowledge on a topic before reading about it (Fisher & Frey, 2009). To navigate this issue, teachers can contrive learning experience that will become background knowledge that all students in their classroom have in common. In this way, as teachers introduce strategies for activating background knowledge or making connections, they will be able to refer to this background knowledge that is shared by all students. Different student experiences and activities can be used to develop this shared background knowledge, including read-alouds, visual aids, and multi-media and other memorable activities.

Read Aloud

Reading aloud to students is a powerful tool for exposing students to new vocabulary, modeling strategies to decipher meanings of new words within text, and initiating meaningful discussions about new terms and concepts (Santoro, Chard, Howard, & Baker, 2008). This includes reading texts aloud that may be above the independent decoding levels of students. It is also an excellent way to build shared background knowledge, because all students will have interacted with the same text. There are a variety of types of reading materials that can be used to motivate students, pique interest in an upcoming topic, or simply help them appreciate reading as something to do for pleasure.

For instance, *Faithful Elephants* (Tsuchiya, 1970) is a picture book that can be used to pique student interest in reading more about World War II. In this book, the story is told of Japanese zookeepers that had to make tough decisions about zoo animals, especially the elephants, because of American actions in World War II. When reading this book, students become interested and involved with the feelings and actions of the zookeepers in regard to the elephants. It often stimulates further interest in World War II because students want to understand what has caused the zookeepers and elephants to come to this point. When teachers use this book to initiate emotional engagement in the topic with students, these learners will have their curiosity triggered about knowing more about the events during World War II that led to the problem in this story.

Teachers can also use shared experiences to build background knowledge about abstract concepts in the curriculum. For example, a teacher could use *The Three Little Pigs* (Marshall, 1984) and *The True Story of the 3 Little Pigs* (Scieszka, 2009) to introduce the concept of point of view in a secondary Language Arts class. Most children are familiar with the original story; however, the teacher will read it aloud to ensure that students who do not know the story have been exposed to it and that those who have heard the story before are thinking about the same version. Then the teacher will read aloud the second picture book that tells the same story from the wolf's perspective. Using these short texts creates shared knowledge that the teacher and students can recall later when studying point of view with more advanced texts.

Narrative picture books are not the only texts that can help create shared background knowledge; nonfiction expository texts can be used as well. The key here is to select short pieces on the topic that students will need shared knowledge about. *Junior Scholastic* or *Time for Kids* are two news and current events magazines with content area information on a range of topics. Articles can be read aloud while students follow along.

An additional use of the read aloud can be simply having students experience having books read aloud for pleasure. For example, teachers can spend a small portion of the day reading aloud higher-level books or novels that students could not read independently. In this way, this wide breadth of reading on various topics exposes students to background knowledge across subject areas and also builds positive and enjoyable reading experiences for students. Times that may be good for this form of read-aloud may be after lunch or recess, when students naturally need transition time to adjust back into structured academic learning. This type of read aloud is particularly important for students who are not being read to at home.

Visual Aids and Multi-media

The use of visual aids and multimedia can also provide rich opportunities to build student background knowledge before reading. Sources can include photographs, diagrams, video clips, and podcasts. Many of the media experiences allow students to interact with ideas and events in a way that is not possible with just printed words. Photographs and diagrams provide illustrations of information that sometimes cannot be recreated with words. With video clips, students can sometimes see actual footage of events about which they will be reading. Likewise, with podcasts, learners can sometimes hear firsthand from authors, politicians, and scientists about different critical ideas. Media in general can help open up meaningful opportunities for building students' background knowledge.

Memorable Activities

Shared background knowledge can also be created through memorable class activities. These activities can include everyday experiences that occur in the classroom, discussions, hands-on activities, and special events that create meaningful shared memories. Because knowledge of words is an important part of students' background knowledge, activities that help build vocabulary knowledge are also important. In this way, teachers can feel confident that all students understand the vocabulary needed to make meaning of what is read.

Building Vocabulary through Language Development and Reading

Student vocabulary can be increased through language development and reading. This includes fostering an awareness of words and enabling wide reading. It also includes teaching students strategies for learning word meanings on their own while reading.

Foster Student Interest and Awareness of Words

Student vocabularies can be enhanced by creating school experiences that draw student attention and interest to words and their meanings. In Chapter 5, the concept of creating a print-rich environment was introduced. This includes visual displays such as word walls. In the early grades, word walls might contain sight words and other newly used words that students are learning to read and spell. Generally, these word walls are organized using the alphabet. As students move into the upper grades, word walls and other word displays are more likely to be around a common topic. For example, in a science classroom, a word display might label the components of a cell. In a math classroom, a word wall might contain words commonly found in word problems.

Another way that word awareness can be fostered is through the use of poetry. Poetry is taught from the earliest primary grades and can be used at different levels with students for fostering word awareness and interest. When they are young, students can be asked to focus in on ideas like alliteration and rhyme that draws attention to sounds at the beginning and end of words. These skills help students develop awareness surrounding certain sound patterns in words. However, as students get older, poetry can be used to help stimulate student interest in more complex word awareness such as the rhythm of the words used to express ideas, the feelings shared through the words, and the inferred meanings that can be understood from the words.

Another fun way to draw student attention to words and meanings is through the use of jokes. One of our favorites goes like this:

Question: Where does a bull keep his important papers?
Answer: In his beef-case!

This riddle requires the listener to use a variety of language skills to appreciate the nuance of the words used and reason a connection between them. Important papers might be kept in a briefcase. "Brief" sounds like "beef." A bull is composed of beef and so logically, he might keep his important papers in his "beef-case." The process of working through jokes and riddles with word play inherently draws student attention to words and their meanings, while having a bit of fun at the same time.

Foster Wide Reading

Reading is one of the primary ways that students learn new words, and in turn, vocabulary knowledge increases student understanding of what they read (Bryant, Goodwin, Bryant, & Higgins, 2003; Cunningham & Stanovich, 1998). Therefore, it is important that students read—a lot. The promotion of **wide reading**, structured time for independent reading at a student's independent reading level, is an important part of vocabulary instruction as well as reading instruction. As you learned in Chapter 7, a commonly used approach to encouraging wide reading is providing a structured independent reading time during the school day, such as sustained silent reading (SSR) or drop everything and read (DEAR). Students should be encouraged to read across topics and genres because it is through this wide reading that they will develop greater word awareness by becoming familiar with a variety of words used within different types of text (Chard & Osborn, 1999). For instance, if students are only reading realistic fiction stories, they will likely only be exposed to one particular set of vocabulary involving this genre. However, students who read biographies and other nonfiction texts will have experiences with vocabulary words of a greater variety and depth because of the specific and technical words authors use within these different genres. In addition, it is important to ensure that texts are available at the students' independent reading levels (which can sometimes vary greatly) or have texts available in a format they can access, such as books on tape or text to speech on a computer.

Foster Students' Independent Learning of Words While Reading

Whether it be textbooks or pleasure reading, students will benefit the most from wide reading when they have strategies to help them infer word meaning from text (Beck, McKeown, & Kucan, 2013; Marzano, Norford, Paynter, Pickering, & Gaddy, 2001). For example, using context cues is a strategy a student can use while reading independently. As you learned in Chapter 7, context cues can be used to help with word identification, but they also help readers infer the meanings of unknown words. The words around the target word can give clues about its meaning as well as the overall meaning of the sentence. When using this vocabulary learning method, many students may only get a partial grasp of a word's meaning.

A more structured approach is the use of vocabulary logs, sometimes called vocabulary notebooks. When using vocabulary logs, students write down unfamiliar words while they read. The idea is not to disrupt the students while engaging in the reading task, but simply to create a record of words on which they need more understanding. After students' reading time is completed, they can go back to their vocabulary log and use their classroom resources, such as a physical or digital dictionary, to find the words' definitions. To help retain word meanings, students will also want to put the definition in their own words or draw a picture or other visual connected with each word's meaning.

Building Vocabulary through Explicit Instruction

Because not all words can be explicitly taught, academic and other important words are purposefully selected for explicit instruction. Instructional approaches include the use of graphic organizers, morphemic analysis, and keyword mnemonics.

Graphic Organizers

Graphic organizers are visual representations of the characteristics of a word that assist them in seeing the connections and relationships between vocabulary being learned and other words they already know (Johnson & Pearson, 1984). They can take a variety of forms, with one of the most common types being the semantic map. Semantic maps can vary in complexity and extend word knowledge by overtly relating a new word to other known words. For example, semantic maps often include other words that have the same meaning (synonyms) and words that have contrasting meanings (antonyms). More advanced maps can include dictionary definitions and references to parts of speech to draw attention to the syntactic uses of the words. Finally, some maps require students to apply their knowledge of the newly learned word by using it in a sentence.

A semantic feature analysis is another type of graphic organizer. The semantic feature analysis allows students to look at multiple vocabulary words, developing detailed understanding of these words' meanings, while finding connections and relationships between them (Anders & Bos, 1986; Baumann, Kame'enui, & Ash, 2003). Typically, this organizer uses a grid where a column going down the left hand side is used to list the key concepts on a particular topic, and then possible characteristics or features of the different concepts are listed in a row across the top of the grid. When completing the semantic feature analysis grid, students work across each concept's row, deciding if the vocabulary word has each particular feature listed on the top row of the grid. If the concept does have the feature, students mark a plus (+). If the concept does not have the feature, students mark a minus (–). With a more advanced concept, both a plus and minus (+/-) are used when the characteristics of the word vary under different circumstances. See Figure 11.4 for an example of how a semantic feature analysis might be used in a science class to help students distinguish important characteristics of different types of energy sources, creating a deeper understanding of the terms *fossil fuels*, *solar energy*, and *wind energy*.

Characteristics	Energy Sources		
	Fossil Fuels	Solar	Wind
1. Is it **renewable**?	–	+	+
2. Does it release **carbon dioxide**?	+	–	–
3. Is it **environmentally friendly**?	–	+	+
4. Is it **cost-effective**?	+/–	+/–	+/–
5. Is it **efficient**?	+	–	–

Figure 11.4 Semantic feature analysis

Morphemic Analysis

Morphemic analysis is another approach for helping students increase their vocabulary knowledge. Just as knowledge of morphemes can be used to help identify words (Chapter 7), it can also be used to help students infer the meaning of those words. This process of using knowledge of word morphemes to infer meaning of a whole word is called **morphemic analysis** (Alvermann, Phelps, & Gillis, 2010).

To effectively use morphemic analysis, students can be taught common word prefixes and suffixes and their meanings. Chapter 7 introduced using affixes as tools for structural analysis to break down words in to smaller decodable pieces. These affixes can also be used in morphemic analysis for their utility for deciphering overall word meaning. Affixes are morphemes, which are the smallest word parts that contain meaning (see Chapter 4). When students are taught the meanings of the four most common prefixes (*anti-*, *in-*, *re-*, and *un-*) and suffixes (*-ed*, *-ing*, *-ly*, and *-es*), they can use this information to begin understanding longer and more complex words. For instance, any time students see a word with *re-*, they could use their knowledge of prefixes to grasp that the overall meaning of the longer target word is something that is repeated. In the same way, if a word ends in *-ed*, students could determine from their knowledge of suffixes that the word refers to something past tense.

Besides understanding affix meanings, students often know base words within longer words because students have seen them often from the time they were beginning readers. At other times, base word morphemes may be more complex. Sometimes these more complex base words have Greek and Latin roots. Students can be taught multiple related words because there are typically whole groups of words that contain the same root (Carnine et al., 2017). An example would be words like *unicycle*, *bicycle*, *recycle*, and *tricycle*, which all have the base word *cycle*, and are derived from the Latin word *cyclus* meaning "circle". All of these words have to do with objects or a process that is circular. By understanding the meaning of this Latin root, as well as having some prefix knowledge, students can understand the meaning of multiple words as well as see the relationships among these words.

Keyword Mnemonics

A particularly effective way to help students learn new vocabulary is through the use of keyword mnemonics (Bryant et al., 2003; Jitendra, Edwards, Sacks, & Jacobson, 2004). On the surface, this strategy may seem counterintuitive because of the number of steps; however, it is very effective for helping students connect new information to what they already know. Consider a stream: if jumping over the stream is your only strategy, it may help you in the narrowest parts but fail you in the wider bends where the shores are further apart. A keyword mnemonic is like stones in the stream that connect the banks of the stream when a new vocabulary word is not at all familiar to the student. In order for the keyword approach to be effective, specific steps must be followed (Mastropieri & Scruggs, 1991).

First, a mnemonic needs to be constructed. For example, if the vocabulary word is the geometry term *ray*, a similar sounding word would be *way*—*way* is an example of a keyword. The next step is to create an image that connects the vocabulary word and the definition using the keyword. This is depicted in the image below (Figure 11.5). The first boy asks *"Which way?"* (the keyword) and the second boy points to a geometrical ray on the road that goes out of sight over the horizon and answers *"Follow that line forever"* (the definition).

Figure 11.5 Keyword mnemonic

A Focus on Mnemonics

Mnemonics are techniques for helping students learn and remember important concepts and vocabulary (Mastropieri & Scruggs, 1991). Often a picture is used in conjunction with mnemonic devices as a visual support.

Letter Strategy

Letter strategy mnemonics use the first letter of a word to spell out a new word that is memorable. One of the strategies presented in the last chapter, Chapter 10, utilized a letter strategy mnemonic. In the RAP strategy, RAP stands for:

Read
Answer
Paraphrase

Acrostics

Acrostic mnemonics use the first letter of each word in a sentence to represent a target word. A commonly used acrostic in math classes is "Please excuse my dear Aunt Sally." The first letter of each word in this sentence helps students remember the correct order of mathematical operations:

parentheses
exponents
multiplication
division
addition
subtraction

The primary benefit of both of these types of mnemonics strategies is that they assist students in efficiently recalling vocabulary words that are already known.

Next, students need to be taught how to retrieve the information. This can be done through a series of self-questions to recall the definition for a vocabulary term. When asked, "*What does ray mean?*" a student will think through the following questions:

1. Question: What word sounds like *ray*?
    Answer: *Ray* sounds like *way*.
2. Question: Think of the picture of *way*. What do you see in the picture?
    Answer: A boy was asking "*which way?*"
3. Question: What else was in the picture?
    Answer: Another boy pointing to a line and answering "*follow that line forever.*"
4. Question: So, what does *ray* mean?
    Answer: "*A line that goes on forever.*"

As long as these steps are followed for constructing and retrieving information, the keyword mnemonic strategy is effective when developed by both teachers and students. This strategy also lends to structured peer practice—called **classwide peer tutoring**.

Activating Background Knowledge

While sometimes students will not have background knowledge on a reading topic, there are other times when students will. For instance, if students will be reading about topics like summer break from school, playing a sport, or making food, they may have previous experiences that may be helpful for them to recall when reading. However, when activating student background knowledge, it is important for teachers to structure and guide students' thought processes. In this way, students can focus on prior knowledge about a topic that is key for reading the target text the teacher has selected. Teachers can use guided questioning to help steer students' retrieval of ideas from student background knowledge. Pre-planning of guided questions by teachers is important so that questions are carefully thought out.

Even when teachers activate appropriate background knowledge, students may not know how to use that knowledge as a tool to help understand the text (Roberts & Duke, 2010). Teachers often use anticipation guides to help students make connections between what they are going to read and what they already know. Anticipation guides are tools that teachers can tailor to a specific text. Anticipation guides can include questions or prompts that illicit thoughtful student responses about similar prior student experiences to what will happen in a reading selection. Anticipation guides are generally used before students begin reading. This personal investment often makes students more engaged in the reading task at hand. After reading, it can also help clarify student misconceptions on a topic as they share their ideas with the class and compare their own experience to what the author has written (Alvermann, Phelps, & Gillis, 2010).

The K-W-L is a more structured type of anticipating guide. With the K-W-L, a student fills in a three-column chart as they engage in a reading task. Before reading, a student completes the first two columns, "*What do I already know about this topic?*" and "*What do I want to know?*" In this way, students are then thinking about their own previous learning and experiences, but also thinking ahead to what else they might want to learn based on their prior knowledge. After reading, the student completes the last column, "*What did I learn?*" which prompts students to make connections between what they learned in the reading and the information they listed in the first two columns of the chart. Readers of *this* textbook complete K-W-L charts in the end of section activities. This enables the reader to experience firsthand how using the K-W-L chart helps with activating background knowledge, setting a purpose for reading, and making connections between new and known information. Through using the K-W-L chart in the section activities, our hope is that readers will be more active and engaged in their reading and learning when using this textbook and supplemental online resources on the same topic. In turn, we hope this will make teaching using the K-W-L chart with K-12 students more meaningful and effective.

Application Vignette: DIVE

Mr. McConnell is a 7th grade science teacher. The students in his class come from a variety of linguistic and cultural backgrounds and many of them are English learners. As Mr. McConnell begins to plan to teach a unit about classifying organisms, he remembers a recent professional development he attended about best practices for English learners. At his training, Mr. McConnell learned about the DIVE method for teaching content. The acronym DIVE stands for *Deliberate planning, Instructional strategies, Vocabulary, and Environment.*

The first component of DIVE is deliberate planning. When developing lesson plans, Mr. McConnell deliberately plans with the needs of his English learners in mind. As he is planning his content instruction, Mr. McConnell reviews his students' WIDA levels in the areas of listening, speaking, reading, and writing (see Chapter 1 for more on WIDA levels). He knows this will help him ensure he is choosing the most effective instructional strategies, teaching both content *and* English language vocabulary. It will also ensure that he has arranged his classroom environment and activities to provide his students with the chance to speak and write using academic language.

The next component of DIVE is the instructional strategies that are best practices for English learners. Given his students' diverse backgrounds, he knows he will need to go beyond *activating* his students' prior knowledge. Instead, he will design activities that *build* the background knowledge of his students. Mr. McConnell may need to use videos and manipulatives to help provide context for the information his students are about to learn.

In addition to considering their background knowledge, Mr. McConnell plans to incorporate scaffolding within his instruction. When he is working with his students, he knows that it is crucial that he uses various forms of representations like visuals, demonstrations, manipulatives, and videos in conjunction with any lecturing. Students who have limited listening and reading proficiency may miss key information presented orally or in text. These same students often have the capacity to understand the concepts when they can actively engage with them. Additionally, some of his English learners tend to understand a concept but have not yet acquired the oral or written proficiency to demonstrate what they know.

In addition to scaffolding his lessons, Mr. McConnell plans to scaffold his questioning strategies. For example, he will turn his questions into sentence starters, like

"*One characteristic we can use to classify organisms is* _____," instead of the broader, overwhelming question, "*How do we classify organisms?*" He will also scaffold his questions from the most basic concepts to the most complex concepts in order to provide a framework for his students' responses.

When he learned the DIVE strategy, Mr. McConnell also learned about how he can target vocabulary with his students. He is aware that his English learners need to both understand and use vocabulary that is content based and process based. For example, the content objective in Mr. McConnell's lesson is that "*students will classify organisms into kingdoms according to characteristics.*" Mr. McConnell realizes that to accomplish this task, many language objectives are also involved. In terms of vocabulary, he knows he needs to make sure his students not only understand the terms *characteristics*, *kingdoms*, and *organisms*, but other terms that may be included in the process like *compare* or *categorize*. English learners need explicit teaching in both the scientific terms and the words included in assignment and lab directions. He plans to actively engage his students in using the target vocabulary by actually speaking and writing, not simply hearing or reading them.

The final area of DIVE is environment. Making sure English learners feel safe in their classroom is a very important factor in language acquisition. Since his training, Mr. McConnell has tried to provide many opportunities for his students to practice speaking and writing about what they are learning in his classroom. To help his students feel comfortable participating orally during class, Mr. McConnell has his students answer questions with choral responses during some units. This gives his English learners the chance to answer aloud without being singled out in front of their classmates. Choral responses also provide peer modeling for students with emerging speaking skills. Another way Mr. McConnell helps his students be successful with communicating orally is by providing plenty of "think time" when he asks questions aloud. This gives his English learners enough time to process his question and formulate their responses. He also provides sentence starters so these students can focus their response on conceptual understanding, rather than on their grammar.

Finally, Mr. McConnell engineers his classroom environment to allow his students to practice using language by creating groups of mixed abilities. By assigning students roles in the groups based on his students' skills, Mr. McConnell can make sure each student can participate successfully at his or her language level. This also allows students to practice writing and speaking in smaller groups, which enables students to be more involved while also learning from their peer models.

More information about DIVE can be obtained by contacting Dr. Meghan Betz at www.timetotalkspeechtherapy.com

References

Alvermann, D. E., Phelps, S., F., & Gillis, V. R. (2010). *Content area reading and literacy: Succeeding in today's diverse classrooms.* Boston, MA: Allyn & Bacon.

Anders, P., & Bos, C. (1986). Semantic feature analysis: An interactive strategy for vocabulary development and text comprehension. *Journal of Reading, 29,* 610–616.

Baker, S. K., Simmons, D. C., & Kame'enui, E. J. (1998). Vocabulary acquisition: Instruction and curricular basics and implications. In D. C. Simmons & E. J. Kame'enui (Eds.), *What reading research tells us about children with diverse learning needs: Bases and basics* (pp. 219–238). Mahwah, NJ: Erlbaum.

Baumann, F. J., Kame'enui, E. J., & Ash, G. W. (2003). Research on vocabulary instruction: Voltaire Redux. In J. Flood, D. Lapp, J. Squire, & J. Jenson (Eds.), *Handbook of research on teaching the English language arts* (2nd ed., pp. 752–785). Mahwah, NJ: Erlbaum.

Beck, I. L., McKeown, M. G., & Omanson, R. C. (1987). The effects and uses of diverse vocabulary instructional techniques. In M. G. McKeown & M. E. Curtis (Eds.), *The nature of vocabulary acquisition* (pp. 147–163). Hillsdale, NJ: Lawrence Erlbaum Associates.

Beck, I., McKeown, M. G., & Kucan, L. (2013). *Bringing words to life: Robust vocabulary development* (2nd ed.). New York, NY: Guilford Press.

Berkeley, S., & Scruggs, T. E. (2010). Current practice alerts: A focus on vocabulary instruction. *Division for Learning Disabilities (DLD) and Division for Research (DR) of the Council for Exceptional Children, Issue 18.*

Berkeley, S., & Taboada Barber, A. (2015). *Maximizing effectiveness of reading comprehension instruction in diverse classrooms.* Baltimore, MD: Brookes.

Bryant, D. P., Goodwin, M., Bryant, B. R., & Higgins, K. (2003). Vocabulary instruction for students with learning disabilities: A review of the research. *Learning Disability Quarterly, 26,* 117–128.

Carnine, D. W., Silbert, J., Kame'enui, E. J., Slocum, T. A., & Travers, P. (2017). *Direct instruction reading* (6th ed.). Boston, MA: Pearson.

Chard, D. J., & Osborn, J. (1999). Phonics and word recognition instruction in early reading programs: Guidelines for accessibility. *Learning Disabilities Research & Practice, 14,* 107–117.

Cunningham, A. E., & Stanovich, K. E. (1998). What reading does for the mind. *American Educator, 22,* 8–17.

Dochy, F., Segers, M., & Buehl, M. M. (1999). The relation between assessment practices and outcomes of studies: The case of research on prior knowledge. *Review of Educational Research, 69,* 145–186.

Dolch, E. W. (1941). *Teaching primary reading.* Champaign, IL: The Garrard Press.

Fisher, D., & Frey, N. (2009). *Background knowledge: The missing piece of the comprehension puzzle.* Portsmouth, NH: Heinemann.

Fry, E., Fountoukidis, D. L., & Polk, J. K. (1985). *The new reading teacher's book of lists.* Englewood Cliffs, NJ: Prentice-Hall.

Goldman, S. R., & Rakestraw, J. A. (2000). Structural aspects of constructing meaning from text. In R. Barr, M. L. Kamil, P. Mosenthal, & P. D. Pearson (Eds.), *Handbook of reading research* (Vol. III, pp. 311–335). Mahwah, NJ: Lawrence Erlbaum Associates.

Jitendra, A. K., Edwards, L. L., Sacks, G., & Jacobson, L. A. (2004). What research says about vocabulary instruction for students with learning disabilities. *Exceptional Children, 70,* 299–322.

Johnson, D., & Pearson P. D. (1984). *Teaching reading vocabulary* (2nd ed.). New York, NY: Holt, Rinehart, & Winston.

Juel, C., & Deffes, R. (2004). Making words stick. *Educational Leadership, 61,* 30–35.

Keene, E. O., & Zimmerman, S. (2007). *Mosaic of thought: The power of comprehension strategy instruction* (2nd ed.). Portsmouth, NH: Heinemann.

Lesaux, N. K., & Marietta, S. H. (2012). *Making assessment matter: Using test results to differentiate reading instruction.* New York, NY: Guilford Press.

Marshall, J. (1984). *The three little pigs.* New York, NY: Grosset & Dunlap.

Marzano, R. J., Norford, J. S., Paynter, D. E., Pickering, D. J., & Gaddy, B. B. (2001). *A handbook for classroom instruction that works* (2nd ed.). Denver, CO/Alexandria, VA: Association for Supervision and Curriculum Development.

Mastropieri, M. A., & Scruggs, T. E. (1991). *Teaching students ways to remember: Strategies for learning mnemonically.* Cambridge, MA: Brookline Books.

Nagy, W., & Stahl, S. (2000). *Promoting vocabulary development.* Austin, TX: Texas Education Agency.

National Reading Panel. (2001). *Put reading first: The research building blocks for teaching children to read.* Jessup, MD: Author.

Phythian-Sence, C., & Wagner, R. K. (2007). Vocabulary acquisition: A primer. In R. K. Wagner, A. E. Muse, & K. R. Tannenbaum (Eds.), *Vocabulary acquisition: Implications for reading comprehension* (pp. 1–14). New York, NY: Guilford Press.

Pullen, P. C., & Cash, D. B. (2017). Reading. In J. M. Kauffman & D. P. Hallahan (Eds.), *Handbook of special education* (2nd ed., pp. 409–421). New York, NY: Routledge.

Roberts, K. L., & Duke, N. K. (2010). Comprehension in the elementary grades: The research base. In K. Ganske & D. Fisher (Eds.), *Comprehension across the curriculum: Perspectives and Practices K–12* (pp. 23–45). New York, NY: Guilford Press.

Sampson, M. B., Rasinski, T. V., & Sampson, M. (2003). *Total literacy: Reading, writing, and learning* (3rd ed.). Belmont, CA: Wadsworth/Thomson Learning.

Santoro, L. E., Chard, D. J., Howard, L., & Baker, S. K. (2008). Making the very most of classroom read-alouds to promote comprehension and vocabulary. *The Reading Teacher, 61*, 396–408.

Scieszka, J. (2009). *The true story of the 3 little pigs.* Paradise, CA/New York, NY: Viking: Paw Prints.

Stanovich, K. E. (1986). Matthew effects in reading: Some consequences of individual differences in the acquisition of literacy. *Reading Research Quarterly, 21*, 360–407.

Tsuchiya, Y. (1970). *Faithful elephants: A true story of animals, people and war.* New York, NY: HMH Books for Young Readers.

Chapter 12

Supporting All Students in Understanding Text

Students Who Struggle with Reading Comprehension

As you learned throughout Section IV, comprehension is the ultimate purpose of reading. However, even with purposeful instruction, some students will struggle to understand what they read. This happens for a variety of reasons. Some students have problems with basic reading skills that impede their ability to access the text that they are trying to understand. Some students do not have, or do not know how to activate, knowledge from prior experiences that they need to make important connections to themselves, other texts, and the world in general (Jennings, Caldwell, & Lerner, 2010). Additionally, some students enter school with limited vocabulary knowledge compared to their peers and this knowledge gap increases exponentially over time (Graves, 2000; Mancilla-Martinez & Lesaux, 2011). Even acquisition of academic language, or the "language of schooling," is difficult for many at-risk learners due to its decontextualized nature, complexity, and unfamiliarity to many students (Berkeley & Taboada Barber, 2015). Finally, many struggling readers fail to approach text strategically, making their efforts at comprehension both inefficient and ineffective. Left unaddressed, challenges with reading increase over time and can impede student motivation to attempt reading tasks and increase anxiety. Compared to peers, minority students, students living in poverty, students who are learning English, and students with disabilities generally have more limited vocabularies and understand less of what they read (Biancarosa & Snow, 2006). Students who are learning English as a second language or who have language-based disabilities are especially at-risk for problems with reading comprehension. Teachers will need to be prepared to address the unique needs of these struggling readers.

Challenges Stemming from English Language Development

For students who are learning English, vocabulary is likely to be delayed as a natural result of the language acquisition process. While social and conversational language development generally develops in the first two years of being immersed in a new language, the acquisition of academic language can take much longer—from five to seven years (see Chapter 1 for more information). However, it is important to note that a student's first language, or L1, can be a source of support for developing semantic abilities in English—their second language, or L2. For example, students who speak Spanish and are learning English may know the Greek and Latin roots common across both languages. To illustrate, the English words *astrology* and *biography* are very similar to the Spanish words *astrología* and *biografía*. These similarities can help bridge semantic understanding between the languages. Most times English learners rely on semantic knowledge from their L1 to facilitate semantic and vocabulary learning in their L2. However, not all students have strong vocabularies in their L1, either because they were too young to develop this knowledge before learning English or because they struggled with semantics in their L1 originally. These students will not have a semantic base to support their acquisition of English.

Challenges Stemming from Disability

Like students who are learning English as a second language, students with disabilities are likely to have a more shallow vocabularies than their typically developing peers. Large numbers of students with language-based disabilities are hindered in their vocabulary development through conversation and reading because of language impairments inherent to their disability and challenges acquiring basic reading skills needed to access text (Wong, 2004). Because these students spend large amounts of working memory decoding words, they often have few resources remaining to understand what the words mean in isolation or as a larger concept (Saenz & Fuchs, 2002). For example, these students may not effectively use context cues to infer the meanings of novel vocabulary terms (Bryant, Ugel, Thompson, & Hamff, 1999).

Further, deficits in memory can impede a student's ability to recall words that are known and needed to efficiently make connections between new and existing knowledge. All of these factors result in a negative cycle of learning called the Matthew Effect where students with "rich" reading skills and vocabulary "get richer" and students with "poor" reading skills and vocabulary "get poorer." Over time, this results in an "achievement gap" between the performance of students with disabilities and their typically developing peers that is tremendously challenging to close. Because students with language-based disabilities, and learning disabilities in particular, have great difficulty acquiring basic reading skills and vocabulary, these students are very likely to struggle to understand what they are reading. Additionally, as you learned in Chapter 1, deficits in these students' working memory impede their ability to integrate information and comprehend text (Swanson & O'Conner, 2009). This is because working memory is needed to get the gist of the reading and hold newly learned information while continuing to process new information. Working memory also plays a role in a student's ability to make inferences and monitor comprehension (Cain, Oakhill, & Bryant, 2004).

Due to memory and processing problems inherent to their disabilities, these students may have difficulty retrieving memories and making connections to the learning task. In addition, many students with disabilities may overuse or misapply their background knowledge. A student that overuses their background knowledge might defer almost exclusively to knowledge and experiences rather than using new information from within the text. In some instances, this prior knowledge will result in a "right answer" to a comprehension question, reinforcing this practice. However, there are other instances where a student may not have correct information in their existing knowledge base or they may believe inaccurate information, called a misconception, about a topic—for example, believing that the sun revolves around the earth. Failing to attend to information presented in text impedes a student's opportunity to learn new information or correct misinformation in their knowledge base (Alvermann, Phelps, & Gillis, 2010; Dochy, Segers, & Buehl, 1999). In either scenario, the student misses the opportunity to make connections between the new and the known, which is how comprehension and vocabulary development occurs.

Struggling readers tend to have difficulty attending to appropriate information. For example, rather than making meaningful connections between new information read and their existing background knowledge, students have a tendency to make **tangential connections**, or connections that are irrelevant to understanding what was read (Roberts & Duke, 2010). For example, relating an unimportant detail from the reading to a personal experience. Similarly, struggling readers have difficulty identifying the main idea of what they have read because instead of honing in on what is most important, they tend to recall points they find interesting (Jennings et al., 2010). Similarly, students with language-based disabilities also have problems with pragmatics that cause them to struggle with comprehension of more complex and abstract ideas in text versus more literal ones. For instance, when a text is using the more complex convention of irony to convey meaning, learners who struggle with pragmatics will have difficulties. For instance, when they read about someone adamantly saying they are *"not tired"* while that person is yawning, they will not understand the contradiction within the text and the implied meaning.

These students are also likely to be unaware of when their understanding has broken down, and even when they are aware that they have not understood, they may not know what to do about it (Gersten, Fuchs, Williams, & Baker, 2001). In other words, these students tend to lack strategies both for basic reading and for comprehension. Even when students learn strategies, without explicit self-regulation instruction, these students are likely to abandon the strategies after instruction ends (Vaughn, Gersten, & Chard, 2000). Students who have a history of academic failure, such as students with learning disabilities, often have faulty beliefs about the causes of academic success and failure (Shell, Colvin, & Bruning, 1995). For example, a student with a learning disability may believe that he got a reading comprehension question correct because the teacher gave him an easy question or he was lucky that day, rather than believing that he was able to answer the question because of his own hard work and use of strategies. Student beliefs about the causes of their academic successes and failures play an important role in student motivation for reading and whether or not self-regulation efforts are sustained (Gersten et al., 2001).

Assessment of Student Understanding of Text

Since reading comprehension is the goal of reading, it is important to monitor all students' comprehension. To do this, teachers ask students to demonstrate their understanding of what they have read either orally or in writing. Initial screening typically occurs through student performance in the general curriculum. When students are not performing as well as expected, the teacher is likely to collect additional information. This information is used to inform instruction. As with basic reading, when students are identified as at-risk, the teacher will also put a plan in place to monitor student progress.

Before learning about specific assessment approaches, it is important to understand common features of comprehension assessments. First, it is important to understand how comprehension questions are asked. When assessing students' comprehension of material read, students are often asked either literal or inferential questions about the reading. **Literal comprehension** questions, also called explicit questions, require students to retrieve information from the text that has been specifically stated within the passage. Answers to these types of questions are specifically stated in text, generally in a single sentence. **Inferential questions**, also called implicit questions, encompass asking students about implied meanings and understandings of text they have read. A correct answer for this type of question is not stated word for word in text, but rather, students need to infer the answer based on information in different places in the text and/or in combination with what they already know. However, implicit questions are not questions that students can answer solely from their background knowledge—answers need to be grounded in the text. Many times literal and inferential comprehension questions are a form of vocabulary assessment. Sometimes with literal comprehension questions, students are asked to find or give the definition or meaning of a specific word found within the passage. Other times, students are asked to figure out implied meaning of pieces of the text or the overall text itself based on the vocabulary or words used.

Comprehension tests can contain items that require literal or inferential comprehension and typically have forced choice or open-ended questions. While forced choice questions involve identification of correct information, open-ended questions involve the student's own production of that information. As you remember from Chapter 5, production tasks are more challenging than identification tasks. With forced choice test questions, students are asked to select an answer from a multiple-choice selection, match questions to answers, or indicate if a statement is true or false. With open-ended test questions, students are asked comprehension questions and then have space where they can write their answers with explanation in their own words. This assesses students' abilities to pull everything together that they have read in a summary or synthesis.

When a student is asked to write a summary, the desired outcome is a written paragraph of the main ideas covered in what was read. To write a cohesive summary, students generally must have a firm foundation in the vocabulary and background information needed to understand the topic about which they are reading. Summaries usually involve writing several sentences, which means students who struggle with writing tasks will also struggle with this type of comprehension prompt. Students who struggle with writing can be asked to summarize orally. In that way, students' writing difficulties do not compound the difficulty of reading comprehension tasks through physically writing. Summary writing can also vary in level of challenge based on whether students are writing narrative or expository summaries. For most students, recalling story-based information is an easier task because they can rely on background knowledge and vocabulary from their everyday lives. With summarizing expository information, students may struggle further because it involves understanding and then using vocabulary on topics that go beyond daily student experiences and may involve complex information. A description of common skill-based assessments is presented next.

Observation/Authentic Assessment

Observation within the classroom environment plays an important role in monitoring strengths and weaknesses of student comprehension. These observations can range from a naturally occurring classroom situation to more structured questioning. Teachers can observe students' reading comprehension by monitoring independent student partner and small group work. This usually occurs during the reading instruction block of the day where students are naturally engaging in reading tasks and discussing books and stories they have read. By circulating amongst pairs and groups, teachers can observe students discussing their reading takeaways and possibly hear what students think is confusing. In these observations, teachers may notice specific discussions about new vocabulary they understood or that confused them within the passage. This observation information is especially critical because of the importance of vocabulary in building students' background knowledge for understanding new ideas (see Chapter 11).

Informal observation of students' comprehension can be more structured as well. Teachers may engage students in discussion about a story or book that students have been reading. In a small teacher-led reading group, the teacher can ask both literal and inferential comprehension questions orally and tally correct responses by individuals. Teachers may also ask students to show how confident they feel about their understanding of a certain topic or vocabulary word by giving a "thumbs up" to show they are very familiar with the concept or word, a "thumbs down" to show they have no awareness, or a "thumbs sideways" if they think they know a little bit about the word or concept but are not confident. Students can also be informally monitored by having them complete assessments where vocabulary words are sorted into categories by understanding level (deep understanding, emerging understanding, no understanding) versus sorting the words into categories by actual word meaning. In this way, teachers can quickly determine which vocabulary words need more instruction.

Additionally, student-made products are often a key way that comprehension is informally tracked. Student reading journals are one mechanism for monitoring comprehension in this manner. One journaling method is a double-entry journal where students note interesting quotes or pieces of information from the text read in the left column and then respond or give their reaction to the quote in the right column. Using this form of journaling, teachers can see what students are noticing in either a narrative or expository text they have read, and then observe how that student is processing that information through their written reactions. Other student products that are useful in monitoring comprehension are concept and story maps. Both of these student products use a form of graphic organizer, where teachers can evaluate students' comprehension by how they complete them. When students complete concept maps, they are typically making connections between ideas they have read within expository text. In this way, teachers can assess if students have grasped the big ideas surrounding a nonfiction topic they have read about as well as what connections have been made.

Informal Reading Inventories

Informal reading inventories (IRIs) are comprehensive informal assessments that provide important information about students' comprehension in addition to their ability to access text. IRIs include comprehension questions about read passages that are both explicit and implicit. In addition, IRIs have a read-aloud feature where students identify the important information from the story in sequential order. An IRI gives teachers specific information about student strengths and weaknesses in comprehension, which helps them know where to begin instruction. Chapter 3 contains an in-depth description of administration and interpretation of IRIs.

Oral Story Retells

A story retell is also used to gauge student understanding of narrative text. In the early elementary grades, this story retell is typically done orally, while at the secondary level a written version of the story retell may be completed. The story retell encompasses important skills that include sequencing and memory. For an accurate retell, students need to possess the cognitive ability to pinpoint important details or events from the story and sequence them in a meaningful way. Student difficulties in either identifying important story details or difficulties in memory with remembering story order can be detected by a teacher during the oral story retell process.

Teacher-made Tests

Teachers can also make their own tests. These tests are usually on a grade-level story or multiple stories students have read, and questions are typically asked in a forced choice manner through multiple-choice, true/false, or fill in the blank. Within these tests, there may also be a few open response literal or inferential comprehension questions. Teachers use these curriculum-based tests to evaluate students' understanding of instructional material read.

A Focus On Prosody Assessment

Prosody is an often-overlooked element of reading fluency. Prosody refers to the quality of the expression of that reading. Specifically, prosody refers to "emphasis, pitch changes, pause placement and duration, and phrasing in accord with syntactic structure so that text is translated aloud with the tonal and rhythmic characteristics of everyday speech" (Klauda & Guthrie, 2008, p. 310). A student who is having difficulty with prosody might display stiff, rigid reading, ignore punctuation, or repeatedly read words or phrases in text. All of these reading behaviors have the potential to interfere with student understanding of the meaning of text. For example, consider reading dialogue in a novel. Understanding the ebb and flow of a conversation between characters would certainly be difficult without the assistance of punctuation guided pauses and appropriate expression!

Within an informal reading inventory, these sorts of prosody issues are noted, but do not count as miscues. A teacher would evaluate the notations holistically and compare the prevalence of prosody issues over time to evaluate whether instruction was helping the student to improve. Another prevalent method is the use of a rubric that captures degrees of proficient prosody.

Computer-based Assessments

When teachers need to assess all of their students' reading progress, more and more schools are using curriculums that incorporate comprehension assessments in a digital format. These computer-based options allow teachers to assess a whole classroom of students simultaneously. In addition, they save teachers time because the tests are automatically scored and visually displayed.

For example, the Star Reading assessments give teachers detailed printouts of student strengths and weaknesses in comprehension skills across both narrative and expository texts. As part of the assessment, the program reports a "zone of proximal development," which is the reading level span where students can read independently. Teachers can use these assessment results to design instruction that targets the identified weaknesses of students (Renaissance Star Reading, 2019). While a Star Reading assessment may be given just a few times throughout the year, it can also be used in conjunction with Accelerated Reader (AR) tests to monitor student comprehension on a more regular basis. AR tests are also computer-based assessments, and they are taken on books that students check out and read from the library based on students' zone of proximal development as determined by a Star Reading assessment. Since students can read and take AR tests on as many books as they read independently, their regular use can help track student reading progress. AR tests cover both fiction and nonfiction and use both literal and inferential comprehension questions. Teachers can use AR tests to monitor student reading progress, moving students up in reading level when consistently scoring 80% or above on tests and down in reading level when test scores are regularly below 80% (Renaissance Star Reading, 2019).

Cloze/Maze Assessments

A Cloze assessment allows teachers to evaluate student abilities to figure out vocabulary and overall meaning of the passages they read. This is accomplished by giving students a passage with some words omitted to determine whether they are able to use context cues,

---

A Focus on Formal Assessment of Reading Comprehension

While this chapter focuses on informal assessments of reading comprehension to inform instruction, there are circumstances where an educator might need information about how a student is doing related to other students of the same age or grade. In these instances, a formal assessment that is norm-referenced is needed. As you remember from Chapter 2, norm-referenced assessments are standardized and require specialized training to administer. These types of assessments cover a wide range of skills related to reading comprehension. Results provide an indication of how a student performed compared to a norming sample of students in the same grade. A formal assessment of reading comprehension would generally be used as a pre and post assessment of a student's performance as well as to determine whether a student's progress is sufficient to close an achievement gap with peers. An example of a formal assessment of reading comprehension is the Gates-MacGinitie Reading Test (GMRT).

Gates-MacGinitie Reading Test (GMRT)	
Test Description:	• Comprehension • Vocabulary
Ages:	K–7 through adult
Administration:	Group or Individualized
Time Required:	75–100 minutes
Publisher:	http://www.riversidepublishing.com/K12academics/

---

syntax and vocabulary knowledge to accurately infer the meaning of the word that has been omitted. The number of words left out can vary, but it is typically every 5th, 7th, or 10th word. While this type of assessment may look like a vocabulary test on the surface, it actually evaluates multiple skills that students need for effective comprehension. Specifically, students need to apply the semantic and pragmatic oral language knowledge they possess in a reading context.

Maze assessments are very similar to a Cloze assessment. The main difference with Maze is that below each blank are three possible word choices, which include the correct word and two other word possibilities. With having word choices below each blank, the content of the assessment becomes an identification task rather than a production task. Thus, Maze provides a similar evaluation of comprehension skills in an easier format.

Instructional Supports for Struggling Readers

In this section of the textbook, you learned that reading comprehension is the ultimate purpose of reading and that it is dependent on a student's ability to decode the printed word. Good readers approach text strategically and actively engage with text before, during, and after reading. Chapter 10 included a range of reading comprehension strategies that can help students understand what they read. Chapter 11 emphasized that comprehension is supported, or thwarted, by the amount of relevant background knowledge and vocabulary that the student possesses. Approaching text strategically is intuitive to good readers, but not for students who struggle. Additional considerations for instruction are needed for these students.

Selection of Instructional Materials

High-quality instruction for comprehension takes into account that the instructional level for decoding of many learners is not the same as their instructional level for comprehension. This can be a difficult challenge to negotiate since it involves teachers creatively figuring out how to select instructional materials that meet students' comprehension needs. For students whose instructional comprehension level is below their instructional decoding level, students will be able to independently decode text at the level where they are working on developing their comprehension skills. However, when a student's comprehension level is higher than the student's decoding level, teachers will need to provide accommodations and/or modify text so that it is accessible to the student. This ensures that the student is exposed to text that allows him or her to develop his higher-level comprehension skills. In these cases, teachers can employ technology like books on tape to help make the text accessible to students.

Quality instruction should also take into consideration any cultural differences of students. Multiple goals can be met by matching instruction with materials that are both culturally sensitive and inclusive. First, teachers are more likely to engage diverse students in a specific learning task when they can identify with the students' cultural identity. Second, the use of these materials can also help to foster cultural awareness and appreciation across all students in a classroom. Often, this will include the cultures of English language learners. Using texts with vocabulary and language familiar to English learners will help these learners continue to make connections between ideas and concepts in their L1 and English as their L2. There are increasing options of texts that represent a variety of cultures, such as Children's Press High Interest Books (https://www.leeandlow.com/imprints/children-s-book-press).

A Focus on Culturally Relevant Materials

Having an awareness that learning can be impacted by cultural background is critical for teachers of reading. Gathering information about students' culture and incorporating these elements into instructional lessons can help further engage these students and bridge understanding of new content.

Teachers can gather information about their students' cultural backgrounds in their classroom by having students complete a short survey that helps them identify and describe their cultural background and related traditions and values associated with it. Then, teachers can take this information and use it to develop ideas for instruction, as well as employ it to drive material selection. Culturally relevant instructional materials can include books, high-interest media materials (such as photographs and videos), and hands-on field trips, activities, and events.

Considerations for Instruction

Just as with early reading and word identification, students who are at-risk for reading problems are likely to need additional supports that may not be necessary for the typical learner. These supports can be **visual** (visual stimuli to support a learning task), **tactile** (physical manipulation of objects), or **auditory** (verbal prompts that help students attend to relevant information). These supports can be used separately or in combination. These types of supports are prominent throughout the last two chapters. For example, graphic organizers are inherently visual supports that make covert thinking and connections visible. Mnemonic strategies and images are also inherently visual with keyword mnemonics relying on an auditory "keyword" to support retrieval of known information (see Chapter 11 for more information). Strategy checklists used to help students monitor strategy use are both visual and tactile—requiring students to check off steps that they have completed. Because comprehension is an internal cognitive process, teachers need to be intentional in providing sensory supports to students to ensure that they are supported in their efforts to become strategic readers.

When students are taught a new comprehension or vocabulary strategy, some students will need more assistance than others to both learn the strategy as well as to use it independently. When **scaffolding**, a teacher (a) explains a new strategy and provides modeling of its usage, (b) structures guided student practice with corrective teacher feedback, and (c) eventually provides opportunities for independent strategy usage with decreasing levels of teacher support during strategy application (Ciullo & Dimino, 2017). This instructional practice allows students who may need more support to incrementally develop independence. In Chapter 10, scaffolding of self-questioning was described, progressing from student use of teacher-generated questions to student generation of an increasing number of their own questions. Scaffolding is important for many students when applying any newly learned strategy, not just self-questioning.

For example, many at-risk students will come to the classroom without meaningful background knowledge to support their learning. As a result, a teacher's attempts to help them activate background knowledge to facilitate connection making will not be effective, and worse, may prompt students to make connections that detract rather than enhance comprehension. For instance, a female student may read an article about Hillary Clinton, and connect with knowing that she has a daughter. While this connection may pique the student's interest, it is not a meaningful connection that will support the student's understanding of the political impact Clinton has had on the United States as a whole, and specifically on women. If the student is just thinking of Hillary Clinton as a mother with a daughter like herself, she will make connections that are not as meaningful and substantive. Many of our students with learning differences may attend to these more overt and surface level connections. Therefore, scaffolding student use of background knowledge by building background knowledge first (as described in Chapter 11) will be critical to some at-risk learners.

Students may also need support to participate fully in class activities intended to help them process information. Often class activities around reading involve responding orally to the reading through class or peer discussions. Teachers can differentiate these activities to ensure that all learners are able to engage in conversations. Some students might not be equipped to immediately participate in whole-class discussions about what has been read, and teachers can use instructional practices that help students prepare for these conversations and discussions. Teachers can begin by using an instructional method called "**think time**." This method involves teachers being aware that some students may take longer to process information and think about content that has been read about or already discussed. When a teacher poses a question or attempts to start a discussion, she can ask her questions in a way that gives students the time they need to think through a response. For example, the teacher might say to a struggling student, "*I'm going to call on you next to tell me three important things that you read.*" Then, the teacher will ask a different student a question and allow the student to respond. Finally, the teacher will return to the struggling student to ask the question she had given him "think time" for. Teachers can also alert a struggling student to upcoming participation demands by giving her an agreed upon signal, such as subtly touching the corner of her desk so the student knows that a question will be asked of her shortly. In this way, the student has time to cognitively prepare to share aloud.

A Focus on Instructional Accommodations

Accommodations do not negate the need for explicit, direct instruction. However, in addition to quality instruction, some students with disabilities will need instructional accommodations in order to make progress in the curriculum or toward IEP goals. Accommodations are changes that are made for individual students and might include changes in time, input, output, and level of support (Hallahan, Lloyd, Kauffman, Weiss, & Martinez, 2005). In the areas of reading comprehension skills, instructional accommodations might include:

- extended time to complete reading assignments (time),
- books on tape or e-reader so students can access grade level text (input),
- text to speech for answering comprehension questions (output),
- structured peer tutoring (level of support).

Additionally, teachers can take the pressure of sharing with the whole class out of the situation entirely by using a method called "think-pair-share." In this situation, a teacher will start discussion at the two-person level. The teacher will first pose a question or idea and ask students to "think" through their own ideas for a few minutes independently. She will then have students "pair" with a partner to discuss their ideas and finally "share" out to the larger group either orally or on personal whiteboards. Teachers will select students' partners carefully to facilitate respectful and thoughtful sharing. The pairs can have several minutes to talk with one another to share their ideas on the initially posed question or idea. This form of sharing is often less intimidating for students because they are given time to think through their ideas on a subject, and they initially have just one person with whom to share their ideas versus the whole class. Teachers can support student pair discussions by circulating, listening, and monitoring what is shared, and then wrapping up the activity by asking groups to share out to the whole class one or two big ideas.

Finally, it is important for teachers to be aware that some practices are more needed for particular at-risk students than others. For example, attribution feedback is particularly important for students with learning disabilities. In a review of the literature involving strategy instruction, providing attribution feedback was one of the critical elements for effective instruction in student reading comprehension strategy application (Berkeley & Riccomini, 2013). Attribution feedback helps these students better understand how to monitor their independent strategy use and generalize their application of that strategy across settings.

As you learned in Chapter 11, morphemic analysis is especially critical for English language learners. Many academic and more complex multisyllabic words in English have Greek and Latin roots. This language characteristic is similar across many European languages, helping English learners connect complex English words to ones in their L1 with similar Greek and Latin roots (Rasinski, Padak, Newton, & Newton, 2011). Therefore, knowing English base words that have Greek and Latin roots can be an important tool for English learners because knowing individual roots can help with understanding multiple vocabulary words.

Additional Learning Opportunities

Vocabulary development that includes student depth of understanding and application for comprehension should involve practice opportunities for any student. For struggling readers with learning disabilities or English language learning needs, these additional learning opportunities across multiple contexts are truly a *need*! Research shows that for deep conceptual understanding of words, typical students need at least 12 different encounters with a word (McKeown, Beck, Omanson, & Pople, 1985) and students who have memory difficulties may require even more. Students with pragmatic difficulties may benefit most when these vocabulary-learning experiences are meaningful across content areas, helping students to apply vocabulary knowledge across subject areas and assisting them in generalizing across contexts (Stahl, 1999). With English learners specifically, it is important that vocabulary learning be supported by discussions involving background knowledge and information with which students are already familiar. In this way, English learners are expanding their vocabulary knowledge by making connections and building from the words they already know, helping develop their English language skills overall for understanding language and comprehending text (Eckerth & Tavakoli, 2012).

Practice is critical for struggling students, so providing supported wide reading opportunities for struggling readers is important. Students who struggle with understanding word meanings and text overall are the same ones that read less (Stanovich, 1986). Teachers can use instructional methods that facilitate and support engaging these students in reading across types of text. Appropriate text selection is a key way teachers can assist these students in reading more. Teachers can help these learners pick out different genres of reading material on their independent reading level. When students are able to find success in reading independently with appropriately leveled books, they will be more likely to engage in further reading. Then, teachers can help students recognize texts at their independent level so they are better equipped to choose their own books, giving an extra layer of independence and freedom in reading choice to students. Especially with older struggling readers, teachers may need to find texts that are of high interest in content, but low enough in reading level to meet these students' needs. Gathering information on students' interests and focusing on books with high-interest content for students can help promote wide reading. Additionally, teachers can incorporate technology, such as Don Johnston's *Readtopia* (2019). This program provides additional reading opportunities involving excerpts from literature, nonfiction texts, and graphic novels. Technology practice opportunities are often desirable by students and allows for controlled practice opportunities when students cannot directly receive instruction from the teacher. Additionally, this program specifically provides a wide breadth of text formats, situated within thematic units that incorporate digital media and focused word study.

Specialized Instruction: Comprehension

Corrective Reading: Comprehension Strands A, B, C

The comprehension strand of *Corrective Reading* is a Direct Instruction program that focuses exclusively on comprehension to build the thinking skills needed for students to more efficiently process information when reading text. The program is designed for poor comprehenders in Grades 3 through Adult. Like all Direct Instruction programs, the comprehension strand requires that students be grouped by ability to progress through a tightly controlled curriculum that ensures mastery by all students.

Each of the levels become increasingly advanced, addressing comprehension skills through instruction in:

- vocabulary knowledge (common words, synonyms/antonyms),
- logical thinking skills (deductions, statement inferences, analogies, classification),
- semantics (*all* versus *every*; *and* versus *or*; *no* versus *don't*),
- sentence writing skills (parts of speech, combining sentences, subject/verb agreement),
- basic background knowledge (months, seasons, holidays, classes of animals),
- memory development (recitation to strengthen auditory memory),
- organizing information (main idea/moral, outlining),
- using source information (reading for specific information, recognizing discrepancies).

For more information:

https://s3.amazonaws.com/ecommerce-prod.mheducation.com/unitas/school/program/corrective-reading-2008/corrective-reading-overview-brochure.pdf

Visualizing and Verbalizing

Visualizing and Verbalizing is a Lindamood-Bell program that focuses specifically on cognitive development, comprehension, and thinking. Lindamood-Bell programs use a sensory–cognitive approach. In these programs, intensive instruction is delivered to students individually or in small groups using multisensory techniques. Program content is structured through sequential lessons that foster concept imagery. Specialized training is needed to deliver instruction. *Visualizing and Verbalizing* uses concept imagery activities to help improve student reading and listening comprehension, memory, oral vocabulary, critical thinking, and writing.

For more information:

https://lindamoodbell.com/program/visualizing-and-verbalizing-program

References

Alvermann, D. E., Phelps, S. F., & Gillis, V. R. (2010). *Content area reading and literacy: Succeeding in today's diverse classrooms*. Boston, MA: Allyn & Bacon.

Berkeley, S., & Riccomini, P. J. (2013). QRAC-the-code: A comprehension monitoring strategy for middle school social studies textbooks. *Journal of Learning Disabilities, 46*, 154–165.

Berkeley, S., & Taboada Barber, A. (2015). *Maximizing effectiveness of reading comprehension instruction in diverse classrooms*. Baltimore, MD: Brookes Publishing.

Biancarosa, G., & Snow, C. (2006). *Reading next—A vision for action and research in middle school and high school literacy: A report to Carnegie Corporation of New York* (2nd ed.). Washington, DC: Alliance for Excellent Education.

Bryant, D. P., Ugel, N., Thompson, S., & Hamff, A. (1999). Instructional strategies for content-area reading instruction. *Intervention in School & Clinic, 34*, 293–302.

Cain, K., Oakhill, J., & Bryant, P. (2004). Children's reading comprehension ability: Concurrent prediction by working memory, verbal ability, and component skills. *Journal of Educational Psychology, 96*, 31–42.

Ciullo, S., & Dimino, J. (2017). The strategic use of scaffolded instruction in social studies interventions for students with learning disabilities. *Learning Disabilities Research & Practice, 32*, 155–165.

Dochy, F., Segers, M., & Buehl, M. M. (1999). The relation between assessment practices and outcomes of studies: The case of research on prior knowledge. *Review of Educational Research, 69*, 145–186.

Eckerth, J., & Tavakoli, K. (2012). The effects of word exposure frequency and elaboration of word processing on incidental L2 vocabulary acquisition through reading. *Language Teaching Research, 16*, 227–252.

Gersten, R., Fuchs, L. S., Williams, J. P., & Baker, S. (2001). Teaching reading comprehension strategies to students with learning disabilities: A review of research. *Review of Educational Research, 71*, 279–320.

Graves, M. F. (2000). A vocabulary program to complement and bolster a middle-grade comprehension program. In B. M. Taylor, M. F. Graves, & P. Van Den Broek (Eds.), *Reading for meaning: Fostering comprehension in the middle grades* (pp. 116–135). New York, NY: Teachers College Press.

Hallahan, D. P., Lloyd, J. W., Kauffman, J. M., Weiss, M. P., & Martinez, E. A. (2005). *Learning disabilities: Foundations, characteristics, and effective teaching* (3rd ed.). Boston, MA: Pearson.

Jennings, J. H., Caldwell, J. S., & Lerner, J. W. (2010). *Reading problems: Assessment and teaching strategies*. Boston, MA: Pearson/Allyn & Bacon.

Johnston, D. (2019). *Readtopia*. https://learningtools.donjohnston.com/product/readtopia/

Klauda, S. L., & Guthrie, J. T. (2008). Relationships of three components of reading fluency to reading comprehension. *Journal of Educational Psychology, 100*, 310–321.

Mancilla-Martinez, J., & Lesaux, N. K. (2011). The gap between Spanish speakers' word reading and word knowledge: A longitudinal study. *Child Development, 82*, 1544–1560.

McKeown, M. G., Beck, I. L., Omanson, R. C., & Pople, M. T. (1985). Some effects of the nature and frequency of vocabulary instruction on the knowledge and use of words. *Reading Research Quarterly, 20*, 522–535.

Rasinski, T. V., Padak, N., Newton, J., & Newton, E. (2011). The Latin–Greek connection building vocabulary through morphological study. *The Reading Teacher, 65*, 133–141.

Renaissance Star Reading. (2019). https://www.renaissance.com/products/assessment/star-360/star-reading-skills/

Roberts, K. L., & Duke, N. K. (2010). Comprehension in the elementary grades: The research base. In K. Ganske & D. Fisher (Eds.), *Comprehension across the curriculum: Perspectives and Practices K–12* (pp. 23–45). New York, NY: Guilford Press.

Saenz, L. M., & Fuchs, L. S. (2002). Examining the reading difficulty of secondary students with learning disabilities: Expository versus narrative text. *Remedial & Special Education, 23*, 31–41.

Shell, D., Colvin, C., & Bruning, R. (1995). Self-efficacy, attribution and outcome expectancy mechanisms in reading and writing achievement: Grade-level and achievement-level differences. *Journal of Educational Psychology, 87*, 386–398.

Stahl, S. A. (1999). *Vocabulary development*. Newton Upper Falls, MA: Brookline Books.

Stanovich, K. E. (1986). Matthew effects in reading: Some consequences of individual differences in the acquisition of literacy. *Reading Research Quarterly, 21*, 360–407.

Swanson, H. L., & O'Conner, R. (2009). The role of working memory and fluency practice on the reading comprehension of students who are dysfluent readers. *Journal of Learning Disabilities, 42*, 529–548.

Vaughn, S., Gersten, R., & Chard, D. (2000). The underlying message in LD interventions research. *Exceptional Children, 67*, 99–114.

Wong, B. Y. L. (2004). *Learning about learning disabilities* (3rd ed.). San Diego, CA: Academic Press.

SECTION IV: APPLICATION ACTIVITIES

Show What You Know!

In this section you learned that some vocabulary words are more critical to explicitly teach because of the role that they play in learning. Can you differentiate between useful words, important words, and difficult words? Complete the activity below to find out!

Directions:

Sort the following third grade vocabulary words into 3 columns: useful words, important words, and difficult words.

1. hold
2. demonstrate
3. together
4. characters
5. only
6. never
7. preview
8. nonfiction
9. about
10. bring
11. theme
12. compare
13. summarize
14. clarify
15. predict
16. fiction
17. narrator
18. own
19. analyze
20. plot
21. setting
22. contrast
23. main idea
24. about

Answer Key: Useful words: 1, 3, 5, 6, 9, 10, 18, 24
        Important words: 2, 7, 12, 13, 14, 15, 19, 22
        Difficult words: 4, 8, 11, 16, 17, 20, 21, 23

Partner Activity/Discussion

In this section you learned a wide range of strategies that can help students to plan, pay attention and problem solve, and process information. Discuss additional considerations for instruction that you will need to keep in mind for at-risk learners.

Learn More: Multimedia Activity

In this section you learned about reading comprehension, prior knowledge, and vocabulary. For this activity, you will go deeper in your learning about one of the topics on the Colorín Colorado website. This national website houses a wealth of resources for educators and families of English language learners in Grades PreK–12, including videos, webcasts, articles, reports, book recommendations, and more! In completing the activity, you will also be exposed to some excellent online resources for a wide range of other topics as well. Have fun learning!

Directions:

1. **Before**

    In the first text box below, list key ideas you know (K) after reading this section of the textbook. In the next text box, write questions about what you want to learn (W) from completing this multi-media activity.

K (**K**now)	What do you already know about this topic? 1. 2. 3. 4.
W (**W**ant to learn)	What do YOU want to learn more about? 1. 2. 3. 4.

2. **During**

    Explore the Colorín Colorado website at https://www.colorincolorado.org/. Use the information you find here to answer your questions!

3. **After**

    After you have finished reading about the areas you wanted to learn more about, look back at what you indicated you knew before starting (K) and wanted to learn (W). Can you now answer the questions? How does this new information connect with what you knew before starting? Write the answers to your questions in the text box below. Be sure to add any additional unexpected information that you learned (L) as well!

L (Learned)	What did you learn? 1. 2. 3. 4.

Section V

Writing and Spelling

Section V: Overview

Writing is intrinsically connected to reading. Just as comprehension is the entire purpose of reading, communicating ideas with others is the purpose of writing. Similarly, spelling is dependent on student skills in decoding and language development. Further, like decoding skills, spelling develops in a predictable developmental sequence. The first chapter in this section focuses on instructional approaches that help students approach writing and spelling in the strategic ways that good writers do. The last chapter in this section presents the characteristics of students who struggle with writing and spelling and describes how to use assessment data to inform instructional choices for these students.

- Chapter 13: The Development of Writing and Spelling
- Chapter 14: Supporting All Students in Writing and Spelling

Guiding Questions

As you are reading, consider the following questions:

- What are the major processes of writing?
- What are the developmental stages of spelling?
- What instructional approaches foster writing and spelling development?
- What challenges do at-risk students have with developing writing and spelling proficiency?
- What assessments are used to informally assess a student's writing and spelling development?
- What additional instructional supports are needed for readers who struggle to develop proficiency with writing and spelling?

Chapter 13

The Development of Writing and Spelling

Fundamentals of the Writing Process

Writing is one of the primary ways that students express ideas and communicate in school. In addition to formal essays, writing is used in a wide range of learning activities—from responding to test items to jotting a note to a classmate. Further, writing is a powerful tool for helping students learn and has an especially beneficial effect on student learning when combined with reading activities (Alvermann, Phelps, & Gillis, 2010). Writing is a complex process and the instructional approaches used to support writing development are multi-faceted.

Types of Composition

There are three primary types of composition that are taught in schools: narrative essays, expository essays, and persuasive essays. A **narrative essay** describes an experience or tells a fictional story. As you learned in Chapter 10, narrative texts contain story grammar elements such as characters, setting, and plot. An **expository essay** is an explanation of a process, a comparison of subjects, or a recounting of another nonfictional event. Expository texts can contain a variety of text structures depending on the purpose of the writing. A **persuasive essay** attempts to convince the reader of an opinion. The most effective persuasive essays contain evidence to support the position taken.

In the early grades when students are just beginning to master sound/symbol relationships, writing is mostly descriptive words and sentences. By the 3rd grade, students progress from writing single sentences to paragraphs of connected thoughts. As students continue through the grades, they will continue to be exposed to the various composition types and by 8th grade, students are formally evaluated on their proficiency with these styles. Regardless of the compositional style, there are common components of written expression that students develop as they gain experience with writing increasingly complex prose.

Components of Written Expression

The purpose of written expression is to communicate ideas in written form. In order for a writer to successfully communicate in writing, the content of the message needs to be clear and the conventions of the language need to be followed.

Content and Clarity

Writing is a subjective process; however, it is generally evaluated based on how clearly the content of the message has been conveyed. Part of this is the value of the idea of the message. A poorly conceptualized idea has little value even when a piece of writing is technically adequate. Another critical component of communicating through writing relates to organization. A reader is more likely to understand writing that is logically organized. A less tangible aspect of writing is the voice of the writer. The writer's choice of words and the rhythm and flow of language used can help convey the tone of the writer.

Mechanics and Conventions

Mechanics and conventions are the "rules" of language and include grammar (syntax) and usage, capitalization and punctuation, and spelling. Common rules for grammar and usage in English include:

- subject/verb agreement,
- pronoun agreement,
- parallel construction,
- consistent verb tense,
- word choice.

In English, a verb must agree with the subject in number, meaning a singular noun would have a corresponding singular verb ("*The cat runs*") and a plural noun would have a corresponding plural verb ("*The cats run*"). In addition, pronouns must agree, meaning a singular noun would have a corresponding singular pronoun ("*The girl took her lunch to school*") and a plural noun would have a corresponding plural pronoun ("*The girls took their lunches to school*"). Parallel construction indicates that similar parts of a sentence need to be in the same form, for example a list of words would all be of the same part of speech ("*I have a dog, a cat, and a fish*") and be of the same tense ("*On the way to school he jumped, skipped, and hopped*"). Consistent verb tense indicates that the tense of writing should remain constant, in other words a writer should not shift between past and present tenses. Finally, word choice refers to correctly using words that are commonly confused (such as *accept* instead of *except*, *they're* or *there* instead of *their*, and *between* instead of *among*).

Capitalization is the purposeful use of uppercase letters in writing. Grammar rules related to capitalization include using an uppercase letter at the beginning of a sentence and to

---

A Focus on 6+1 Traits of Writing

6+1 Traits of Writing is an instruction and assessment approach used to help students with the writing process. The following traits are the focus:

1. *Ideas*—the main message,
2. *Organization*—the internal structure of the piece,
3. *Voice*—the personal tone and flavor of the author's message,
4. *Word Choice*—the vocabulary a writer chooses to convey meaning,
5. *Sentence Fluency*—the rhythm and flow of the language,
6. *Conventions*—the mechanical correctness.
6+1. *Presentation*—how the writing actually looks on the page

Each trait is accompanied by a rubric that is used by both teachers and students within writing instruction and assessment, creating a common vocabulary within classroom instruction and clear expectations for student writing products.

For more information see: https://educationnorthwest.org/traits

signify proper nouns (people, places, things). Punctuation includes the following punctuation marks and their corresponding rules for usage:

- end punctuation (periods, question marks, exclamation points),
- semi-colons, colons, commas,
- apostrophes,
- quotation marks,
- dashes, hyphens.

Punctuation is an important part of conventions, because correct use of punctuation can clarify the writer's intended meaning.

Spelling is also a part of conventions. Accurate spelling fosters clarity of expression, while inaccurate spelling can impede understanding. You will learn more about the developmental progression of spelling acquisition in the next section.

Developmental Spelling Stages

Just as proficient readers have an array of strategies to help themselves decode text, proficient spellers possess an array of strategies to help themselves **encode**, or spell, words. Decoding and encoding are reciprocal processes, meaning that decoding fosters improvement in encoding and vice versa. In addition to their knowledge of sound/symbol relationships (phonics), good spellers use visual, morphological, and semantic knowledge to help themselves spell words.

As you learned in Chapter 7, words can be categorized as phonetically regular words, phonetically irregular words, and sight words. Phonetically regular words follow predictable phonetic patterns based on the most common sounds of letters and/or groups of letters and their corresponding sounds. For example, the words *cat*, *baseball*, and even longer words like *understated* and *subtraction*, are phonetically regular. Phonetically irregular words, like *friend*, *have*, and *become* do not have predictable letter/sound correspondence. Sight words occur frequently in text and are comprised of both regular and irregular words. Just as students are taught different approaches for how to identify each type of word, there are different approaches for teaching students to spell each type of word.

Although there is not complete agreement about the number of stages that a student progresses through as spelling develops, research indicates that spelling develops hierarchically and sequentially just as language and decoding skills do (Beirne-Smith & Riley, 2009). Further, just as with decoding errors, students tend to be consistent in the errors that they make when spelling (Hodges, 1982). As such, analysis of these errors can provide insight into the stage of the student's spelling development and where to focus instruction.

Precommunicative Stage

As you learned in Chapter 5, when children are very young, their first attempts to communicate can include scribbles, pictures, and letters that are not properly formed or related to their phonological sounds. Throughout this stage, students are learning letters—particularly the letters in their own names, developing their phonological awareness of words and sounds, and potentially writing a few meaningful words that they have memorized—such as *mom* (Bear, Invernizzi, Templeton, & Johnston, 2016). A variety of terms are used to describe this stage of spelling, including **precommunicative stage**, preliterate stage, emergent spelling stage, and prephonetic stage. Student writing in this stage is sometimes referred to as "pretend writing." The images below depict samples of student writing in this stage.

On its face, Photo 13.1 may appear to be meaningless scribbles. However, when asked, the child indicates that his drawing represents "cars racing," and describes how three different colors of cars were racing down the road. At this early juncture, the student is using oral language skills in conjunction with beginning drawings to construct meaning, showing a beginning bridge between his oral language and a form of written communication.

Photo 13.1 "cars racing"

In Photo 13.2, the child is slightly further along in his written communication. His drawing has distinct figures that look like people and he indicates that the picture represents "Mommy and me." Even without additional narrative description from the child, it can be seen that the picture is conveying meaning involving two individuals who care about one another through the arms in the picture stretching out towards one another. In this drawing, more meaning is conveyed through the written drawing with less support needed in terms of oral language.

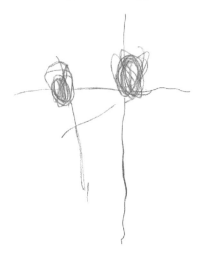

Photo 13.2 "Mommy and me"

In Photo 13.3, the student has attempted to write his name, which is one of the first actual words a student will typically learn to write. One's own name is a memorized word that is highly meaningful to an individual and used frequently. In this sample, the student has written his name, "Anthony." The letter formation for several letters is approximated rather than traditional spelling, especially in terms of the way the student formed the letter "n." Additionally, the student has an emerging idea that written letters should progress from left to right, but he is still developing visual–spatial awareness as evidenced by the letters that are stacked on top of one another. In this case, the writing itself contains the meaning entirely, and while the student actually spoke his name while writing, it is not needed for understanding the written communication.

Photo 13.3 "Anthony"

In this last example (Photo 13.4), still in the precommunicative stage, a student has written a string of letters that are a combination of correctly and incorrectly formed letters to describe the buildings he has drawn. The student has mastered many correctly written letters that progress from left to right across the page, but he is still working on the formation of the uppercase letters "N," "M," and "E" specifically. Embedded within the letter string is the sight word "DAD" in all uppercase letters. At this point, the student is refining uppercase letter formation and is beginning to use these letters in memorized sight words.

Photo 13.4 "This is my dad's house"

Semiphonetic (or Early Letter Name) Stage

In the **semiphonetic spelling stage**, also called the early letter name stage or the alphabetic spelling stage, a student attempts to spell words using predominant sounds and then first and last consonants. For example, in the word *dog*, the student might write the letter of the dominant sound they hear (in this case, the letter "d"), or the letter "t" to represent the word *toy*.

In this stage, students predominantly use the names of letters to represent the sounds that they hear in words. For example, the student might write the letter "r" to represent the word *are*.

At this stage, students also begin to produce sounds at the beginning of words first, followed by ending sounds, and in the next stage, medial vowel sounds. Notice that this is the same developmental sequence that occurs when students are developing phonological awareness (see Chapter 5). It should be noted that when students are first beginning to demonstrate these sound/symbol correspondences in their writing, they will be missing many of the letters needed to spell the word completely accurately. Student efforts in this stage are referred to as "invented spelling" (Beirne-Smith & Riley, 2009). Students generally enter the early letter name stage as they are being taught to read in their kindergarten year (Bear et al., 2016). The images below depict samples of student writing in this stage.

In Photo 13.5, the student is attempting to write, "We are going to P.E." In this sample, the student represents each word with the initial sound heard in each word. The ending "P.E." has likely been copied from a visual classroom schedule of special electives. The learner has progressed to demonstrating an awareness and emerging proficiency with sound/symbol relationships. However, to fully understand the message, the teacher relies on oral dialogue with the student in the moment in order to connect the child's thought process and specific meaning to the initial consonants written.

Photo 13.5 "We are going to P.E."

In Photo 13.6, the student has gone on a trip to the zoo and is describing some of the animals he saw on that trip, finishing the sentence starter from the teacher "I see_____." In this example, the student's spelling is further developed, and he is towards the end of the letter name stage. While the child does not yet know how to correctly spell *turkey* and *tiger*, his phonetic approximations are close to the actual words, with the student showing awareness of some word sounds at the beginning, final, and medial positions.

Photo 13.6 "I see turkeys and tigers"

Phonetic (or Middle/Late Letter Name) Stage

In the **phonetic spelling stage**, also called the middle or late letter name stage, students begin to correctly spell short vowels within syllables in addition to consonants. For instance, words like *pen*, *not*, and *man* would be spelled correctly. Students may occasionally display small errors with similar sounding short vowel sounds, such as transposing the letters "e" and "i." While in the early letter name stage, the student may have spelled these same words as "p" for *pen* (only identifying the beginning consonant), "nt" for *not* (missing the medial vowel sound), and *men* for *man* (mistaking the medial vowel sound). In the later part of the phonetic stage, the student would begin to correctly identify both beginning and ending sounds, as well as have increasing success with medial sounds for short vowel words. However, students may not yet correctly identify long vowel sounds with silent letters, writing "mad" instead of *made* or "fet" instead of *feet*. At this stage, students will spell sight words correctly, such as *the*, *for*, and *you*. Students display rapid growth through the middle and late letter name stages during the primary grades (Bear et al., 2016). The images below depict samples of student writing in this stage.

In Photo 13.7, the girl pictured is correctly spelling a short vowel sound word with magnetic letters. At the beginning of the phonetic stage, students may use both print and other manipulatives, such as foam and magnetic letters, to master construction of short vowel sound words. These types of activities help students gain competency with beginning, medial, and ending sounds of these short vowel words.

Photo 13.7 "This says 'sit.'"

In the second example (Photo 13.8), the student has intended to write, "The chipmunks wake up and gather their food." The student correctly spells sight words and short vowel sound words, and uses invented spelling to write "chmks" to represent *chipmunks*. The student does not appear to have mastered long vowel spellings, writing "wak" for *wake*. The student also shows signs of difficulties with ambiguous vowel constructions by spelling "ther" for *their* and "fud" for *food*. These areas will continue to develop in later stages.

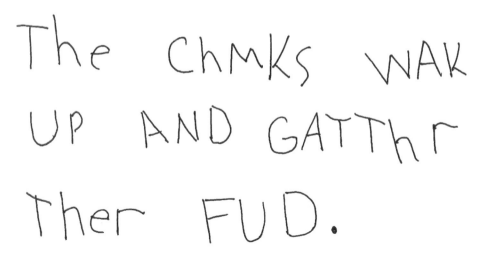

Photo 13.8 "The chipmunks wake up and gather their food."

The third example in Photo 13.9 is later within the phonetic stage where the learner is describing "a party hat" as a "a prte hat." In this sample, the sight word "a" and the short vowel word *hat* are clearly mastered. While the more advanced vowel sounds in *party*, which involve a medial r-controlled vowel as well as using "-y" as an /ē/ sound, have not yet been internalized and applied by the student.

Photo 13.9 "a party hat"

Within Word (Transitional Speller) Stage

In the **within word stage**, also called the transitional speller stage (Bear et al., 2016), students begin to experiment with long vowel and ambiguous vowel spelling patterns. Students generally enter this stage toward the end of 1st grade and continue to progress through this stage until about 4th grade. Students will take more time to move through this stage, with students who are struggling to learn to decode when reading being likely to stay in this stage for a longer period of time. The images below depict samples of student writing in this stage.

The student's poem in Photo 13.10 illustrates experimentation with ambiguous vowels, spelling "iglo" for *igloo*, "nudle" for *noodle*, "octipos" for *octopus*. Note that all consonants and clearly heard vowel constructions are spelled accurately.

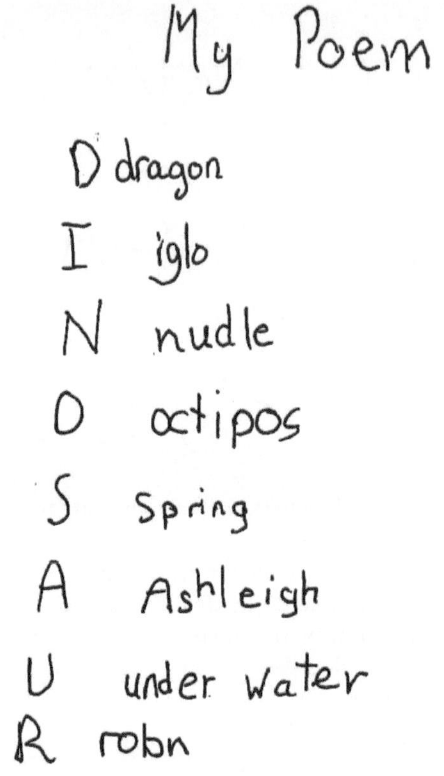

My Poem

D dragon
I iglo
N nudle
O octipos
S spring
A Ashleigh
U under water
R robn

Photo 13.10

In the second example in Photo 13.11, an excerpt is taken from a student's science note taking on African elephants as part of instruction on endangered animals. The student displays mastery of many sight words and short vowel sound words as well as words with more complex consonant and vowel sound constructions. However, the student is struggling with homophones, writing "there" for *their*.

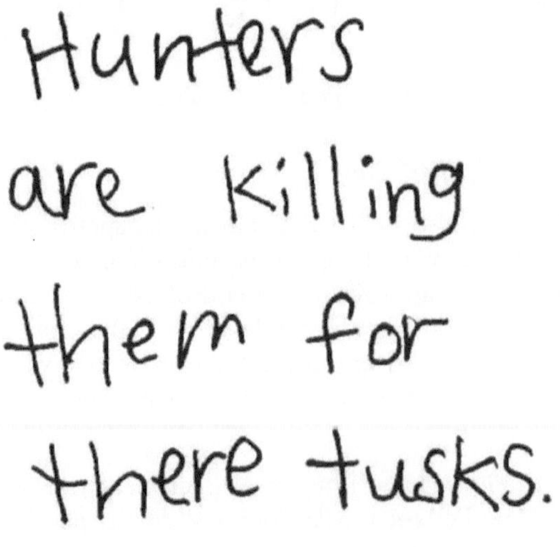

Hunters
are Killing
them for
there tusks.

Photo 13.11 "Hunters are killing them for their tusks."

Syllable Juncture Stage

In the next stage, **syllable juncture** or syllables and affixes stage, students begin to experiment with spelling multisyllable words with an increasing number of syllables, and words with prefixes and suffixes. Students generally enter the syllable juncture stage in upper elementary or middle school. The images below depict samples of student writing in this stage.

In Photo 13.12, the student has written a sentence where sight words and short vowel sound words are all spelled accurately, but the student is still experimenting with spellings for multi-syllabic words, writing "amarc" for *America*. At this stage, students also may make errors when spelling words with **inflectional endings**—endings that change a word's meaning, such as *-s, -ed, or -ly*.

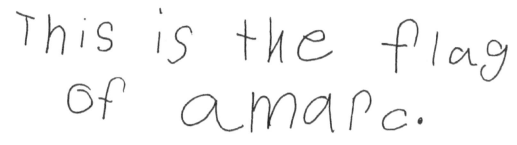

Photo 13.12 "This is the flag of America."

Photo 13.13 illustrates a student who has yet to master the spelling rules for adding suffixes, writing "diveing" for *diving*. Specifically the student has not correctly added the suffix to a "silent e" word by removing the silent "e" before adding the *-ing* ending.

Photo 13.13 "I would go scuba diving."

Derivational Constancy Stage

The most advanced stage of spelling is **derivational constancy**, also called derivational relations. In this stage, students spell most words correctly but are still becoming proficient with derived forms of base and root words as well as the internal morphology in syllables. Depending on a student's rate of development, a student could enter this stage in middle school, high school, or college (Bear et al., 2016). Development in this stage often extends into adulthood, where even adults who are no longer in school misspell words in this stage. Errors in this stage are more advanced in nature than in previous stages, and typically surround spelling unstressed syllables in words like *simultaneously* and *inaccurately*. Similar sounding prefixes or suffixes may be misspelled as well. The sample in Photo 13.14 depicts a student's writing sample in this stage.

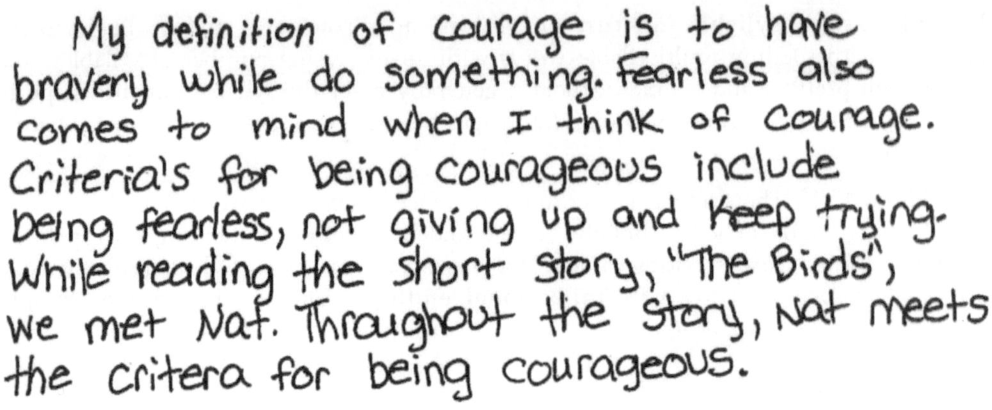

My definition of courage is to have bravery while do something. Fearless also comes to mind when I think of courage. Criteria's for being courageous include being fearless, not giving up and keep trying. While reading the short story, "The Birds", we met Nat. Throughout the story, Nat meets the critera for being courageous.

Photo 13.14

Within this writing sample, the student is using the words *courage* and *courageous*, which are both words at the derivational constancy level. With both words, the student spells them correctly showing an understanding of the base word *courage* and then the process of adding the "-ous" morpheme/suffix to the base word to change it from a noun to an adjective. Since the student employs correct spelling in both cases, it can be observed that she understands not only the physical process of adding the ending but also the semantic change that is made by this addition. Additional information that the student understands the meaning of both *courage* and *courageous* can also be seen from the appropriate use of both words syntactically and semantically in the context of the overall writing.

The Writing Process

Cox (2008) aptly describes writing as "a rather messy process" (p. 233). However, messy as it is, all writers go through a similar five-step process when composing text:

- brainstorming,
- drafting,
- revising,
- editing,
- publishing.

These steps are not necessarily linear, but rather, are recursive in nature. For example, a student may draft and revise one section of a paper, repeat the process for the next section, and then finally edit the entire thing. Another student might make a first draft and then revise several times before editing the final version. In schools, students receive direct instruction and practice in this recursive process. Following is a description of the general steps.

Brainstorming is the first step in the writing process and it involves thinking about the writing topic and what the writer already knows. Sometimes what students already know about the topic is from something that they have read or learned in class. Brainstorming might also include thinking about vocabulary that might be used.

Drafting is the process of putting to paper words and connected sentences that represent the ideas that were brainstormed in the planning phase. At this stage, the emphasis is on communicating meaning rather than displaying completely accurate writing conventions. Even after brainstorming, creating a first draft can be a difficult task for some students;

however, it is a critical part of the writing process. Without a first draft, improvements and refinements cannot occur.

Revising is the process of "revisiting" a draft to ensure that the writing conveys the meaning that the writer intended. Revision might include major changes to make the organization clearer or relatively smaller changes such as adjusting word choice for clarity or emphasis.

Editing is the process of proofreading and correcting any errors related to writing conventions—grammar, spelling, or punctuation. Editing marks are used for this purpose (see Figure 13.1).

Capitalization & Punctuation Marks	Other Proofreading Marks
Capitalize i walked down the street.	Start a new paragraph I walked down the street. ¶Next, I stopped at the store.
Make lower case I walked down the Street.	Insert a word quickly I walked down the street.
Add a period I walked down the street⊙	Delete a word I walked down the he street.
Add a comma Next⌟I walked down the street	Reverse word order I walked down the street long.
Add quotation marks He said, I walked down the street.	Spelling error sp I walked down the treat

Figure 13.1 Proofreading marks

Publishing is the process of making a finished piece of writing public. This might be creating a final clean draft for display or reading the piece of writing aloud to an audience. Sometimes published products are word processed or include illustrations.

Writing Strategies

Just as students understand more of what they read when they approach text strategically, students are better able to express their thoughts in writing when they approach writing strategically. Because writing is a complex, multi-step process, a student will need a wide range of strategies in their learning "tool belt." In Chapter 10, reading comprehension strategies were conceptualized as the 4 Ps: plan, pay attention and problem solve, and process information. As shown in Figure 13.2, strategies for writing can be conceptualized in a similar way.

Planning occurs before readers begin writing and helps them to create their first draft. When teaching students any strategies it is important to include overt reference to:

- *why* to use a strategy,
- *how* to use a strategy,
- *when* to use a strategy.

These components help to foster self-regulation, the cyclical process students use to sustain their efforts to attain a learning goal (Zimmerman, 2000).

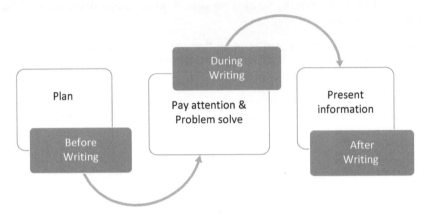

Figure 13.2 The 4 Ps of the writing process

Paying attention and problem solving happens as students are working to improve the clarity of their ideas and expression through revision and editing. It is important to foster students' self-monitoring of their performance during the writing process. In the case of writing, this means self-evaluating how well the piece of writing communicates the intended ideas. Instructional approaches common in classrooms generally utilize feedback from multiple sources: student self-evaluation, feedback from peers, and feedback from the teacher. These feedback sources are important for students as they work to improve their writing.

Finally, when students have created their final draft, strategies for presenting their writing are important because communicating ideas with others is the point of written expression. Selecting an appropriate audience for the writing and effective dissemination outlets are both areas where strategies can help students communicate more effectively.

Instructional Approaches

As you have learned in this chapter, writing is a complex process and correspondingly, instruction to help students improve their writing is multi-faceted. In this section, instructional approaches will be presented for spelling, followed by strategies for the larger writing process.

Fostering Acquisition of Spelling

Spelling is the encoding of language and is a reciprocal process to decoding. Both processes are developmental with reading supporting spelling development and vice versa. Therefore, it is not surprising that the most effective instructional approaches for fostering spelling acquisition are similar in nature to instructional approaches for decoding.

Word Study

Spelling instruction for phonetically regular words is usually most effective when connected to the sound patterns the student is learning to read. Word study is an example of instruction that follows this approach. **Word study** includes instructional activities that help students recognize the different sound pattern construction similarities of targeted spelling words (Bear et al., 2016).

When using word study, students are given a group of words that can be broken into categories by the sound-pattern construction. Students are given a jumbled group of words that can be separated into categories by target sound patterns the words possess—called word sorts. There are many types of word sorts, including sorting by common sounds or spelling patterns. By sorting the words, students' attention is focused in on the targeted patterns, which helps them remember and spell these words. Grouping the target words by sound or spelling patterns also helps students generalize across multiple words, helping students learn multiple words at once.

Student progression through word study aligns with their developmental spelling level. Students at the letter name stage, for example, might be working on sorting words that start with the /d/, /c/, and /f/ sounds or sorting words from common word families (*top, mop, hop*, and *chip, ship, lip*). Older students in the more advanced syllable juncture stage might be sorting to distinguish between words with the same sound /shun/ but different spellings. For example, words like *comprehension, confusion*, and *erosion* would be sorted together because /shun/ is spelled with "-sion." *Exploration, dehydration*, and *graduation* would be another word group sorted together because here /shun/ is spelled with "-tion."

When completing word sorts, students can physically manipulate and sort words into groups using cards. The other option is to use technology to help with the word sort task using the drag-and-drop function of the mouse, placing words with similar sound patterns in separate groups or word lists. The focus of word sorts is not memorization but recognizing how to spell a word by the letter/sound pattern used for a particular sound construction.

Memorization Strategies

For words that are phonetically irregular, memorization strategies are effective. With these strategies, students simply memorize the accurate spelling of target words. While there are many different strategies that could be chosen, they all have similar qualities. In general, memorization strategies involve multiple structured practice opportunities, the idea being that the repetition will help students remember accurate word spelling. Additionally, the strategies typically have immediate feedback built in for spelling accuracy, so any spelling errors are noted and corrected right away.

One specific spelling memorization strategy is Cover, Copy, Compare (CCC) (Joseph et al., 2012). When using this strategy, the teacher selects up to ten targeted spelling words and gives them in written list form to students. Students then start at the top of the list and study each individual word. After students have spent time reading and looking at a word, they fold the paper over to **C**over the target word and attempt to **C**opy the target word without looking at it. After the student has attempted to spell the word, they unfold the paper and **C**ompare their written attempt to the original word. If their attempt is correct, they proceed to the next word. If their attempt is incorrect, they complete the CCC process again a second time for the target word. The student then continues the CCC process for all the words on the spelling list.

Structural Analysis

Strategies used for learning multi-syllabic words are typically ones involving structural analysis. While there are many different spelling strategies that employ structural analysis components within them, the hallmark of all of these strategies is using base words and affixes to break down words for correct spelling. As a result, structural analysis strategies would only be used to target spelling of longer multi-syllabic words. Across the different types of strategies employing structural analysis, students will work on learning word spelling by understanding the spelling of syllables and word parts of longer words.

When presented with a new spelling word, a student would analyze that word, looking for any prefixes or suffixes, as well as identifying the base or root word, which is oftentimes a shorter word the student may have learned to spell previously. The student learns to spell the longer overall word correctly by accurately spelling each individual word part. For instance, if students are learning to spell the word *unnoticeable*, they would break it in to "un-," "notice," and "-able." They would first ensure they knew how to spell both the prefix and suffix, which are shorter and less complex, and then focus on how to spell the base word. When spelling the entire word, the student would practice accurate spelling through constructing the word by adding each correctly spelled word part. Overall, structural analysis strategies help students spell by breaking down longer words into smaller word parts which are more easily spelled.

Fostering Acquisition and Self-regulation of Writing Strategies

It is important for teachers to help students learn an array of strategies to help with the writing process. Additionally, research tells us that how teachers go about helping students learn strategies is just as important as the strategies themselves (Mastropieri, Scruggs, & Graetz, 2003; Swanson, 1999; Vaughn, Gersten, & Chard, 2000). In Chapter 10, you learned that effective strategy instruction includes:

- modeling,
- guided practice,
- independent practice,
- feedback (corrective feedback and strategy feedback).

Figure 13.3 depicts how these concepts are related.

Modeling involves overtly demonstrating a skill or process, often while thinking aloud to illustrate internal thinking—referred to as a "think-aloud." Guided practice allows students to practice a strategy or skill with scaffolded teacher support and corrective feedback that supports accurate application. Finally, independent practice gives students opportunities to replicate application of the skill or strategy with minimal teacher support and feedback that reinforces independent strategy use.

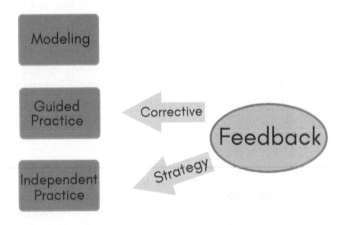

Figure 13.3 The instructional process

In addition to feedback from a teacher that reinforces correct application of strategy use, students will receive feedback about the content, clarity, and conventions of their writing from a variety of sources during the writing process that helps them to improve their writing. You will learn more about this in the remainder of the chapter.

Strategies that Help Students Plan

There are many ways to help students be planful when getting started with their writing. Common strategies support students in the brainstorming and drafting processes. These strategies help students generate and develop their ideas for writing.

Strategies for Brainstorming

Brainstorming is part of the writing process that students often forget to do without prompting. Brainstorming strategies can help students in generating, organizing, and showing connections between their ideas. Brainstorming can be either unstructured or structured. Unstructured brainstorming might include mentally listing or jotting down ideas to focus the writer's thinking. Structured brainstorming might involve using a graphic organizer or an outline as a way to help organize thoughts that might be used in the writing. Graphic organizers typically employ the use of visual aids to help students map out their thoughts on a topic, showing the relationship between the main idea and related details.

Strategies for Drafting

After brainstorming ideas for writing, students will need to draft their ideas in complete connected sentences. This task can be a particularly challenging one for students. As you learned in Chapter 10, narrative and expository text structures have different characteristics. Just as this impacts how a reader approaches reading comprehension, it also affects how a writer approaches the composition of these types of text.

Quickwrites is a strategy that can help students when writing narrative stories (Mason, Kubina, & Taft, 2011). When using Quickwrites, a student is given a prompt that may be of high interest. Students are then given a short time frame to write as much as they can about the prompt, typically 1–5 minutes in length. As with reading comprehension, self-questioning can be a useful strategy for helping actively engage students. With Quickwrites, students can be taught to ask and answer "W" questions (*who, what, when, where, why*) or questions that are sensory or emotion based, such as:

- What does it look like?
- What does it sound like?
- How does it make you feel?

The focus of this writing strategy is to have students write full sentences on a topic that can later be revised and edited.

POW TREE is an example of a drafting strategy that can support students with expository writing from the brainstorming through the drafting stage (Graham & Harris, 2003). The first part of the strategy can be used with any piece of writing following the acronym POW:

- **P**ick your topic,
- **O**rganize your ideas on that topic,
- **W**rite and say more about the topic.

The first part of the strategy facilitates the student figuring out what they are going to be writing about and approaching that writing in a way that meaningfully uses their ideas to write sentences. When students are writing their first sentences, the strategy's emphasis is on writing as much as they can on their topic.

The second part of the strategy is focused specifically on essay writing and provides a guide for structuring ideas when drafting using the acronym TREE:

- **T**opic sentence,
- **R**easons (at least three or more),
- **E**nding,
- **E**xamine.

This ending part of the strategy helps students think about what pieces they need to write for their essay and reminds them that going back to review what they have written should be part of the process.

Strategies that Help Students Pay Attention and Problem Solve

Students are better able to clearly communicate their ideas in writing when they actively engage in the aspects of the writing process that require them to refine their initial writing draft—revising and editing. Many strategies can help support students as they work through these processes.

Strategies for Revising

Revising is the first step in fine-tuning a student's initial writing draft. When revising, a student is evaluating how well their original draft conveyed their intended meaning. Changes made in this stage are intended to repair conceptual or organizational problems. Revising is a difficult skill for students to acquire because students must evaluate their own original writing. Without explicit instruction, students can be unsure about what they should be doing during the revision portion of the writing process. There are varieties of approaches that can be used to support student development in the revising stage. Teachers can help students by clearly teaching them what types of changes to focus on when revising and how to make these changes. Students can be instructed to focus on evaluating whether their writing conveys their intended meaning, incorporates all their key ideas, and uses an organizational structure that is easily understood.

Besides explicit instruction, students benefit from teacher and sometimes peer feedback on how they are revising. The nature of writing is an iterative process where a student writes, then revises, and then writes again based on revisions, with this sequence often having multiple passes. With each writing endeavor being a new application of the writing process, students benefit from feedback not only on how to make revisions in general but also on specific revisions for each new piece of writing. The feedback can come from both peers and a teacher. Teachers can provide structured revision checklists for this purpose for students to use in evaluating one another's writing and then discussing the changes. Then, teachers can provide additional feedback using the same checklist, or they can share feedback with the student based on what is currently being covered during instruction.

Writing Workshop is a more structured approach to help students with the revision stage of the writing process. During a Writing Workshop, time is allotted for all the stages in the writing process. During the time designated for revising, students can be paired and given

Photo 13.15

time to read, evaluate, and then discuss one another's work. There is usually time allotted for students to meet with the teacher individually, as depicted in Photo 13.15, or in small groups to get teacher feedback on revisions. Using the Workshop approach helps students see the writing task as an ongoing project where their writing meaningfully improves as time is spent on each stage in the process.

Within the Writing Workshop approach, time management by the teacher is key so that time is used appropriately during each writing process stage rather than being wasted unnecessarily with too much time spent where it is not needed. Additionally, both teacher and peer feedback during the revision discussions need to be focused. A checklist with a few key items for each writing project can guide peer feedback, and these checklist items can be changed depending on the nature of the project. Teacher feedback on revisions can also be targeted to current instruction or narrowed to just a few key revision practices.

Strategies for Editing

The second phase of "pay attention and problem solve" within the writing process involves editing. With editing, students are looking through their writing to correct any mistakes they have made with writing conventions. Many times students may not know what to look for to pinpoint these errors or may feel overwhelmed by the number and types of errors. As a result, students can benefit from structured guidelines on what they should be looking for in terms of errors.

A helpful strategy for the editing phase is COPS. Within COPS, the learner is directed to evaluate their writing for: **C**apitalization, **O**verall Appearance (handwriting, margins, and indentations), **P**unctuation, and **S**pelling (Telaumbanua & Al-Hafizh, 2013). This strategy helps students know what they should be looking for generally when reviewing any piece of writing. Students can use the strategy to self-evaluate their own writing or the writing of peers during peer review. Teachers can also use this strategy in writing conferences with students to help guide editing. Following COPS, students can be empowered to complete the editing process by themselves or with peer support, which can be motivating when working through the writing process. While the strategy is a supportive resource, it is general in nature, and teachers may want to incorporate more specific discussion points in peer and teacher feedback. As such, teacher-developed supplemental resources and checklists may be needed.

Strategies that Help Students Present Information

Publishing involves a range of options for presenting information. Oftentimes students share what they have written by rewriting their final draft in their best handwriting. At times, students may share this final written copy by reading it aloud to others. Because this part of the process can be intimidating to students, strategies can help them to be more successful.

One of the most commonly used strategies for helping students present their information is the use of technology. Using technology in the form of word processing to type up the final draft of their writing ensures students' writing will be clear and easy to read. Additionally, multiple copies of the typed version of a student's writing can be made and shared with others more easily than a handwritten version. One drawback of using technology is that sometimes the time it takes for students to type their written work can bog down the writing process, with too much time spent on the presentation step. Used as a tool for visual clarity and developing student typing skills, technology can be used as a valuable tool in presenting or sharing student writing.

References

Alvermann, D. E., Phelps, S. F., & Gillis, V. R. (2010). *Content area reading and literacy: Succeeding in today's diverse classrooms.* Boston, MA: Allyn & Bacon.

Bear, D. R., Invernizzi, M., Templeton, S., & Johnston, F. R. (2016). *Words their way: Word study for phonics, vocabulary, and spelling instruction* (6th ed.). Upper Saddle River, NJ: Pearson.

Beirne-Smith, M., & Riley, T. F (2009). Spelling assessment of students with disabilities. *Assessment for Effective Intervention, 34,* 170–177.

Cox, C. (2008). *Teaching language arts: A student-centered classroom* (6th ed.). Boston, MA: Pearson.

Graham, S., & Harris, K. R. (2003). *Students with learning disabilities and the process of writing: A meta-analysis of SRSD studies.* New York, NY: Guilford Press.

Hodges, R. E. (1982). Research update: On the development of spelling ability. *Language Arts, 59,* 284–290.

Joseph, L. M., Konrad, M., Cates, G., Vajcner, T., Eveleigh, E., & Fishley, K. M. (2012). A meta-analytic review of the cover-copy-compare and variations of this self-management procedure. *Psychology in the Schools, 49,* 122–136.

Mason, L. H., Kubina Jr., R. M., & Taft, R. J. (2011). Developing quick writing skills of middle school students with disabilities. *The Journal of Special Education, 44,* 205–220.

Mastropieri, M. A., Scruggs, T. E., & Graetz, J. E. (2003). Reading comprehension instruction for secondary students: Challenges for struggling students and teachers. *Learning Disability Quarterly, 26,* 103–116.

Swanson, H. L. (1999). Reading research for students with LD: A meta-analysis of intervention outcomes. *Journal of Learning Disabilities, 32,* 504–532.

Telaumbanua, Y. P., & Al-Hafizh, M. (2013). Using the COPS strategy in teaching writing a narrative text to junior high school students. *Journal of English Language Teaching, 2,* 423–429.

Vaughn, S., Gersten, R., & Chard, D. J. (2000). The underlying message in LD intervention research: Findings from research syntheses. *Exceptional Children, 67,* 99–114

Zimmerman, B. J. (2000). Self-efficacy: An essential motive to learn. *Contemporary Educational Psychology, 25,* 82–91.

Chapter 14

Supporting All Students in Writing and Spelling

Students Who Struggle with Writing and Spelling

Just as comprehension is the entire purpose of reading, communicating ideas with others is the purpose of writing. However, even with purposeful instruction, some students will struggle with written expression. Proficient writers have prior experiences and vocabulary knowledge that help support expression of their ideas, while struggling writers may be lacking in these areas. The writing of some students is impeded by problems that they have with spelling. Spelling acquisition is difficult for many at-risk learners who also struggle with developing basic reading skills. This is because decoding and spelling are constrained by the same cognitive and linguistic processes inherent in the acquisition of language (Hodges, 1982). As such, students who are learning English as a second language or who have language-based disabilities are especially at-risk for problems with spelling and written expression.

Challenges Stemming from English Language Development

Students who are learning English as a second language develop spelling skills more slowly than their native English-speaking peers do. Like with decoding, one of the challenges is due to the orthographical differences between students' first language (L1) and English (see Chapter 6 for more information). Some students' L1s use the Roman alphabet as English does, but their L1s may be more systematically phonetic than English, which has many phonetic irregularities. Additionally, many students' L1s do not use the same alphabet as English. For example, Russian follows the Cyrillic alphabet and Chinese uses characters that comprise individual meaning units versus letters tied to sounds. Orthographic differences, such as the ones highlighted here, can cause challenges for students learning to write and spell individual words.

Additional challenges stem from simultaneously trying to learn how to speak, read, and write in English. While native English speakers often learn to read and spell simultaneously, they have their oral language knowledge as a foundation when building these skills. With English language learners, they do not have strong oral language skills in English on which to rely. Sometimes they do not even have reliable English oral language models, with parents and community members sometimes speaking in slang or using incomplete English pronunciations of words. With this limited oral language knowledge and exposure, sometimes connections between reading words and writing words in English may seem to have a more covert than overt relationship for English language learners. Thus, effectively using more complex and narrowly focused vocabulary as well as more complex sentence structures in writing may be especially difficult. For instance, many languages use morphemes that indicate number and tense in ways that do not align with English. Differences may be seen in sentence structures as well. For example, many European languages have adjectives placed following a noun, versus before a noun as in English. Because they have missed years of English oral language experiences, students with English learning needs can experience difficulties in writing English at the letter/sound level, the word level, and sentence level.

It is also important to keep in mind that English language learners may not experience even growth of abilities across skill areas. Students may have the oral language abilities to express themselves, but their ability with printed language may not be at the same level. When this disconnect happens, students may be able to share more aloud than in writing, which can be frustrating to them. Additionally, students may evidence a strength in personal narrative writing because they have developed proficiency with BICS more quickly, but still struggle with expository writing in which CALP plays a larger role because academic English takes longer for growth and development. (For more on BICS and CALP, see Chapter 1). Understanding and utilizing subject area vocabulary to read and communicate about content can take several years for English language learners to develop competency. Therefore, it may take more time for these students to correctly incorporate the rich vocabulary they are learning from text into their writing.

Cultural differences in social situations, such as proximity in conversations, body language information, and gestures can cause difficulties in students' ability to correctly perceive language information and appropriately interpret language cues. These linguistic misunderstandings related to pragmatics are more often seen when students' L1 norms do not align with those in English. Examples of pragmatic information difficulties can be seen with students from some Asian and Indian cultures, where making eye contact can be seen as disrespectful depending on the social situation or gender, while in English culture, making eye contact is seen as a sign of listener and speaker attention. Additionally, in Hispanic and Middle Eastern cultures, proximity and spatial boundaries are much closer than is typical of English speakers. Intonation and pitch differences can also cause pragmatic difficulties and can be seen among English, Asian, and Spanish speakers because tone and inflection can change the meaning of the words conveyed. All of these differences in pragmatics across languages and cultures can lead to difficulties in English learners fully understanding English language usage. This can impede student participation and benefit from instructional activities involving peer and teacher writing conferences, as well as employing appropriate contextual language usage in their own writing.

Challenges Stemming from Disability

Students with language-based disabilities have a more difficult time acquiring writing skills than their typically developing peers (Graham, Harris, & McKeown, 2013). In fact, they significantly underperform their peers in the quality of text written (quality, organization, voice, ideation, and output), including text production skills (sentence fluency, handwriting, spelling, and grammar), knowledge about writing, and motivation to write (Graham, Collins, & Rigby-Wills, 2017). These problems are difficult to remediate when they stem from language-based learning disabilities (Beirne-Smith & Riley, 2009).

Students with language-based disabilities have significant difficulty with reading tasks related to phonology and acquisition of the alphabetic principle (see Chapters 1, 6, and 9). These same difficulties also impede spelling development causing them to lag behind their typically developing peers in moving through the developmental spelling stages presented in Chapter 13 (McNaughton, Hughes, & Clark, 1994). Specifically, students with language-based disabilities do not effectively use their knowledge of sound/symbol relationships to encode words, resulting in errors such as omitted or substituted vowels (Darch, Kim, Johnson, & James, 2000). Just as with word identification, memory problems also impede students' abilities to remember words and word parts (Moats, 1995).

As has been established in Chapters 6 and 12, students with language-based disabilities have vocabularies that are more limited and shallow than their typically developing peers. This discrepancy in word knowledge begins in the earliest grades and widens over time. Because students cannot use words in their writing that do not exist in their speaking vocabularies, it is not surprising that these students display less conceptually sophisticated writing than their peers. Similarly, students with language-based learning disabilities tend to lack metalinguistic awareness, meaning that while listening and reading, they do not adequately attend to the morphological nuances of words and the syntax within sentences. As such, their writing is generally deficient in these areas as well.

Written expression development can also be impeded by pragmatics problems, which involve understanding and using language in social contexts. Many students with disabilities can struggle with pragmatics in social situations that involve oral language, which can impede their ability to benefit from group learning situations in the classroom such as peer writing groups. For example, a student may make comments that are inappropriate or irrelevant during conversations with others. At other times, students may display problems with word choice that leads to miscommunication with peers. For instance, a student may say that he was "*destroyed by a friend*" rather than saying he was "*upset by a friend*." Additionally, these students may also have problems with interpreting nonverbal communication and misinterpret body language during oral communication. All of these concerns can detract from students' abilities to understand and use peer feedback during classroom writing activities involving writing groups and Writing Workshops. These pragmatic concerns can also carry over to students' written expression with students struggling to accurately convey their ideas and feelings in writing.

Another concern students with learning disabilities often have in writing is difficulty with organization. Challenges these students have with self-regulation make it difficult for them to make and follow through on a writing plan. Initially, students may have difficulty developing a plan that focuses their ideas, or they may get "stuck" at this stage experiencing a "block" in being able to begin putting their ideas to paper. Difficulties with expressing their ideas in writing may, at least in part, be due to uneven oral language development. Further, students may be frustrated by this inability to fully convey their ideas in writing. Another related concern is that some students have difficulties with the physical production of printed text, known as **dysgraphia**. Students with dysgraphia can have difficulties with letter formation, spacing, and fluency in handwriting. At times these challenges may be so

A Focus on Dysgraphia

Dysgraphia is a type of learning disability that impacts students' writing development, including spelling, handwriting, and expressing ideas in writing. Although dysgraphia can be present in students with dyslexia, they are not always comorbid. As you learned in Chapter 9, dyslexia is a neurological impairment that affects the phonological components of language.

Students with dyslexia may have trouble mastering basic and then more complex spelling patterns because of underlying problems in language and reading. Additionally, students with dysgraphia may have difficulty with letter formation, which may make basic spelling patterns difficult to physically form. This can result in letter reversals later than would be expected developmentally or writing that is deviant in other ways, such as inappropriate letter size or spacing between letters or words. In addition, it can be laborious for these students to express ideas or to copy writing from an existing source—taking notes, for example. Dyslexia may also keep students from accurately conveying their language ideas in writing because ordering and organizing ideas may be difficult.

Refer to the International Dyslexia Association for more information: https://dyslexiaida.org/

A Focus on Specialists Who Support Students with Written Language

Speech–Language Pathologists

Speech–Language pathologists, called SLPs, work with students with written language disorders. These professionals have specialized knowledge of the systems of language and how they relate to spoken and written language. SLPs play a role in the diagnosis, assessment, and provision of written language interventions.

Occupational Therapist

Occupational therapists, called OTs, provide support for students with significant problems with handwriting. These professionals have specialized knowledge needed to evaluate students' fine motor abilities that hinder handwriting (muscle strength, endurance, coordination, and motor control). OTs provide support for handwriting development and adaptations when appropriate.

---

severe that writing production needs to be supported with assistive technology through word-processing or speech-to-text programs.

Assessment of Student Spelling Skills

Spelling provides important insights into students' phonological development as well as being an important component of writing in general. For this reason, it is important for teachers to assess student progress in this area on an ongoing basis. When evaluating student spelling, teachers can complete an error analysis just as they can do for student word recognition and fluency monitoring.

Across any type of spelling assessment, it is critical for teachers to mark and determine the nature of student spelling errors. From these errors, teachers can determine if there are any patterns in specific student spelling mistakes. For example, teachers will often see that the same phonemic difficulties students experience when reading decodable words also carry over to spelling these same words. Since word recognition in reading and spelling are closely linked, errors in reading specific phonetically irregular sight words will often be reflected in spelling as well. Conducting an error analysis on a given spelling assessment helps the teacher identify gaps in sight word knowledge and specific phonological difficulties that can be targeted in spelling instruction as well as determine if parallel instruction is needed with decoding in reading.

Teachers analyze student writing to look for patterns in student spelling errors. For example, students might misspell:

- shorter phonetically regular words,
- beginning, ending, or medial word sounds,
- complex vowel constructions,
- affixes (adding or deleting endings like -s, -ed, or −ing),
- multi-syllabic words (deleting or adding syllables).

Students can also make mistakes spelling phonetically irregular words that are sight words. These errors are important to pick out because they can indicate a lack of student memorization of specific phonetically irregular words for spelling. Lastly, teachers can also note student spelling errors with homophones, which are words that sound alike but are spelled differently and can only be determined by how a word is used in the context of a sentence.

Observation/Authentic Assessment

Informal evaluation of student writing products created during authentic academic activities can provide important insights into students' orthographic knowledge. There are numerous types of writing throughout the school day that provide opportunities for teachers to informally assess students' spelling development, including written answers to questions or prompts, narratives, letters, and journal entries.

Because students tend to make consistent errors in spelling, analyzing their daily spelling can give an indication of a student's stage of spelling development. However, care should be taken when drawing conclusions based solely on an authentic piece of student writing. Evaluating spelling in authentic settings may not be a completely accurate representation of a student's abilities. For example, Bear and colleagues (2016) highlighted the following scenarios that might skew the interpretation of a student's spelling:

- Students may have used word walls or other environmental print as a reference for how to correctly spell a word.
- Students may only attempt to spell words that they are already confident they know how to spell accurately.
- Students may not make their best effort to spell correctly if they are concentrating on expressing their ideas.

As such, it is important to use a variety of data sources to get the most complete picture of a student's spelling development.

Teacher-made Spelling Tests

Teacher-made spelling tests are another data source for monitoring student spelling development. One of the difficulties teachers have is determining which words to teach and then assess for student proficiency. With word recognition, students are expected to read memorized phonetically irregular sight words accurately as well as fluently decode phonetic words. Since spelling is the inverse of word recognition, it is also important for students to know how to spell these sight words as well as phonetically regular words. When constructing teacher-made spelling tests, it is recommended that both phonetically regular words and sight words be incorporated at the ratio of 80:20 of phonetic words to sight words. Generally, spelling tests are administered with the teacher saying the word, saying the word in a sentence, and saying the word again in isolation, while the student spells the word. The student in Photo 14.1 is taking a spelling test.

Informal Spelling Inventories

In an informal spelling inventory, spelling lists are administered that contain words specific to a developmental spelling stage. See Table 14.1 for commonly used informal spelling inventories. Informal spelling inventories often include a screener to help determine the stage level of the assessment that should be given. This is comparable to the use of a word list in an informal reading inventory. Next, students are asked to spell words consistent with the targeted developmental stage. Student spelling is scored using features of words targeted for

Photo 14.1

that particular spelling stage. For example, in the Developmental Spelling Analysis (DSA), there are controlled spelling lists for each of the developmental stages: letter name, within word, syllable juncture, and derivational constancy. Within each of these lists, specific spelling features are highlighted. For example, spelling patterns featured in the within word list include: long vowels with a vowel–consonant–"silent e" pattern; r-controlled vowel patterns; other common long vowels; complex consonants (scr, qu, ck); and ambiguous vowels including digraphs and diphthongs. Scoring of the DSA includes special consideration to errors in the features instead of, or in addition to, correct spelling of the word (depending on the scoring conventions used).

Table 14.1 Informal Spelling Inventories

Informal Spelling Inventories	Approximate Grade Level
Primary Spelling Inventory	kindergarten through 3rd grade
Elementary Spelling Inventory	1st through 6th grade
Upper Level Spelling Inventory	5th through 12th grade

Adapted from: Bear, D. R., Invernizzi, M., Templeton, S., & Johnston, F. R. (2016). *Words their way: Word study for phonics, vocabulary, and spelling instruction* (6th ed.). Upper Saddle River, NJ: Pearson.

Informal spelling inventories are comparable to informal reading inventories in that they provide information about whether words are easy, too difficult, or just right for instruction (Invernizzi, Abouzeid, & Gill, 1994). In Chapter 3, this was referred to as the "Goldilocks principle" (see Figure 14.1). Within a list of 25 words specific to a developmental stage, the student is considered independent if he spells 23 out of 25 words correctly, indicating that the student has a firmly developed understanding of the sound patterns at this developmental stage. The stage would be considered instructional for the student if the student scored between 12 and 21 words correctly, indicating that the student is inconsistent with the phonetic sound features of the stage. A stage would be considered frustrational if the student

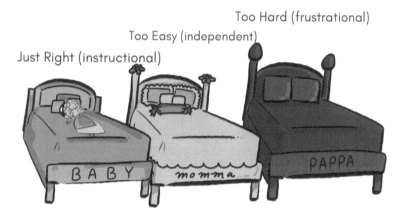

Figure 14.1 The Goldilocks principle

spelled 11 or fewer words correctly, indicating that the student has little knowledge of the phonetic features of words at this stage and may be guessing with spelling attempts. These collective data are used to cater instruction to individual student needs.

Instructional Supports for Struggling Spellers

In Chapter 13, accurate spelling was discussed as the foundational skill set for written communication. For students to develop effective spelling skills, they should progress through the developmental stages of spelling, correctly spelling progressively more complex words as their skills develop. Chapter 13 also discussed different ways students can remember target spelling words through memorization strategies, and also how to use sound patterns to decode phonetically regular words. For some students who struggle with spelling, additional instruction will be needed to more specifically address student needs.

Selection of Instructional Materials

Teacher selection of instructional materials can be especially critical for students who struggle with spelling. It is helpful for teachers to choose spelling words that are meaningful to students. Approximately ten spelling words is an appropriate number of words for students to focus on and master within a weekly period. Besides selecting a manageable number of target words, teachers will also want to ensure the words chosen for instruction and their instructional methods match. For instance, as mentioned earlier in this chapter, an appropriate ratio of decodable words to sight words is eight to two. If a teacher is choosing to focus her teaching on the decodable spelling words in a unit, it is important that she focus her instruction on sound pattern recognition or structural analysis for more complex words. When a teacher is spending time teaching irregular sight words, she will want to implement instruction that focuses on memorization strategies because these words do not follow a predictable pattern. It would be ineffective for teachers to engage in sound pattern instruction for irregular sight words, and using memorization to remember decodable words would be an overwhelming task because of the sheer volume of words that would need to be committed to memory. Additionally, teachers want students to hear and recognize learned sound patterns in novel words, which will not be supported by simply memorizing individual decodable words.

Considerations for Instruction

Just as with the areas of reading, students who are at-risk for spelling problems are likely to need additional supports that may not be necessary for the typical learner. These supports can be **visual** (visual stimuli to model accurate spelling), **tactile** (physical manipulation of letters or words), or **auditory** (verbal prompts that help students attend to target sounds). In the previous chapter, many of these supports were discussed in terms of strategies for spelling instruction. For instance, one of the strategies discussed was word sorts where students visually discriminate between words with different spelling patterns. Word sorts can also often be structured for tactile manipulation by putting the words on cards that can be moved around when being grouped and sorted. Most memorization strategies that were discussed try to incorporate all three levels of prompts within practice opportunities to help ensure that students have multiple word exposures using various modalities. The structural analysis strategies that were highlighted often employ tactile elements where students draw lines or use other hands-on methods of breaking longer words into their multiple parts. Many times when engaging in structural analysis, teachers can provide auditory prompts that help students segment longer words into syllables by pausing in between syllables while saying the word aloud.

While spelling word selection is an important consideration for all students, it is particularly important for at-risk students. Careful selection of words by sound relationship helps students to retain correct word spelling more easily, while a large of group of words unrelated by sound construction is often difficult for students to remember because of the cognitive load on students' memory for words that must simply be memorized. Additionally, students benefit from connections that can be directly made between their spelling and oral language and decoding skills. Students can learn how to spell the same words they are learning to read simultaneously so they are focusing on the same sound constructions. However, their spelling skills can further benefit from knowledge they may have of oral language and structural analysis skills for reading. For instance, if students are focusing on spelling words in a particular unit with -s, -ing, and -ed endings, teachers can use direct connections to oral language and decoding for this skill.

In some classes, all students will have the same spelling words and will receive instruction and participate in practice opportunities as a whole class. However, some students who struggle with spelling may require small group instruction. To set up small group instruction, teachers can use part of their small group time within their literacy block to target spelling as well as reading skills. Within this small group setting, teachers can more easily monitor individual student spelling progress. With a smaller teacher–student ratio in the small group setting, teachers can provide targeted instruction on specific student spelling difficulties, allowing for immediate feedback on practice opportunities within the small group setting. In the small group environment, struggling students often feel more comfortable asking questions and engaging in practice opportunities at their spelling level. Additionally, by providing spelling instruction in small group format, teachers can more easily use spelling word lists targeted to specific student learning needs.

Additional Learning Opportunities

Additional learning opportunities with spelling can be provided through computer-assisted instruction (CAI). CAI allows students to engage in meaningful and engaging practice while it frees up the teacher for other instruction. There are multiple websites targeting spelling available online, such as *Spelling City* (https://www.spellingcity.com/), which allows teachers to input teacher-selected spelling words for individual students or whole classes. Once the teacher has the spelling words uploaded into the website, students can engage in various games where they practice spelling words using activities like word searches, fill in the blank, and alphabetizing words. For students who are struggling with spelling, CAI can provide ongoing support, with teachers having the ability to monitor student progress while engaging in online practice activities until reaching the desired mastery level.

Specialized Instruction: Spelling

Many times students with spelling difficulties will need a more direct and explicit approach to spelling instruction.

Words Their Way

Words Their Way is a developmental spelling program that builds from short CVC words to longer and more complex words with roots and endings. This spelling program is constructed to align with four developmental spelling stages:

- *Letter Name*—the simplest CVC constructions to variations of this construction involve beginning and ending blends and digraphs.
- *Within Word*—complex vowel constructions within the middle of the target words include various multi-vowel sound constructions in the center of target words.
- *Syllable Juncture*—multisyllable words include syllables formed in different ways.
- *Derivational Constancy*—words in this stage are formed using base words or roots, which are often from Greek and Latin, combined with prefixes and suffixes forming more complex words.

For more information: https://www.pearson.com/us/higher-education/series/Words-Their-Way-Series/2281883.html

---

Assessment of Student Writing Skills

Writing is the way that students express their ideas and thinking through print. Because this is one of the primary mechanisms for students to demonstrate their learned knowledge in school, it is important for teachers to assess the progress of all students to ensure that they are making adequate improvements over time. Assessments of writing should span multiple genres of writing, just as reading comprehension assessments can be designed to span reading many genres of text. Writing assessment can involve assessments structured with writing prompts and rubrics, as well as teacher-made tests. By structuring assessments across writing types like essays, narratives, letters, and journals, a teacher can determine specific student strengths and weaknesses by type of writing, as well as whether there are specific student writing difficulties that span all the writing genres. Information gathered from these writing assessments is then used to inform instruction. As with reading skills, when students are identified as at-risk in writing, the teacher can put a plan in place to monitor student progress.

Unlike other areas of literacy, a writing evaluation or assessment is generally not a structured test but simply asking students to write on a topic or prompt. The important parts of the writing assessment are both the **writing prompt** and **rubric**. The prompt gives a student guidance about what to write, and the writing rubric is typically a detailed evaluation grid specifying the needed writing elements with an evaluation mechanism, usually numerical, for evaluating student competency with those specific elements.

Observation/Authentic Assessment

Writing is often evaluated in authentic contexts through written products that are naturally developed as part of academic learning activities. For instance, students may be asked to write stories in a similar style to one they have read in class. By reviewing this written narrative, teachers can evaluate student writing competency by simply evaluating a work product that is produced by the students as part of their overall literacy instruction. Another example is **dialogue journaling**. In this journal format, a teacher and student are alternating in writing journal entries. Typically, this type of journaling is done with narrative text, but it can also be used with expository text. In dialogue journaling, the teacher initially raises questions about different aspects of what has been read in class, and the student responds to these questions in paragraph form. Teachers follow up with entries that give students feedback that reinforces clear understanding and provides clarification on other information as needed. The dialogue journal is a written conversation between a student and teacher about text.

At times, looking at student breadth of writing is critical to understand the students' current writing abilities and their developmental progression. This authentic assessment of writing is called the **writing portfolio**. It can include pieces of writing students have

A Focus on Formal Assessment of Written Expression

While this chapter focuses on informal assessments of spelling and written expression to inform instruction, there are circumstances where an educator might need information about how a student is doing related to other students of the same age or grade. In these instances, a formal assessment that is norm-referenced is needed. As you remember from Chapter 2, norm-referenced assessments are standardized and require specialized training to administer. These types of assessments cover a wide range of skills related to written expression. Results provide an indication of how a student performed compared to a norming sample of students in the same grade. A formal assessment of written expression would generally be used as a pre and post assessment of a student's performance as well as to determine whether a student's progress is sufficient to close an achievement gap to peers. An example of a formal assessment of written expression is the *Test of Written Language, 4th Edition* (TOWL-4).

Test of Written Language (TOWL)	
Test Description:	• Vocabulary • Spelling • Punctuation • Logical Sentences • Sentence Combining • Contextual Conventions • Story Compositions
Ages:	9–0 through 17–11 years
Administration:	Group or Individualized
Time Required:	60–90 minutes
Publisher:	https://www.proedinc.com/Products/12850/towl4-test-of-written-languagefourth-edition.aspx

naturally made as part of their academic learning, but the span covers months of time and can contain work samples from a variety of content areas and writing genres. The critical ideas behind the portfolio are that students' writing will be evaluated developmentally through work samples over time, and then for competency across academic areas to evaluate students' ability to use written language to express what is being learned.

Teacher-made Tests of Writing Skills

At times there is a need for teacher-made tests of writing. Most times these teacher-made tests focus on conventions of writing versus the content of writing. Included in these tests of writing conventions can be grammar, spelling, capitalization, and punctuation. Teacher-made tests should be focused on evaluating student skill abilities on what has been recently taught through instruction as well as reviewing previously taught skills with which teachers want students to maintain competency.

Instructional Supports for Struggling Writers

In Chapter 13, a structured process for writing involving brainstorming, drafting, revising, editing, and publishing was discussed. Chapter 13 also addressed how strategy instruction can be employed within each writing process stage to develop students' writing skills. For students to develop effective writing skills, they must be able to approach writing strategically in a process-oriented manner. For some students who struggle with writing, additional instruction will be needed to focus in on specific student areas in need of development.

Selection of Instructional Materials

Thoughtful selection of writing materials can be an important factor in developing students' writing. When writing is a difficult task for students, carefully chosen writing prompts that stimulate students' interests can be key in garnering students' engagement and persistence in the writing task. For instance, high-interest visuals such as images of natural disasters, comical situations, or unusual creatures can be provided to students with their text-based writing prompts as springboards for student thinking on a topic. Another way of engaging struggling writers is by providing choice in writing prompts instead of requiring the use of one specific prompt. Text-based resource materials that include target vocabulary and information can also be valuable supports for teachers to provide when students are given technical expository writing prompts.

Considerations for Instruction

A critical consideration for teaching struggling writers is spending time frontloading instruction. Struggling writers benefit from instruction that sets them up with assistive writing tools before beginning writing tasks. In this way, activating student background knowledge is important. Students are better able to write on a topic if teachers have spent time initially with students, helping them reconnect with relevant background knowledge they may have before they begin writing. Additionally, working with students to make a word bank of important vocabulary to incorporate when writing about a topic can help students with the cognitive load of retrieving these words when writing. Thus, more of students' focus can be on the writing task itself. Students may also benefit from accessing source material before writing. For instance, if a class is asked to write about a topic with which students may have varying levels of background information, such as poisonous snakes, they will benefit from reading information about the topic before they write about it. While writing about the topic, students will be able to tap into this newly acquired knowledge and refer to the reading material as a resource when trying to get their ideas down on paper.

As you learned in Chapter 13, graphic organizers give students a visual for ideas that they have in their head so they can concretely see how many ideas they have on a topic. The visual support can also help struggling writers in the retrieval process for details they may want to include as well as helping them see how their ideas are related or unrelated to one another. However, brainstorming with a graphic organizer can take time, and the time spent on this beginning organization may be disproportionate to other key steps in the writing process. Additionally, graphic organizers lend themselves to single words or short phrases which are not always easily converted into whole sentences during the drafting phase. It is important for teachers to use graphic organizers in a way that helps students visually connect their thoughts on a topic, while not allowing these organizers to bog down the writing process. A computer-based tool that can help teachers and students in generating many different types of graphic organizers for writing is *Kidspiration* (http://www.inspiration.com/Kidspiration). This web-based program allows users to select different visuals, including lines and shapes to help write, connect, and organize thoughts for writing.

You also learned in Chapter 13 that one of the best ways to develop student writing is to give them feedback on their written expression. However, teachers often make the mistake of correcting and giving feedback on every student writing error or inconsistency across both content and conventions. For all writers, and struggling writers in particular, this level of feedback is likely to negatively affect students' writing motivation. When giving students feedback on their writing, it is best to focus feedback on skills that are currently being taught in addition to specific skills that teachers have been reviewing or expect students to already have mastered. Typically, targeting one to two new skills related to content and one to two new skills related to conventions will give students constructive feedback for how to improve without overwhelming them. For instance, if a student is struggling with using commas and capital letters (conventions), spelling of multi-syllabic words (conventions), including main ideas (content), and using supporting details (content), the teacher could choose to focus in on capital letters and main ideas, having one area from both content and convention to target for evaluation and feedback.

A Focus on Instructional Accommodations

Accommodations do not negate the need for explicit, direct instruction. However, in addition to quality instruction, some students with disabilities will need instructional accommodations in order to make progress in the curriculum or toward IEP goals. Accommodations are changes that are made for individual students and might include changes in time, input, output, and level of support (Hallahan, Lloyd, Kauffman, Weiss, & Martinez, 2005). In the areas of writing and spelling, instructional accommodations might include:

- extended time to complete writing assignments (time),
- computer-assisted instruction for spelling practice (input),
- use of a keyboard or voice-to-speech software (output),
- word banks during writing activities (level of support).

Supports that help students self-regulate their use of strategies can be especially helpful to students who have challenges with the self-monitoring aspect of the writing process. For example, students can use strategy guide sheets for cueing if they struggle to remember strategy steps when applying them in novel writing situations. Teachers can also help support writing strategy usage through attribution feedback that prompts students to use strategies that they have learned rather than relying solely on the teacher for corrective feedback. Students may also benefit from scaffolding instruction in a way that begins to move them toward more independent application of particular writing strategies.

Additional Learning Opportunities

When thinking about additional learning opportunities in writing, this extra practice does not necessarily mean that the student produces more final written products. However, students who struggle with writing may need additional time as they work through each step in the writing process. As a result, they may get many practice opportunities in the beginning stages of writing, like in the brainstorming and drafting stages, but may not get as many opportunities as other students in practicing the higher-level skills within the revising and editing stages. They may also not get as many opportunities to successfully publish or get their writing to the final draft stage, which can add to student frustration with the writing process. The teacher's task with struggling writers is really to provide additional opportunities for the students to practice writing skills at every stage of the writing process. Struggling writers need just as much, if not more, practice in critically thinking about their own writing and making changes within it during the revision stage. They also need chances to practice detecting and correcting their written expression errors through

---

Specialized Instruction: Writing

Many times students with writing difficulties will need a more direct and explicit approach to writing instruction.

The Strategic Instruction Model (SIM)—Writing Strategies Series

The Strategic Instruction Model (SIM)—Writing Strategies Series is a program that can be used to teach students the writing skills required in most state standards lists across Grades 2 through 12. It builds off the SIM approach to overall literacy, which uses explicit instruction and evidence-based practices to develop students' critical thinking and problem solving skills approach to reading and writing.

Within the *Writing Strategies Series*, there are four different levels that incorporate both paper-based curriculum and digital media supports:

- Fundamentals in the Sentence Writing Strategy,
- Proficiency in the Sentence Writing Strategy,
- Paragraph Writing Strategy,
- EDIT Strategy.

There are also supplemental materials with both paper and digital components that further develop thematic writing and writing mechanics.

For more information: https://sim.ku.edu/writing-strategies

the editing stage. Additionally, teachers can make the final stage of publishing more accessible through word-processing and text-to-speech technology, which can boost students' positive feelings, attitudes, and motivation about writing.

References

Bear, D. R., Invernizzi, M., Templeton, S., & Johnston, F. R. (2016). *Words their way: Word study for phonics, vocabulary, and spelling instruction* (6th ed.). Upper Saddle River, NJ: Pearson.

Beirne-Smith, M., & Riley, T. F (2009). Spelling assessment of students with disabilities. *Assessment for Effective Intervention, 34*, 170–177.

Darch, C., Kim, S., Johnson, S., & James, H. (2000). The strategic spelling skills of students with learning disabilities: The results of two studies. *Journal of Instructional Psychology, 27*, 15–26.

Graham, S., Collins, A. A., & Rigby-Wills, H. (2017). Writing characteristics of students with learning disabilities and typically achieving peers: A meta-analysis. *Exceptional Children, 83*, 199–218.

Graham, S., Harris, K. R., & McKeown, D. (2013). The writing of students with LD and a meta-analysis of SRSD writing intervention studies: Redux. In L. Swanson, K. R. Harris, & S. Graham (Eds.), *Handbook of learning disabilities* (2nd ed., pp. 405–438). New York, NY: Guilford Press.

Hallahan, D. P., Lloyd, J. W., Kauffman, J. M., Weiss, M. P., & Martinez, E. A. (2005). *Learning disabilities: Foundations, characteristics, and effective teaching* (3rd ed.). Boston, MA: Pearson.

Hodges, R. E. (1982). Research update: On the development of spelling ability. *Language Arts, 59*, 284–290.

Invernizzi, M., Abouzeid, K. M., & Gill, T. (1994). Using students' invented spellings as a guide for spelling instruction that emphasizes word study. *Elementary School Journal, 95*, 155–167.

McNaughton, D., Hughes, C. A., & Clark, K. (1994). Spelling instruction for students with learning disabilities: Implications for research and practice. *Learning Disability Quarterly, 17*, 169–185.

Moats, L. C. (1995). *Spelling: Development, disabilities, and instruction*. Baltimore, MD: York Press.

SECTION V: APPLICATION ACTIVITIES

Show What You Know!

In this section, you learned that approaches for teaching and assessing phonetically regular words is different than the approaches for teaching and assessing phonetically irregular and sight words. Can you differentiate these types of words? Complete the activity below to find out!

Directions:

Construct a spelling list that follows the 80% 20% rule. First, determine whether each word is phonetically regular or irregular. Then select eight regular words and two irregular words for your spelling list.

1. cow
2. mat
3. pig
4. barn
5. rooster
6. friend
7. horse
8. cat
9. dog
10. silo
11. house
12. tractor
13. chick
14. milk
15. peas
16. truck

Answer Key: regular words—1, 2, 3, 4, 5, 8, 12, 13, 14, 15, 16
        irregular words—6, 7, 9, 10, 11

Partner Activity/Discussion

In **Appendix D**, you will find the brainstorming and first draft of a 4th grader's writing. Review the student's work and discuss the strengths and weaknesses of the student. Next, discuss teaching strategies for supporting the student with revising, editing, and publishing.

Learn More: Multimedia Activity

In this section you learned about spelling and writing. For this activity, you will go deeper in your learning about one of the writing topics by exploring the IRIS Center website. The site houses a wide range of resources including learning modules, case studies, professional development activities, fact sheets, information briefs, interviews, and videos. In completing the activity, you will also be exposed to some excellent online resources for a wide range of other topics as well. Have fun learning!

Directions:

1. **Before**

   In the first text box below, list key ideas you know (K) after reading this section of the textbook. In the next text box, write questions about what you want to learn (W) from completing this multi-media activity.

K (**K**now)	What do you already know about this topic? 1. 2. 3. 4.
W (**W**ant to learn)	What do YOU want to learn more about? 1. 2. 3. 4.

2. **During**

   Explore the IRIS Center website at https://iris.peabody.vanderbilt.edu. Use the information you find here to answer your questions!

3. **After**

   After you have finished reading about the areas you wanted to learn more about, look back at what you indicated you knew before starting (K) and wanted to learn (W). Can you now answer the questions? How does this new information connect with what you knew before starting? Write the answers to your questions in the text box below. Be sure to add any additional unexpected information that you learned (L) as well!

L (Learned)	What did you learn? 1. 2. 3. 4.

Appendix A

Typical Developmental Profile for a 5th Grade Student

Case 1	Independent	Instructional	Frustrational
Word List	4	5	6
Decoding	4	5	6
Comprehension	4	5	6

CWPM = 120

[Typical 5th grade fluency: 110–139 CWPM (50th percentile)]

Atypical Developmental Profiles for 5th Grade Students

Case 2	Independent	Instructional	Frustrational
Word List	4	5	6
Decoding	4	5	6
✗ Comprehension		1	2

Case 3	Independent	Instructional	Frustrational
✗ Word List	1		2
✗ Decoding		1, 2, 3	4
✗ Comprehension	5, 6, J.H.		

Case 4	Independent	Instructional	Frustrational
Word List	4	5	6
Decoding	4	5	6
Comprehension	4	5	6

CWPM = 65

Appendix B

Activity I

Activity Leader Directions

1. Draw the picture to the right on a whiteboard.
2. Ask the other participants to copy this diagram onto their own individual whiteboards.

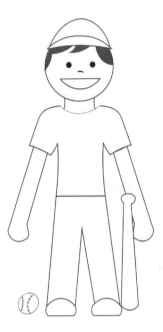

3. Read the rhyme below one at a time allowing time for the participants to ERASE each item as directed. If participants shout out the answers, direct them to erase their answers rather than saying them out loud.

You will have no fun at all,
unless you erase the _____.
              (ball)
You may feel like you need a nap
once you've erased his baseball _____.
                       (cap)
No matter where you're at,
please erase his baseball _____.
                 (bat)
First thing you need to do
is erase one _____.
            (shoe)

You will want to stick like glue,
after you erase his other _____.
                    (shoe)
Wow! Look at those ants!
You'd better erase his _____.
                (pants)
No one will get hurt
if next you erase his _____.
               (shirt)
Before you go off to bed,
be sure to erase his _____.
               (head)

4. Ask everyone to show their whiteboards, which should be completely erased.

Activity inspired by: Fitzpatrick, J. (1997). *Phonemic awareness: Playing with sounds to strengthen beginning reading skills.* Cypress, CA: Creative Teaching Press.

Activity 2

Activity Leader Directions

1. Read the rhymes below one at a time allowing time for the participants to DRAW each item as directed. If participants shout out the answers, direct them to draw their answers rather than saying them out loud.

When drawing a doll, it is said,
first you should draw her _____.
                     (head)
Get down off that chair!
It's time to draw her _____.
                (hair)
You are very wise,
if next you draw two great big _____.
                     (eyes)
No matter where she goes,
she's going to need a button _____.
                     (nose)

It may take a while,
but next she needs a _____.
                (smile)
Boy, this room's a mess!
You'd better draw a fancy _____.
                   (dress)
Cows live on farms.
Time to draw two _____.
              (arms)
Before you go,
she needs a great big _____.
                (bow)

2. Ask everyone to show their whiteboards and show them the picture below.

Activity inspired by: Fitzpatrick, J. (1997). *Phonemic awareness: Playing with sounds to strengthen beginning reading skills.* Cypress, CA: Creative Teaching Press.

Appendix C

1. In English, 26 letters are used to represent 44 sounds

   a. true
   b. false

2. A syllable must:

   a. contain at least one vowel
   b. not contain a vowel
   c. contain at least one consonant
   d. not contain a consonant

3. How many phonemes are in the word *chick*?

   a. one
   b. two
   c. three
   d. four

4. How many phonemes are in the word *knife*?

   a. one
   b. two
   c. three
   d. six

5. How many phonemes are in the word *sox*?

   a. one
   b. two
   c. three
   d. four

6. Which word is a closed syllable?

   a. low
   b. sofa
   c. dough
   d. none of these

7. What is the onset in the word *chair*?

   a.   ch
   b.   air
   c.   a
   d.   ai
   e.   hair

8. What is the rime in the word *crust*?

   a.   c
   b.   cr
   c.   u
   d.   ust
   e.   rust

9. Which is a consonant blend?

   a.   ch (as in *chair*)
   b.   st (as in *street*)
   c.   sh (as in *sheet*)
   d.   ph (as in *phone*)

10. Which is a digraph?

   a.   pl (as in *please*)
   b.   sn (as in *sneeze*)
   c.   ch (as in *cheese*)
   d.   tr (as in *trees*)

11. Which is a diphthong?

   a.   oa (as in *boat*)
   b.   ou (as in *out*)
   c.   oy (as in *toy*)
   d.   oo (as in *book*)

12. Which word contains a schwa sound?

   a.   hated
   b.   rising
   c.   choose
   d.   chicken

13. The second syllable in the nonsense word *alantish* would be expected to rhyme with:

   a.   fish
   b.   ball
   c.   rant
   d.   none of these

14. The open syllable in the nonsense word *moham* would most likely rhyme with:

   a.   do
   b.   dough
   c.   ram
   d.   lah

15. The letter "c" most commonly makes the sound /c/ as in:

    a. cello
    b. cite
    c. rice
    d. corn

16. The word *if* ends with the same sound as:

    a. the ph in *graph*
    b. the f in *of*
    c. the v in *violin*
    d. none of these

17. When "a" and "i" are in the same syllable, it makes the same vowel sound heard in:

    a. mat
    b. mate
    c. mid
    d. none of the above

18. What word has the same sound as the underlined letters in *th͟ink*?

    a. weather
    b. bath
    c. this
    d. all of the words above
    e. none of the words above

19. What word has the same sound as the underlined letters in *j͟am*?

    a. gem
    b. age
    c. gin
    d. all of the words above
    e. none of the words above

20. What word has the same sound as the underlined letters in *bo͟o͟k*?

    a. look
    b. blood
    c. food
    d. all of the words above
    e. none of the words above

Inspired by: Fox, B. J. (2014). *Phonics and word study for the teacher of reading: Programed for self-instruction* (11th ed.). Boston, MA: Pearson.

Appendix D

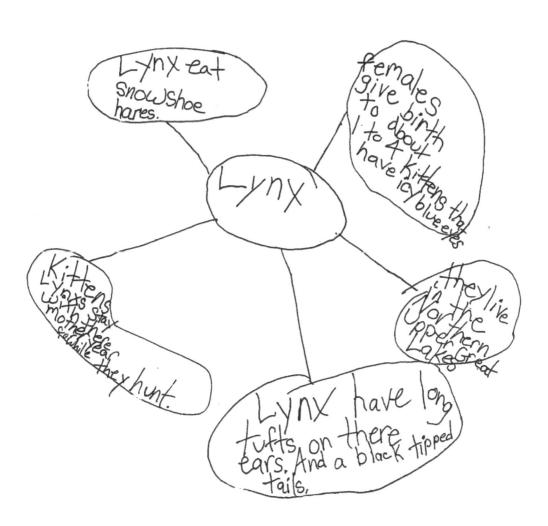

All about Lynx

Do you know what eats snowshoe hares, and has about 1 to 4 kittens has icy eyes, and a black tipped tail? Did you say Lynx? Your right Lynx have icy eyes, a black tipped tail, eats snowshoe hares, and has 1 to 4 kittens. Lynx live in the Northern Upper Great Lakes. They are related to lions, tigers, bobcats, cheetas and jaguars. Lynx kittens stay with their mother for 1 year while hunting to learn from their mom. Can you beleive that only 1 year! Isent that amazing! If I were little it would take me a lot of time. Just beleive me! Lynx have long puff things on their ears. Their ears are very tuff. They have razor long teeth! They have redish for and pointy ears. Lynx have sharp claws to catch their pray. To catch their pray they have to hide and when its the right time they will spring out.

Index

accommodation 12; for accessing text 151; for comprehension 202; for oral language & early reading development 100; for writing & spelling 240

adequate yearly progress (AYP) 24

affix 111; and instruction 118–119

age equivalent 24

at-risk student 4–12

auditory processing 92; 142

auditory support: for basic reading 150–151; for comprehension 200–201; for early reading 98; for spelling 236

authentic assessment 25; for basic reading skills 144; for comprehension 196; for early reading 94; for spelling 233; for writing 237

automaticity 114

background knowledge 36; in an IRI 44; and instruction 178–190

base word 111; and instruction 119

basic interpersonal communication skills (BICS) 7; L1 supporting L2 66

big book 76; and instruction 76, 83

blending 80; for decoding 116–117, 131, 152; for phonemic awareness 79–80

bound morpheme 56; and affixes 111, 119; in other languages 90–91

brainstorming 220; assessment application 243; and instruction 225–226, 240

circle time 76; and instruction 78

classwide peer tutoring 188

cloze assessment 198–199

closed syllable 111

code-switching 8

cognitive academic language proficiency (CALP) 7; L1 supporting L2 66

communication 54–55

compound word 119; and instruction 118–119

comprehension monitoring 163; and comprehension instruction 170–172

computer-assisted instruction (CAI) 152; for basic reading skills 152; for spelling 236–237

computer-based assessment: for basic reading skills 146; for comprehension 198

concepts of print 68; assessment of 94–96; and instruction 76, 99

connected text 113

connection making 178–179; for comprehension 173–175; tangential connections 194–195

consonant 109

consonant cluster 109

content: core language element 56

context cue 115; assessment of 144; and basic reading instruction 122; and at-risk readers 143, 150; and vocabulary acquisition 184

controlled text 114

conventions: for writing 211

criterion-referenced assessment 25

culture 5

culturally relevant material 200

Cummins' quadrant 9

curriculum-based assessment 26

curriculum-based measure 26

decodable text 134

details 164; and comprehension instruction 172

diacritical marks 109

diagnostic assessment 24

dialogic reading 77; for instruction 77–78

dialogue journal 238

difficult words 180

digraph 109

diphthong 109

Direct Instruction 125–127

drafting 220; and writing instruction 225

dysgraphia 231

dyslexia 125, 142

early reading screener 94

editing 221; and writing instruction 227

educational history 20

Elkonin boxes: for decoding 116; for phonemic awareness 81

encoding 212

engagement 118

English learner 6–10; and basic reading skills 141; and comprehension 193; and early reading 90–92; and spelling and writing 229–230

environmental factors 20